Acknowledgements

Pulling together all the information needed for a book such as this requires contributions from various groups at Sun as well as from the AOL/Netscape Alliance team. Without the cooperation and dedication of the people from these groups, we would not have been able to produce this book.

First, we would like to thank the Sun BluePrints team for coming up with the concept of the book, providing edits, reviewing its content, and walking it through the production process. We especially want to express our gratitude for all the hard work and long hours Cathy Miller put in, always with a cheerful disposition. The BluePrint management team of Barb Jugo, Bill Sprouse, Jeff Wheelock, and of course Chuck Alexander, were instrumental by supplying the resources and encouragement necessary to take the book from concept to completion.

Next, we would like to recognize the members of the product teams from both Sun native LDAP engineering and iPlanet Directory Server technical marketing for providing input and reviews. David Huntley from iPlanet marketing provided guidance throughout the whole process while Ludovic Poitou from iPlanet Directory Server engineering spent many hours of his own time reviewing material and provided numerous corrections and enhancements.

Finally, we would like to express our appreciation to the folks at Sun Professional Services, notably James Lick and Dianne Fallier, who reviewed the book and provided invaluable feedback.

Contents

Acknowledgements   iii

Preface   xxiii

1. **Solaris Naming Services Overview   1**

   Definition of a Naming Service   1

   Definition of a Directory Service   2

        Directory Service versus Database Servers   3

        Proliferation of Directory Services   3

   Solaris Directory Services—Historical Perspective   4

        Network Information Service   4

        NIS+   5

        Domain Name System   6

        Solaris Naming Service Switch   6

   LDAP Background   7

        Brief History of LDAP   7

        LDAP Goals and Specifications   8

   Solaris LDAP Implementation   8

   Factors to Consider When Deploying LDAP   9

2. **Solaris Naming Services Architecture   11**

   Evolution of Solaris Naming Services   11

NIS and Files Coexistence   12

NIS and DNS Coexistence   13

Solaris Naming Service Switch   13

NIS Architecture Overview   16

NIS Client Server Architecture   16

How NIS Clients Bind to the NIS Server   17

NIS Maps   17

NIS High Availability Architecture Features   19

NIS+ Architecture Overview   20

NIS+ Client Server Architecture   21

How NIS+ Clients Bind to the NIS+ Server   22

NIS+ Tables   23

NIS+ Interaction with DNS   24

NIS+ High Availability Architecture Features   25

Solaris DNS Architecture Overview   25

DNS Client Architecture   26

DNS Server Architecture   26

DNS High Availability Features   27

LDAP Architecture Overview   27

LDAP Information Model   27

LDAP Naming Model   29

LDAP Functional Model   31

LDAP Security Model   32

LDAP Replication   33

Comparison with Legacy Naming Services   35

3. **Security Models   37**

Authentication versus Authorization   37

Traditional Solaris Authentication   38

How UNIX Passwords Work   39

NIS+ Credentials   40

Alternative Authentication Mechanisms   41

LDAP Authentication (Simple Authentication)   41

CRAM-MD5   42

Kerberos   45

Secure Socket Layer Authentication   49

Security Infrastructure   50

iPlanet Directory Server SASL   50

Solaris PAM Framework   52

PAM Module Types   52

How PAM Works   53

PAM Configuration File   54

Generic pam.conf File   57

PAM LDAP Module   61

How PAM and LDAP Work   63

4.   **iPlanet Directory Server Installation and Configuration   67**

Product Architecture   67

Administration Domains   68

Configuration Data   68

Login Accounts   69

Netscape Console   69

Planning the Installation   70

Installation Procedure   72

Performing a Typical Installation   74

Installation Defaults   78

Starting the Netscape Console   80

Verifying the Installation   81

Installation File Navigation   82

Postinstallation Procedures   83

Changing Common Installation Configuration Parameters   87

Importing Directory Data   89

Reinstalling iPlanet Directory Server   92

Installation Troubleshooting Tips   92

Directory Replication   93

Planning Directory Replication   93

▼   Setting up Replication   94

Verifying Replication   98

Troubleshooting Replication Problems   98

Modifying the Supplier Initiated Agreement   98

Setting up a Secure System Using SSL and Certificates   98

Planning a Secure Server Configuration   99

Running the Certificate Setup Wizard   99

Rebooting the Secure Server   103

Changing the Trust Database Password or PIN   103

Using SSL for Replication   104

iPlanet Directory Server Startup Files   104

Script Generation Program   105

Installing the NIS Extensions   108

5.   **Solaris 8 Native LDAP Configuration   111**

Definition of Native LDAP   111

Native Solaris LDAP Implementation   112

Solaris LDAP Client Profiles   113

NIS Domain   114

Authentication Method   115

Proxy Agent   116

Directory Information Tree   117

Loading Data   118

Naming Context   118

Server Configuration Procedure   119

Tools and Techniques   119

Importing LDIF Files from the Command Line   123

Summary of Steps Required   123

▼   Step 1. Modifying `slapd.user_at.conf`   124

▼   Step 2. Modifying `slapd.oc.conf`   125

▼   Step 3. Modifying `slapd.user_oc.conf`   126

▼   Step 4. Changing Password Store to Crypt Format   128

▼   Step 5. Adding New Containers   129

▼   Step 6. Modifying Self-Entry Modification   133

▼   Step 7. Setting VLV Control ACI   133

▼   Step 8. Adding the Proxy Agent Entry   134

▼   Step 9. Setting Password Read Permission for `proxyagent`   135

▼   Step 10. Generating the Client Profile   135

▼   Step 11. Creating Indexes   137

▼   Step 12. Creating Virtual List View Indexes   137

▼   Step 13. Creating Sample Test Entries   139

▼   Step 14. Populating the LDAP data   139

Client Configuration   140

How LDAP Clients Initialize   140

LDAP Client Initialization Example   144

Troubleshooting Tips   144

    Unresolved Host Name   145

    Unable to Reach Systems in the LDAP Domain Remotely   145

    Sendmail Fails to Deliver/Receive Mail To/From Remote Users   145

    Login Does Not Work   145

6.   **NIS Extensions Configuration   147**

Overview   147

    What the Extensions Are   148

    Storing NIS Information in LDAP   150

    NIS Extensions Initialization   154

    Initialization Checklist   157

▼   Initialization Procedure   158

    Postinstallation Verification   158

7.   **Capacity Planning and Performance Tuning   161**

Server Sizing   161

Directory Considerations   162

    Directory Size   162

    Directory Access   163

    Security Requirements   163

    Replication Strategy   164

Capacity Planning Methodology   164

    Calculating Directory Database Size   164

    Summary of Disk Storage Requirements   168

    Memory Sizing   170

    Summary of Memory Usage   171

    Estimating CPU Usage   172

LDAP Test Suite   172

Results of Experimentation   174

Configuration   174

Simple Read Test with Persistent Connection   175

Read Test with Nonpersistent Connection   175

Modify Tests   176

Authentication Tests   177

Qualitative Observations Based on Test Results   177

Performance Tuning   178

Definition of Indexing   178

Indexing Summary   184

Caching for Performance   184

Directory Caches   184

Evaluating Sizing Factors   185

Setting the Database Cache Size   186

Setting Entry Cache Size   186

Sizing the Database and Entry Caches   187

Tuning Cache Sizes   188

Setting the All IDs Threshold   190

Tuning the All IDs Threshold Value   191

Setting Search Limit Parameters   191

Considering Data Design Issues   193

Designing an LDAP Client   195

Removing Unnecessary Plug-ins   195

Tuning Write Performance   196

Tuning Import Performance   199

Troubleshooting Checklist   200

8.   **Deploying Highly Available LDAP Data Services   203**

iPlanet Directory Services 4.12 HA Architecture Models   203

High Availability Strategy   204

Overview of Sun Cluster 2.2 Software   210

Logical IP Addresses   211

Data Services for Sun Cluster   212

Building a Sun Cluster with HA LDAP Data Services   212

LDAP Fault Monitor   213

iPlanet Directory Server 4.12 Installation   214

Configuring the Sun Cluster HA for iPlanet Data Services   215

LDAP Cluster Deployment Options   216

Asymmetric (Hot Standby Model) HA   216

Active Server Model   218

Redirecting LDAP Client Requests   218

9.   **Preventive Maintenance   219**

Directory Log Files   219

Access Log   219

Viewing the Access Log   221

Access Log Configuration Options   222

Error Log   224

Viewing the Error Log   224

Audit Log   225

Managing Database Transaction Logging   226

Changing the Location of the Database Transaction Log   227

Changing the Database Checkpoint Interval   228

Enabling Durable Transactions   228

Backing Up and Restoring the Directory Database   229

Backing Up the Database from the Directory Server Console   230

Backing Up the Database from the Command Line   230

Restoring the Database from the Directory Server Console   231

Restoring Your Database from the Command Line   231

Deleting Database Backups   232

Restoring Databases That Include Replicated Entries   232

Placing a Database in Read-Only Mode   232

Exporting and Importing the Database with LDIF   233

Exporting Databases to LDIF from the Command Line   234

Importing Databases from LDIF   235

10.   **Managing Directory Services   237**

Establishing Access Control Policies   237

LDAP Security Model Review   238

Access Control Instructions   238

Creating Access Control Instructions   240

▼   Adding a New ACI through the Directory Server Console   241

Managing the Directory Schema   242

The Schema Files   243

How Schema Files Are Read   245

Modifying the Schema   245

▼   Creating Attributes from the Directory Server Console   246

▼   Creating Object Classes from the Directory Server Console   247

Monitoring the Directory Server   248

Monitoring Resources   248

▼   Monitoring Server Performance from the Directory Server Console   251

Monitoring the Server from the Command Line   251

Monitoring Database Activity   253

Monitoring the Database from the Directory Server Console   255

Monitoring the Database from the Command Line   256

Managing with SNMP   258

Using LDAP MIB   260

Managing the LDAP Directory Server with BMC PATROL   264

iPlanet Directory Server KM Overview   264

Introduction to BMC PATROL   265

Checking Memory Usage with pmap   270

11.   **Directory Services Consolidation   273**

Benefits of Consolidation   273

LDAP as a Consolidation Choice   274

Consolidation Approaches   274

Consolidation of LDAP-Enabled Applications   274

LDAP Gateways   276

LDAP Synchronization   276

Password Synchronization   277

NIS Extensions for Solaris   277

NT Synchronization Service   277

iPlanet Meta-Directory Server   278

How Meta-Directory Works   278

Meta-Directory Connectors   279

Deploying iPlanet Meta-Directory   280

Unified Login and Single Sign-on   281

Kerberos and LDAP   281

SiteMinder   281

iPlanet Directory Access Router   284

iDAR Overview   284

iPlanet Directory Access Router Feature Set   285

12.   Microsoft Windows Interoperability   289

Windows NT Interoperability   289

Windows NT Security Model   290

How the NT User Account Information Is Made Available to Solaris
Server   290

Mapping NT User Account Information to LDAP   291

How the Synchronization Service Works   291

Windows 2000 Interoperability   294

Active Directory Services Architecture   294

Information Model   296

Security Model   298

Access Model   299

Replication Model   300

How Active Directory Clients Interact with Servers   301

How Applications Access Active Directory Services   302

Solaris Directory Services and Active Directory Services Interactions   302

Signing On Only Once   303

Joining a Windows 2000 Tree or Forest   303

Specifying LDAP Referrals   303

Using Windows Services in UNIX 2.0   304

A.   Using Netscape Communicator as an LDAP Client   305

B.   LDAP Standards Information   309

C.   Additional Information   323

D.   LDAP v3 Result Codes   329

E. **Schema Information** 337

    IETF Schemas 337

    RFC 2307 Network Information Service Schema 337

    RFC 2307 Draft Objectclasses 341

    Mail Alias Schema 343

Glossary 351

Index 359

Figures

FIGURE 2-1   Naming Service Switch Functions   14

FIGURE 2-2   Major NIS Components   16

FIGURE 2-3   Creation of NIS Maps   18

FIGURE 2-4   NIS Client Failover with the Broadcast Method   19

FIGURE 2-5   NIS Client Failover with the Specified Server Method   20

FIGURE 2-6   NIS+ Architecture   22

FIGURE 2-7   NIS+ Security Process   23

FIGURE 2-8   Sample Directory Information Tree   28

FIGURE 2-9   Full Tree Replication   34

FIGURE 2-10   Subtree Replication   34

FIGURE 3-1   `Login` Program Text String Converting to a Hashed String   39

FIGURE 3-2   CRAM-MD5 Authentication   43

FIGURE 3-3   PAM and the Relationship Between Applications, Library, and Modules   54

FIGURE 3-4   `pam_ldap` Structure   62

FIGURE 4-1   Layout of the `NetscapeRoot` Portion of the Directory Tree   69

FIGURE 4-2   Diagram of Component Interactions   70

FIGURE 4-3   **Netscape Console**   80

FIGURE 4-4   Layout Diagram   82

FIGURE 4-5   **Login to Directory** Window   88

FIGURE 4-6   **Manager** Tab   88

FIGURE 4-7   **Import Database** Window   91

FIGURE 4-8   **Consumer Settings** Tab   95

FIGURE 4-9   **Supplier Settings** Tab   95

FIGURE 4-10   **Source and Destination** Form   96

FIGURE 4-11   Creating an LDIF File   97

FIGURE 4-12   **Certificate Setup Wizard** Generating a Certificate Request   100

FIGURE 4-13   **Certificate Setup Wizard** to Install a Certificate   102

FIGURE 4-14   **Encryption** Tab   102

FIGURE 4-15   **Change Key Password**   103

FIGURE 4-16   Specification of SSL   104

FIGURE 5-1   **Property Editor** View Window   121

FIGURE 5-2   **Set Access Permissions** Window   121

FIGURE 5-3   **Select Attributes** Window   122

FIGURE 5-4   **Password** Tab   129

FIGURE 6-1   NIS Data Accessibility   149

FIGURE 6-2   Data Synchronization   149

FIGURE 6-3   Typical Subtree   152

FIGURE 6-4   **Directory** Tab   159

FIGURE 7-1   Simple Read Test with Persistent Connection   175

FIGURE 7-2   Nonpersistent Connections vs. Persistent Connections   176

FIGURE 7-3   Effects of Additional CPUs   176

FIGURE 7-4   Authentication Performance of the Directory Server   177

FIGURE 7-5   Built-in System Indexes   180

FIGURE 7-6   Automatically Created Indexes   181

FIGURE 7-7   **Select Attribute** Window   183

FIGURE 7-8   **Database** Tab Statistics   189

FIGURE 7-9   **Performance** Tab Information   192

FIGURE 7-10   **Expanded Plugins** Icon   196

FIGURE 8-1   Single-Master, Directory-Replication Architecture   205

FIGURE 8-2   High-Performance, Single-Master, Directory-Replication Architecture   206

FIGURE 8-3   Master and Replication Directory Hub Architecture   207

FIGURE 8-4   Basic Referrals Mechanism   208

FIGURE 8-5   Replication Referrals Mechanism   209

FIGURE 8-6   Referral Search beyond the Local Division   210

FIGURE 8-7   Typical Sun Cluster HA Configuration   211

FIGURE 8-8   A Directory Server Asymmetric High Availability Model   217

FIGURE 9-1   Access Log Tab and the Resulting Details   222

FIGURE 9-2   Access Log Tab and Parameter Settings   223

FIGURE 10-1   **Rights** Pop-up Menu in the **Set Access Permissions** Window   241

FIGURE 10-2   **Create Attribute** Window   246

FIGURE 10-3   **Create Object Class** Window   247

FIGURE 10-4   **Performance Counters**   251

FIGURE 10-5   Database Output Example   256

FIGURE 10-6   Example of a Simple SNMP Environment   259

FIGURE 10-7   Basic PATROL Architecture   266

FIGURE 10-8   Basic iPlanet Directory PATROL Architecture   268

FIGURE 10-9   **IMS4 Directory Services Knowledge Module** Icon   268

FIGURE 10-10   Directory Knowledge Modules   269

FIGURE 10-11   Resource Summary Modules   270

FIGURE 11-1   SiteMinder Single Sign-on   283

FIGURE 12-1   **Directory Server Settings** Tab   293

FIGURE 12-2   Active Directory Services Major Components   295

FIGURE 12-3   Active Directory Namespace   297

FIGURE 12-4   Access Control Process in Windows 2000   299

Tables

TABLE 2-1   `hosts.byname`   **17**

TABLE 2-2   `hosts.byaddr`   **18**

TABLE 2-3   NIS+ Tables   24

TABLE 2-4   Solaris Versions of BIND   26

TABLE 2-5   `posixAccount` Attributes   30

TABLE 2-6   Naming Service Feature Comparison   35

TABLE 3-1   PAM Configurations   55

TABLE 3-2   PAM Abbreviations   63

TABLE 3-3   PAM Authentication   64

TABLE 3-4   PAM Update of Password   64

TABLE 5-1   Directory Information Tree   117

TABLE 6-1   NIS-Specific Attributes   150

TABLE 6-2   New Object Classes   151

TABLE 6-3   Generic Mapping Rules   153

TABLE 7-1   Disk Storage Requirements   168

TABLE 7-2   Typical Memory Usage   171

TABLE 7-3   Sample Test Matrix   173

TABLE 7-4   Server Configuration   174

TABLE 7-5   Types of Indexes and Types of Searches   179

TABLE 7-6   System Indexes   180

TABLE 7-7   Default Indexes   181

TABLE 7-8   Cache Parameters   189

TABLE 7-9   Relative Costs of Index Types   197

TABLE 7-10   Location of Files That Can Be Updated   198

TABLE 10-1   Server Performance Monitoring   249

TABLE 10-2   Current Resource Usage Table   249

TABLE 10-3   Connection Status Table   250

TABLE 10-4   Database Performance Metrics   253

TABLE 10-5   Database Cache Information   254

TABLE 10-6   File-Specific Table   255

TABLE 10-7   Displayed Parameters   258

TABLE 10-8   Operations Table   261

TABLE 10-9   Entry Table   263

TABLE 10-10 Interaction Table   263

TABLE 12-1   Windows NT to LDAP Mapping   291

Preface

This book is one of an on-going series of books collectively known as the Sun BluePrints™ program. The *Solaris™ and LDAP Naming Services* BluePrint describes best practices for planning and deploying naming services based on the Lightweight Directory Access Protocol (LDAP). The introduction of native LDAP in the Solaris 8 operating environment provides powerful capabilities but is based on a model unfamiliar to most Solaris system administrators. Understanding general LDAP concepts and the specific Solaris implementation is key to successful deployment of resilient enterprise-wide naming services.

Sun BluePrints Program

The mission of the Sun BluePrints Program is to empower Sun customers with the technical knowledge required to implement reliable, extensible, and secure information systems within the data center using Sun products. The Sun BluePrints Program is managed by the Enterprise Engineering Group, which is part of the Customer Quality and Availability organization. This group provides a framework to identify, develop, and distribute best practices information that applies across the Sun product lines. Technical subject matter experts in various areas contribute to the program and focus on the scope and usefulness of the information.

The Enterprise Engineering Group is the primary provider of the technical content of the Sun BluePrints Program that includes books, guides, and online articles. Through these vehicles, Sun can provide guidance, installation and implementation experiences, real-life scenarios, and late-breaking technical information.

The monthly electronic magazine, Sun BluePrints OnLine, is located on the Web at `http://www.sun.com/blueprints`. To be notified about updates to the Sun BluePrints Program, please register yourself on this site.

Who Should Use This Book

This book is primarily intended for two types of readers: IT planners and system administrators. IT planners who must decide how to implement their future corporate naming services infrastructure will find the chapters *Capacity Planning and Performance Tuning*, *Directory Services Consolidation*, and *Microsoft Windows Interoperability* useful. System administrators will find helpful installation and management tips in the chapters *iPlanet Directory Server Installation and Configuration*, *Solaris 8 Native LDAP Configuration*, *NIS Extensions Configuration*, *Deploying Highly Available LDAP Data Services*, and *Preventive Maintenance, Managing Directory Services*.

Before You Read This Book

You should be familiar with basic Solaris system administration functions and possess some understanding of NIS or NIS+ and DNS. Some knowledge of LDAP concepts is helpful, but not required.

How This Book Is Organized

This book contains the following chapters and appendixes.

Chapter 1, "Solaris Naming Services Overview," introduces to naming service concepts and the Sun implementation of these concepts in the Solaris operating environment. The chapter discusses how the Solaris naming service infrastructure evolved into what it is today and why naming services are important.

Chapter 2, "Solaris Naming Services Architecture," explains how naming services are *plugged into* the Solaris operating environment and how Solaris clients interact with naming services. The Solaris Naming Service Switch is discussed in detail. An overview of NIS and NIS+ features is presented and contrasted with the Solaris 8 LDAP implementation.

Chapter 3, "Security Models," details the role naming services and directories play in authentication services. The Solaris Pluggable Authentication Module (PAM) infrastructure is discussed in detail to show how new authentication methods, such as LDAP binding, are integrated. When to deploy them and how the various authentication methods such as Public Key Infrastructure (PKI), Kerberos, and UNIX crypt work is discussed.

Chapter 4, "iPlanet Directory Server Installation and Configuration," describes how to install and configure the core components of the iPlanet Directory Server that ships with the Solaris 8 operating environment. Configuration tips that improve the directory performance and availability are included.

Chapter 5, "Solaris 8 Native LDAP Configuration," explains how to configure the iPlanet Directory Server to support the LDAP features in the Solaris 8 operating environment. A discussion of the directory schema extensions required to support Solaris 8 LDAP clients is presented.

Chapter 6, "NIS Extensions Configuration," describes how to configure the iPlanet Directory Server to support the NIS extensions and how to bulk-load NIS maps into the directory. How the iPlanet Directory Server running the extensions interacts with real NIS servers is explained.

Chapter 7, "Capacity Planning and Performance Tuning," presents heuristics, based on past deployments and benchmark results, for sizing a directory. Procedures for optimizing directory server performance are included.

Chapter 8, "Deploying Highly Available LDAP Data Services," describes when to cluster the iPlanet Directory Server and how to deploy Sun Cluster software running the Data Services for LDAP. Alternative methods, such as directory replication, to clustering are presented along with deployment scenarios.

Chapter 9, "Preventive Maintenance," explains how to perform routine directory maintenance such as pruning log files and backing up the directory database. How to examine the directory log files and spot potential problems is presented.

Chapter 10, "Managing Directory Services," discusses the use of the iPlanet Directory Server tools to perform routine directory management functions like setting access control policies, updating the directory schema, and monitoring the health of the directory server. SNMP management with the LDAP Management Information Base (MIB) and deployment of BMC PATROL to monitor the iPlanet Directory Server are explained.

Chapter 11, "Directory Services Consolidation," presents an overview of the iPlanet Meta-Directory Server and describes how it can be used to unify disparate data sources. Creating a single-sign-on environment with SiteMinder is also explained.

Chapter 12, "Microsoft Windows Interoperability," explains how the iPlanet Windows NT Synchronization services can be deployed to provide an unified login between Windows clients and the iPlanet Directory Server. Windows 2000 Active Directory Services is introduced, followed by a discussion of how it can interoperate with the Solaris 8 operating environment.

Appendix A, "Using Netscape Communicator as an LDAP Client" is a procedure for extending the LDAP features in Netscape Communicator so directory data can be viewed and searched.

Appendix B, "LDAP Standards Information" lists RFCs and other standards that define LDAP.

Appendix C, "Additional Information," lists sources of helpful information and LDAP related tools.

Appendix D, "LDAP v3 Result Codes" describes error messages that iDS generates.

Appendix E, "Schema Information" describes the LDAP object classes and attributes required to support native Solaris LDAP.

Glossary is a list of terms and acronyms used frequently in describing naming, directory, and authentication services.

Ordering Sun Documents

The SunDocs^{SM} program provides more than 250 manuals from Sun Microsystems, Inc. If you live in the United States, Canada, Europe, or Japan, you can purchase documentation sets or individual manuals through this program.

Accessing Sun Documentation Online

The `docs.sun.com` Web site enables you to access Sun technical documentation online. You can browse the `docs.sun.com` archive or search for a specific book title or subject. The URL is `http://docs.sun.com/`.

Typographic Conventions

The following table describes the typographic changes used in this book.

Typeface or Symbol	Meaning	Example
AaBbCc123	The names of commands, files, and directories; on-screen computer output	Edit your `.login` file. Use `ls -a` to list all files. `machine_name% You have mail.`
AaBbCc123	What you type, contrasted with on-screen computer output	`machine_name%` **su** `Password:`
AaBbCc123	Command-line placeholder: replace with a real name or value	To delete a file, type `rm` *filename*.
AaBbCc123	Book titles, new words or terms, or words to be emphasized	Read Chapter 6 in *User's Guide*. These are called *class* options. You *must* be root to do this.

Shell Prompts in Command Examples

The following table shows the default system prompt and superuser prompt for the C shell, Bourne shell, and Korn shell.

Shell	Prompt
C shell prompt	`machine_name%`
C shell superuser prompt	`machine_name#`
Bourne shell and Korn shell prompt	`$`
Bourne shell and Korn shell superuser prompt	`#`

## CHAPTER 1

Solaris Naming Services Overview

Naming services, like NIS and NIS+, have long been an integral part of the Solaris operating environment. Now, for the first time in over 10 years, Sun is introducing a new naming service into the Solaris operating environment to provide functionality equivalent to that of NIS and NIS+. Unlike its predecessors, the new LDAP naming service stores its data in a *directory* that is accessible from a standard network protocol. The directory not only stores operating system information, but it also makes an excellent repository for application data.

Just as TCP/IP and HTTP became the foundation of corporate intranets and extranets in the 90s, directory services based on the standard Lightweight Directory Access Protocol (LDAP) will be requirements in the next millennium. Although legacy Solaris directory services like NIS and NIS+ still play an important role in an organization, the emergence of LDAP as an industry standard creates opportunities for directory service consolidation and data sharing among applications.

Realizing that LDAP technology is new to many Sun customers, we present in this Sun BluePrint™ the information system administrators and system planners need to start exploring Solaris LDAP deployment possibilities. This introduction starts with a definition of what exactly a naming service is, followed by an overview of the familiar legacy Solaris naming services.

Definition of a Naming Service

In simple terms, a naming service provides a convenient way of looking up complex information by using user-friendly names. Although computers often required information to be stored in a structure containing numeric identifiers, computer users and application developers do not necessarily want to know the internal representation of the data. Instead, they like to see it in a more human-readable form.

A prime example of the benefits of a naming service is the translation of Internet protocol (IP) addresses to computer names. IP addresses are hard to remember and can frequently change as computers are moved from one subnet to another. By providing a mapping of names to IP addresses, the naming service ensures that users who reference a computer by its name will always be using the correct IP address. If IP addresses change, applications and scripts that reference the computer name are unaffected, since the naming service simply remaps the name to the new IP address.

The information maintained by a naming service can be stored in a simple data structure like a two-column table or in complex data records. The network protocol used to access the naming service varies. It can be proprietary or based on open standards. The security methods used to protect data maintained in a naming service can range from none—totally unprotected—to one requiring strong authentication. Finally, high availability features such as data replication can be a feature of the naming service and can be implemented in different ways.

The native Solaris LDAP naming service has characteristics that are quite different from previous naming services. The most distinguishing characteristic is how information is stored. Rather than storing data in simple tables, this new naming service stores data as *entries* within a *directory*. The entries are represented by complex objects that can be searched by specification of any item contained in the entry. Because of this characteristic, LDAP naming services are referred to as directory services.

Definition of a Directory Service

When you think of directories, the first thing that comes to mind are publications, such as the Yellow and White Pages, used to locate people and businesses. To find the phone number of a person, you search a directory by thumbing through the pages and following the alphabetical listing until you locate the person's surname. To locate a business, you search the alphabetical listing of business categories. Once the desired entry is found, you simply make note of the phone number adjacent to it.

Computer, or *online*, directory services work in a similar way. Instead of searching through a hard copy in the form of a phone book, you type in keywords or select menu items with the mouse. The results of your query are then displayed on the computer screen. In some cases, such as validation of a user's identity, the results of online directory searches are transparent to the user.

The main differences between traditional hard-copy directories and online directories are the complexity of searches and the dynamic nature of the information stored in the online directory. While a phone book may only be updated once a year, online directory services are updated constantly. Changes must be made readily available to users or else outdated or erroneous data might be referenced.

Another distinguishing feature of online directories is their flexibility. Unlike printed directories, the type of information contained in them can be easily extended. Additional data fields, such as a person's pager number, can be added without the need to republish the whole directory.

While it is intuitive how to use the information you retrieve from a phone book, the data in an online directory is often accessed by an application program and not by an actual person. An agreed-on set of rules on how to use the data must be established. These rules are referred to as the directory *schema* and are discussed in later chapters.

Directory Service versus Database Servers

A directory service sounds a lot like a relational database but there are some distinguishing characteristics of each. Although both are used for storing data that can later be retrieved by keyword searches, the most significant difference is the nature of the data. The data stored in a database is typically updated frequently but might only be searched periodically. For example, an accounts receivable database might be updated whenever a sale is made but is only searched once a day when daily sales reports are generated. This type of environment requires fast and efficient write speeds.

The type of data stored in directory services is usually the opposite. Data might be updated infrequently, for example, when new user accounts are added, but is searched often, for example, whenever someone logs in to an account. In some cases, the read-to-write ratio can be 1000 to 1 or greater. Therefore, directory services are optimized for read access and, in that area, perform much better than databases. Another feature of a directory service is the ease with which data can be distributed across multiple computers. While such distribution is feasible with databases, it is rarely deployed because of significant performance problems.

Proliferation of Directory Services

With the introduction of client-server applications in recent years came the requirement to store information about the users who access these products. For example, a messaging server must maintain a database of all email users and the location of their mailboxes. Likewise, a secure web-based application must maintain account information about its users.

As the number of users accessing network-based applications increased, the size of the data store required to support the products increased. Maintaining information in a flat file would not be efficient, so some form of directory service was required.

Since it couldn't be assumed that the underlying operating system would have a suitable directory service, middleware products each ship with their own directory service.

If a server was used to run multiple middleware products, then multiple directory servers had to be installed. In many cases, the same information was kept in these different directories, which in addition to being hard to manage, can result in data being out of sync. The introduction of standards-based directory servers helps to alleviate this problem.

Solaris Directory Services—Historical Perspective

To better understand the role naming services play in the Solaris operating environment today and evaluate the role they may play in the future, it is worthwhile to take a look at the evolution of Solaris naming services. We start with the Network Information Service (NIS) and work up to the native LDAP in the Solaris 8 operating environment.

Network Information Service

In 1985, Sun introduced NIS, which was one of the first widely deployed UNIX-based naming services. The main reason for creating NIS was to provide centralized administration of operating system data. Prior to NIS, each computer on a network had to maintain its own table of users and host information that was required when sharing resources with other computers in the network. The tables were kept in text files and had to be manually updated on every computer when new information was entered or updated. This situation created an administrative nightmare.

NIS stores information in maps that are accessible by all computers in the network through remote procedure calls (RPCs) rather than storing information in simple text files. The information in these maps is arranged in data pairs and referenced by RPC of the form `getXbyY`. For example, the `gethostbyname` call returns the IP address of a specified host.

NIS clients bind to an NIS server when they boot. Clients bind to a server either by sending a broadcast to locate the nearest NIS server or by binding to one of a number of servers contained in a list. If a particular NIS server is down, the client will attempt to bind to an alternative server.

NIS maps can reside on two types of servers: *master* or *slave*. An NIS map can only be updated on the NIS master server. The NIS slave servers contain read-only replicated NIS maps that are propagated to them by the master server. Maps are propagated in their entirety whenever any changes are made on the master.

NIS maps are generated from data contained in text files, which, by default, are the files found in /etc. For security reasons, it is recommended that the default location be changed. Multiple NIS maps are generated from a single file, which contains the same data, only in reverse order. This order is necessary because of the way data is structured in NIS maps, which is in the form of a key-value pair. For example, one NIS map uses the host name as a key to obtain an IP address, and a second NIS map is used as a key to obtain a host name from an IP address.

Although NIS resembles a directory service, it lacks many of the key features you have come to expect. The data structure used is primitive and not easily extensible. Access control features are limited, and the replication model is inefficient.

Even though the first implementation of NIS was developed 15 years ago, it is currently the most widely deployed Solaris naming service. A successor to NIS called NIS+, which corrected a number of flaws in the NIS architecture, was introduced some 10 years ago, but NIS remains the naming service of choice for most Sun customers.

NIS+

Sun recognized that the NIS architecture contained a number of deficiencies and proceeded to improve it with the creation of NIS+. The enhancements NIS+ provided included:

- Hierarchal name space
- Client authentication
- Flexible data structure

While these enhancements were significant, there was no easy way to convert all NIS servers to NIS+ servers. The architecture of NIS+ dictated a top-down approach that required cooperation between all the IT departments within a corporation. Also, the administration of NIS+ was far more complex because directory trees that could span multiple machines had to be maintained along with public keys for authentication. For these and other reasons, NIS+ was not widely adopted by the Sun customer base.

However, many of the concepts introduced in NIS+ are similar to those found in LDAP-based directory services. If you have been exposed to NIS+, then some of the features contained in the LDAP-based directory services are already familiar to you.

Domain Name System

The Domain Name System (DNS) was developed to address a problem similar to that addressed by NIS. However, the focus of DNS was primarily on resolving host names to IP addresses—an issue that became a major concern as the Internet grew in size. The NIS model was not suitable since it did not support a hierarchal namespace as is required to accommodate large numbers of IP addresses spanning multiple companies and organizations.

NIS also maintains information about operating system services and user account information, so it cannot be replaced with DNS. However, there is a certain amount of overlap because both services can be used to resolve host names to IP addresses. NIS servers are equipped with a DNS forwarding feature so the two naming services can coexist. If a host name cannot be resolved by the NIS server to which the NIS client is bound, then the request is passed on to a DNS server.

Since DNS is so entrenched in the Internet, it is unlikely that it will be replaced any time soon. The most likely scenario is that businesses will continue to maintain their IP addresses in DNS and use LDAP-based directory servers for other data. Although DNS continues to be enhanced, mostly in the area of automatic registration of IP addresses, there are no foreseeable plans to make it a general-purpose directory service.

Solaris Naming Service Switch

Since a number of naming services are available for the Solaris operating environment, Sun developed the concept of universal naming. This means that an application does not have to be aware of which naming service is actually running. Instead, the application talks to a naming API, which is naming service independent. The API consults the Solaris Naming Service Switch to determine which naming service to search and in which order to search.

Although the Solaris Naming Service Switch was developed as a tool to cope with the coexistence of multiple directory services present in the Solaris operating environment, it can also be used to provide client-side failover. For example, if the NIS directory service is unavailable, then local files located in /etc will be consulted instead. See Chapter 2, "Solaris Naming Services Architecture" for a more in-depth discussion on the Solaris Naming Service Switch.

LDAP Background

Since the focus of this Sun BluePrint is about deploying LDAP-based directory services in the Solaris operating environment, some background information on the history of LDAP and the goals it attempts to achieve is helpful.

Brief History of LDAP

Early naming services such as Sun's NIS and NIS+ were designed for a specific purpose, such as storing information about system resources and user accounts. As mentioned previously, access to the NIS and NIS+ directories by applications is accomplished through an API designed for that purpose. The API specifies a set of procedure calls that can be either local or remote. Although this method works well in a homogeneous Solaris operating environment, accessing these directories from other platforms requires that the Sun-specific RPC toolkit be ported to that platform.

Recognizing the need for a general-purpose directory service that could be used by applications running on multiple platforms to locate network objects, two standards bodies, CCITT and ISO, developed a specification for one. Rather than basing access to the directory service on RPCs, an industry-standard directory-access protocol was created. The first incarnation of that protocol was X.500.

Besides specifying an access protocol, the X.500 specification defined a rigid set of rules for defining object names so they could be easily located. While the concepts behind the X.500 specification were good, some of the implementation details were not. The X.500 specification dictated that the underlying protocols conform to the ISO protocol stack and not to TCP/IP. Also, the rigid rules set forth in the specification created potential bottlenecks and headaches for the implementors.

Realizing that X.500 was cumbersome to use and hard to implement, the standards bodies created a *lightweight* version of the specification, called LDAP. Since LDAP overcame most of the deficiencies of X.500, it was adopted as an emerging industry standard. iPlanet E-Commerce Solutions, a Sun-Netscape Alliance, produced the iPlanet Directory Server with Solaris extensions, and Microsoft has adopted LDAP in its Exchange server and Active Directory.

LDAP Goals and Specifications

The main goal of the LDAP specification is to provide interoperability between different vendor implementations while providing a great amount of flexibility in the type of information stored in the directory. The LDAP standard defines four models to use as a development guide.

- The LDAP *information* model defines the kind of data you can put into the directory.
- The LDAP *naming* model defines how you organize and refer to your directory.
- The LDAP *functional* model defines how you access and update the information in your directory.
- The LDAP *security* model defines how you protect information in the directory from unauthorized access.

Unlike NIS, which provided little security, LDAP requires that users be authenticated when they access the directory. This authentication takes place when the LDAP client *binds* to the LDAP server. The authorization can be performed by a simple name-password pair or a more sophisticated method by extending the LDAP security mechanism. Alternatively, anonymous authentication can be turned on to allow anyone to bind without supplying a name or password.

Although the LDAP specification defines how clients interact with LDAP servers, it does not specify how to build an LDAP server. One of the first implementations of an LDAP server was SLAPD, which was developed at the University of Michigan. The source code for SLAPD was put in the public domain and formed the basis for commercial LDAP servers such as Netscape Directory Server and Sun Directory Server. The examples used in this Sun BluePrint are based on the iPlanet Directory Server that runs in the Solaris operating environment and is a derivative of those two LDAP implementations.

Solaris LDAP Implementation

Most of the growth in deployments of LDAP servers to date has been to support LDAP-enabled applications that are usually deployed as a component of E-Commerce sites or corporate intranets. A typical example is an email application such as the iPlanet Messaging Server. Because these types of applications are tightly coupled to a directory server, they are usually shipped with one. The reason is that a vendor cannot assume that an LDAP server will be available on the target operating system. As mentioned earlier, this situation contributes to the proliferation of directory servers.

So, how does the Solaris operating environment address this issue? The Solaris 8 operating environment has been made LDAP *aware*. While the Solaris operating environment can still function without an LDAP directory server, the infrastructure is in place for applications to take advantage of whatever LDAP directory server is plugged in. This Sun BluePrint assumes that the LDAP server deployed is the iPlanet Directory Server, but that is an assumption, not a requirement. An LDAP tag has been added to the Solaris Naming Service Switch so applications running on Solaris clients can access the LDAP directory without modification.

Sun has also embraced LDAP as a strategic technology to replace some of the functions of legacy NIS and NIS+ naming services. It might not make sense to place all the data contained in NIS maps in an LDAP directory server, but user account information is certainly a natural fit.

Obviously, consolidating thousands of Sun user accounts from NIS/NIS+ to LDAP is not a simple task and requires a great deal of planning. You can choose among several approaches a way to move your user account data into an LDAP directory. Chapter 11, "Directory Services Consolidation" describes the most popular methods.

Factors to Consider When Deploying LDAP

You should consider a number of factors when planning to deploy Sun enterprise-wide directory servers. Choosing the right directory server software and hardware platform to run it on is one of the first steps. Once the directory server is installed, tune it for peak performance. To keep the directory server running smoothly, implement proper maintenance procedures. Another key factor is planning for the consolidation of legacy Solaris directory services with LDAP-based ones.

The Solaris 8 operating system provides an LDAP infrastructure that can accommodate a variety of directory servers. Since the iPlanet Directory Server is bundled with the Solaris 8 operating environment, it is an obvious choice. Extensions that allow synchronization with NIS servers are also available for the iPlanet Directory Server. However, there are other LDAP directory servers that work quite well with the Solaris 8 operating environment such as the Novell's eDirectory Server for Solaris.

One of the key factors to a successful deployment is sizing the server on which to run the directory server. As the size of the directory database is likely to grow, configuring a server with plenty of room for expansion is key. How to determine the optimum server is not always an easy task. A directory server is much like a database server; it needs to be properly tuned to deliver peak performance.

Knowing what parameters to fine tune and when will help prevent bottlenecks. See Chapter 7, "Capacity Planning and Performance Tuning" for guidelines to tuning.

Knowing how to keep the directory server properly maintained and how to spot trouble before it happens will keep the server running smoothly. Preventive maintenance and performance monitoring need to be performed on a regular basis. See Chapter 9, "Preventive Maintenance" for additional information.

Consolidation of legacy directory services will not take place overnight. In most cases, a phased approach is the best choice. Careful planning will enable this to be a zero-downtime migration. See Chapter 11, "Directory Services Consolidation" for guidelines to consolidation.

## CHAPTER 2

Solaris Naming Services Architecture

The Solaris operating environment provides a sophisticated infrastructure that supports a variety of naming services. The architecture on which it is based is extensible and able to accommodate new naming services without the need for a rewrite of important operating system utilities that access naming services. The Solaris 8 LDAP naming service plugs into this architecture and is thus accessible to system utilities that formerly had only NIS, NIS+, and DNS available.

Reading this chapter is not an absolute requirement for deployment, but if you become familiar with some of the architectural nuances, you can better understand the deployment strategies presented in later chapters. Each naming service has its own unique characteristics which may dictate how you deploy them. Although the focus of this BluePrint is LDAP, it is helpful to understand the feature set of legacy Solaris naming services to see how this new technology compares.

Evolution of Solaris Naming Services

The UNIX operating system was developed to operate in a timesharing environment where users access the server via physically attached ASCII terminals. Users typically accessed only one server, so information about user accounts, group memberships, and so on, only needed to be maintained on that server. Storing that information in a text file worked quite well.

The Berkeley version of UNIX introduced the notion of distributed computing built on top of the TCP/IP protocol. Computers running the UNIX operating system could now easily communicate with one another. However, for things to work smoothly, information about users and other systems in the network needed to be maintained on each server. Storing this data in text files meant that any time something changed, the text files on every server needed to be updated.

In 1985, Sun Microsystems produced NIS (Network Information Service), one of the first UNIX-based distributed naming service as a replacement for storing information in text files. The text files would be converted to binary maps that would only be stored on selected computers, called NIS servers, in the network. The other computers in the network would contact the NIS servers when they needed access to the information.

However, some text files still needed to be maintained for two reasons: 1) some data was required during the booting process before access to the network was established and 2) there had to be a way to log in if the computer was disconnected from the network. Moreover, some mechanism was required so that the operating system utilities could search both text files and NIS, since NIS could not completely replace the text files.

The introduction of NIS presented a new system administration model, by which information was administered from a central repository and not all administrators were granted permission to update it. Since some users still wanted to be able to manage local accounts and system information, they needed some way to do this without administering of NIS maps.

NIS and Files Coexistence

To solve the problem of providing a centrally administered naming service while maintaining some local control, Sun's first implementation of NIS searched the local files before the NIS naming service was consulted. A special character was inserted into the text files to tell the operating system when to start searching the NIS maps. Any line beginning with a "+" character was the signal to contact NIS. For example, the /etc/host file would look like this:

```
127.0.0.1 localhost
129.148.181.130 tiger
129.154.86.22 galaxy
+
```

In this example, the /etc/hosts file would be searched for the specified host. If the host specified is not tiger or galaxy, then the NIS host map is searched. If the host name does not appear in the NIS map either, an error is returned.

Note – The "+" character only has an effect when the Solaris 1 operating environment is running. It will have no effect if the Solaris 2 or later operating environment is running except when run in the Solaris 1 compatibility mode.

NIS and DNS Coexistence

About the same time that Sun introduced NIS, standards for a universal naming system were being defined in RFC 1034 and RFC 1035. Later, implementations of this specification called the Domain Naming System (DNS) began to appear, like the Solaris in.named program, which was derived from Berkeley Internet Name Demon (BIND), found in Berkeley UNIX. Although NIS worked well to store host names and IP addresses of computers within an organization, DNS could scale much better and gained industry-wide adoption.

Companies deploying NIS tended to store the host name and IP addresses of their Sun workstation and server networks in NIS maps, but used DNS to look up names of computers outside of the network. To enable the two naming services to interoperate, Sun added a DNS forwarding capability to the NIS server.

The way DNS forwarding works is that if a search is made in an NIS map that has this feature enabled, the search request is passed on to a DNS server for resolution if the host name is not found. To implement this idea, the hosts.byname and hosts.byaddr maps must have the YP_INTERDOMAIN key in them. Creation of this key requires a simple modification to the NIS Makefile.

The alternative to enabling DNS forwarding is to include DNS as an option in the nsswitch.conf file which is described in the next section. It is not advisable to use both schemes together because redundant searches are performed if the name cannot be resolved, that is DNS will be searched twice.

Solaris Naming Service Switch

With the release of the Solaris 2 operating system, Sun introduced a new naming service called NIS+ and an infrastructure for managing the coexistence of multiple naming services. With NIS and DNS already widely deployed, and NIS+ added to the mix, some mechanism for easy interoperability was required. The DNS forwarding mechanism and "+" notation used in NIS maps were not easily extensible to new naming services like NIS+.

To support the switch, Sun programmers developed a new Application Programming Interface (API) that system utilities and other applications could use instead of talking directly to the naming service. Programs written to this API do not need to know the implementation details of the naming service they are accessing. The switch also gives the system administrator the flexibility to choose which naming services are consulted and in which order.

Solaris Naming Service Switch Architecture

The main components that constitute the architecture are the Network Services libraries, the policy configuration file, and interfaces to the available naming services. A special tag identifies the location where the requested information is actually stored. As shown in FIGURE 2-1 the available tags are files, nis, nisplus, dns, compat (for passwd), with ldap added to the Solaris 8 operating environment.

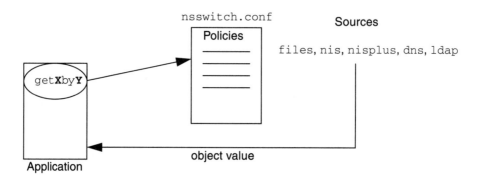

FIGURE 2-1   Naming Service Switch Functions

FIGURE 2-1 shows the flow of information when an application calls the Network Services libraries. These library calls are in the form of getXbyY, for example, gethostbyname(), and are independent of any naming service. When the application makes the call, the library routine consults the nsswitch.conf file to determine which naming services to consult. The specified naming services are then searched in order until a match is found or a NOTFOUND error is returned.

nsswitch.conf File

The policies that determine which naming service sources are searched and in what order reside in the /etc/nsswitch.conf file. Sample configuration files that favor a particular naming service are provided with the Solaris operating environment in the /etc directory. These files are copied and automatically used as the nsswitch.conf file when a primary naming service is chosen during the Solaris installation process.

An example of the configuration files that favor nis follows.

```
#
# /etc/nsswitch.nis:
#
# An example file that could be copied over to /etc/nsswitch.conf; it
# uses NIS (YP) in conjunction with files.
#
# "hosts:" and "services:" in this file are used only if the
# /etc/netconfig file has a "-" for nametoaddr_libs of "inet" transports.

# the following two lines obviate the "+" entry in /etc/passwd and /etc/
group.
passwd:      files nis
group:       files nis

# consult /etc "files" only if nis is down.
hosts:       nis [NOTFOUND=return] files
ipnodes:     files

networks:    nis [NOTFOUND=return] files
protocols:   nis [NOTFOUND=return] files
rpc:         nis [NOTFOUND=return] files
ethers:      nis [NOTFOUND=return] files
netmasks:    nis [NOTFOUND=return] files
bootparams:  nis [NOTFOUND=return] files
publickey:   nis [NOTFOUND=return] files

netgroup:    nis

automount:   files nis
aliases:     files nis
```

The objects for which search policies can be set appear on the left. The search order, or policy, appears to the right of the object. In the case of the passwd object, the local /etc/passwd file is checked first for the user's name, and if the name is found, the password is returned. If the user's name is not found in the /etc/passwd file, the nis passwd map is searched.

The tag NOTFOUND=return is used to direct the switch to look only in the naming services listed to the left unless these services are not operational. In the sample file, files would only be consulted if nis is not responding. This tag speeds up search times by eliminating unnecessary searches and at the same time provides a backup if the primary naming service is down.

NIS Architecture Overview

Even though the first implementation of NIS appeared almost 15 years ago, NIS is still the most widely used Solaris naming service, and the basic architecture has not changed. This section looks at how NIS clients interoperate and how information is stored and updated in NIS.

NIS Client Server Architecture

Deployment of NIS consists of one or more servers and clients that access the servers. Clients and servers communicate with each other by the Remote Procedure Call (RPC) mechanism. NIS client and server implementations are available on many different platforms and can interoperate with one another.

FIGURE 2-2 shows the major components of NIS.

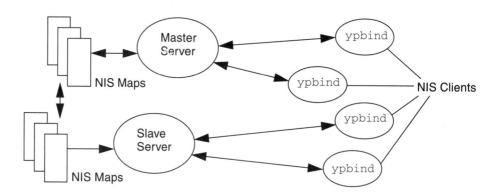

FIGURE 2-2   Major NIS Components

NIS uses a master-slave model by which all updates to NIS maps are performed on the master, then propagated to the slave servers. The propagation can be performed in either a push or pull manner, that is, either initiated by the master or by the client.

The map transfer protocol was not designed to accommodate large maps. Instead of only propagating incremental changes, entire maps are transferred. Careful planning of scheduling policies for map transfers is advisable to prevent overloading of a network during peak time.

How NIS Clients Bind to the NIS Server

A system running the Solaris operating environment typically becomes an NIS client at installation, although it could be configured as one later. A client is only required to supply two pieces of information: 1) the domain name it is joining and 2) how to locate the NIS server(s).

The domain name of the NIS client must exactly match the domain name of the NIS server to establish a connection. Unlike DNS domain names, NIS client names are case sensitive. A Solaris system can belong to both an NIS and a DNS domain. These domains could have the same or different names. The connection from client to server is referred to as *binding* which takes place at boot time. An NIS client can potentially bind to either an NIS master or an NIS slave server. There are two methods for locating a NIS server to bind to.

- Broadcast method — Send out a broadcast message and bind to the first server that responds.

- Specified Server method — Specify a server or list of servers to bind to.

The Broadcast method only works if there is an NIS server on the same subnet. The Specified Server method works regardless of where the NIS server resides. "NIS High Availability Architecture Features" on page 19, discusses the pros and cons of using each method.

NIS Maps

NIS uses a flat namespace where a series of maps reside. Each NIS domain contains its own set of maps. There is no relationship between maps or between NIS domains. The maps contain a pair of entries: the first is the keyword and the second is the value retrieved. TABLE 2-1 and TABLE 2-2 show examples of two different NIS maps.

TABLE 2-1   `hosts.byname`

Keyword	Value
tulip	192.9.200.1
geranium	192.9.200.2
sunflower	192.9.200.3
marigold	192.9.200.4

TABLE 2-2 `hosts.byaddr`

Keyword	Value
192.9.200.1	tulip
192.9.200.2	geranium
192.9.200.3	sunflower
192.9.200.4	marigold

In the preceding examples, the two maps contain the same information, but in different order. This ordering is necessary so a search can be performed both on a host name and an IP address. So that the two maps do not get out of sync, they are automatically created together whenever the map data is updated.

Creating NIS Maps

NIS maps are converted from text files to a binary dbm file by the `makedbm` command as shown in FIGURE 2-3.

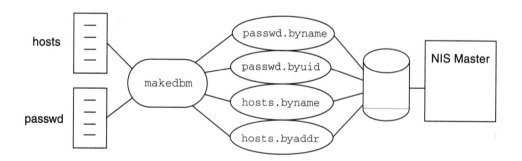

FIGURE 2-3 Creation of NIS Maps

In FIGURE 2-3 the source, or master, for the NIS maps is contained in text files shown on the left. The best practice is to create a copy of one of these files and only edit the copy. These files should be stored in a secure area and backed up frequently.

Once the source files have been created, the `makedbm` command is used to generate the new maps. To make things easier to administer a default, `Makefile`, is provided to perform the `makedbm` operation for the standard NIS maps.

Note – Updates to NIS maps are always performed on the NIS master server that owns the map.

Although it is possible to have NIS maps owned by different masters within a domain, joint ownership is not advisable. In this scenario, an NIS server could act as a master to some maps and as a slave to others. Keeping track of which server is master to which maps could be an administrative nightmare, so it is best to make one server master of all the maps.

NIS High Availability Architecture Features

The main high availability feature of NIS is master-slave data replication. All updates are performed on the master, then propagated to the slaves. If one of the NIS servers fails, an NIS client can bind to another one. However, if the master NIS fails, no updates can occur until it comes back online or another NIS master is created. This may seem like a severe restriction, but in practice the information stored in NIS maps is relatively static, so a few hours of downtime is usually acceptable.

How the NIS client handles the failover from one NIS server to another is determined by the method it uses to bind to its NIS server. FIGURE 2-4 and FIGURE 2-5 illustrate how NIS client failover is handled with both the Broadcast and Specified Server methods.

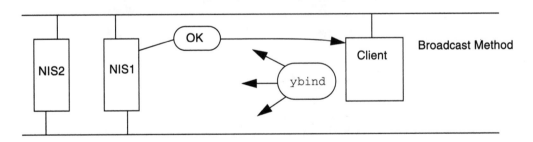

FIGURE 2-4   NIS Client Failover with the Broadcast Method

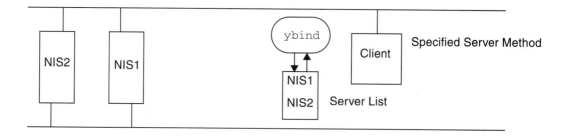

FIGURE 2-5   NIS Client Failover with the Specified Server Method

In the Broadcast method, the NIS client sends out a broadcast to locate an NIS server in the domain of which it is a member. The client then binds to the first server that responds to the broadcast. If the NIS server to which the NIS client binds to fails, then the next time an NIS look up is performed, the operation will time out and the client will issue another `ypbind` broadcast.

In the Specified Server method, the NIS client maintains a list of potential NIS servers. When the client boots, it attempts to bind to the first server in the list. If that server is unavailable, then the client attempts to bind to the next server in the list and so on. The downside of this method is that the time-out period can be lengthy, which gives the impression that the service is down.

A form of load balancing can be achieved with the Broadcast method since the least busy NIS server will respond to the clients `ypbind` request. The disadvantage is that multiple NIS servers must reside on each subnet.

NIS+ Architecture Overview

Sun introduced NIS+ as part of the Solaris 2 operating environment as a replacement for NIS. Several deficiencies in NIS were addressed in the NIS+ architecture. These included:

- Lack of hierarchal namespace
- Weak authentication
- No incremental updates between master and slaves

At the time NIS was developed, Sun's major business focus was the technical computing market. A typical network of Sun systems consisted of a couple of servers and maybe 20-30 workstations that were used by engineers working on the same design project. Verifying the authenticity of a NIS client was not an issue since networks were small and everyone knew who was attached to it.

Because not many companies were wired end to end, the number of names stored in NIS maps was limited and there was little interaction with groups in different locations. A flat namespace, where one NIS domain is not related to another, was sufficient, and since the number of NIS map entries was relatively small, propagating whole maps from master to slave servers was not a major problem.

However, as Sun moved into corporate data centers and companies began creating wide area networks (WANs), networks became larger and the need for a more scalable business-wide naming service became obvious.

NIS+ Client Server Architecture

The architecture of NIS+ is similar to that of NIS in that both naming services employ a master server, in which updates are made, and slave servers or replicas, in which a mirror of the data contained on the master is maintained. However, the similarity ends there.

NIS+ supports two types of masters:

- Root domain master
- Subdomain master

The root master, as the name suggests, acts as the top node in the hierarchal tree. Below the root masters are subdomain masters with other subdomain masters below them. At each level, replica servers can exist to provide redundancy for that section of the tree.

Note – An interesting feature of NIS+ is that the subdomain master is actually a client to the master above it, with the exception of the root master. The ramification of this is that NIS+ must be deployed in a top-down fashion since the domain above it must be configured before a subdomain master is configured.

Propagation of changes from master to replicas is different from NIS. Instead of pushing an entire map when changes are made, NIS+ propagates only the incremental changes. FIGURE 2-6 shows the NIS+ architecture.

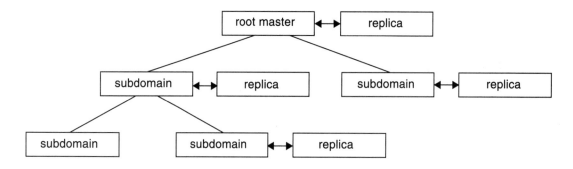

FIGURE 2-6 NIS+ Architecture

How NIS+ Clients Bind to the NIS+ Server

Unlike NIS, which does not authenticate its clients, NIS+ implements the notion of credentials. Two types of credentials exist in the NIS+ world:

- User credentials
- Workstation credentials

The process of creating credentials is quite complex and is beyond the scope of this book. Essentially, the process creates a private/public key pair and stores it in a secure area. During authentication only the public key is passed between the sender and the receiver. Data encrypted with one's private key can be decrypted with one's public key.

Unlike NIS client requests, NIS+ servers perform authentication to see who is sending the request, then authorize that user to perform specific types of access such as read, write, or modify. To gain access to the NIS+ tables, users must provide their credentials, that is in the form of `UID@domainname`. The exchange of credentials is protected by public and private key encryption. If the user is logged in as `root`, then additional credentials that identify the workstation must also be provided.

FIGURE 2-7 summarizes the NIS+ security process.

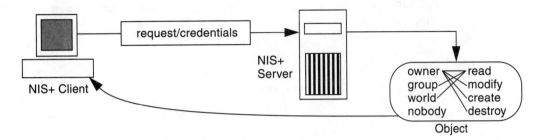

FIGURE 2-7 NIS+ Security Process

As shown in FIGURE 2-7, the following steps take place:

1. The client sends a request for access to the namespace along with its credentials.

2. The server authenticates the client's request by examining the sender's credentials.

3. The server examines the object's definition to determine access rights granted to the sender, or *principal*, as it is called.

4. The server then determines the class of principal: Owner, Group, World, or Nobody.

5. The server determines access rights granted to the principal's class.

6. If the access rights granted to the principal's class match the type of operation, the operation is performed.

NIS+ Tables

NIS+ stores information in tables that have a column-entry structure rather than the key-value structure of NIS maps. A client can access information not just by a key, but by any column that is searchable. This approach eliminates the need to create maps that have duplicate information.

The NIS+ tables in TABLE 2-3 come preconfigured and can be populated with the information shown.

TABLE 2-3 NIS+ Tables

Table Name	Information Contained
Hosts	Network address and host name of workstations in the domain
Bootparams	Location of the root, swap, and dump partition of diskless client in the domain
Passwd	User account information for or about every user in the domain
Cred	Credentials for principals who belong to the domain
Group	The group password, group ID, and members of every UNIX group in the domain
Netgroup	Netgroups to which workstations and users in the domain belong
Mail_Aliases	Information about the mail aliases of users in the domain
Timezone	Time zone of every workstation in the domain
Networks	Networks in the domain and their canonical names
Netmasks	Networks in the domain and their associated netmasks
Ethers	Ethernet address of every workstation in the domain
Services	Names of IP services used in the domain and their port numbers
Protocols	List of IP protocols used in the domain
RPC	RPC program numbers for RPC services available in the domain
Auto_Home	Location of all users' home directories in the domain
Auto_Master	Automounter map information

NIS+ Interaction with DNS

Unlike NIS, NIS+ has no automatic forwarding feature. To forward requests from NIS+ to DNS, the Naming Service Switch on the client must be configured to search DNS for hosts resolution.

Note – If an NIS+ server is run in NIS compatibility mode, the Naming Service Switch on the NIS+ server needs to be configured to search DNS.

NIS+ High Availability Architecture Features

The availability architecture for NIS+ is similar to that of NIS, but with the following key differences:

- Initialization of NIS+ clients
- Propagation of updates from master to replicas
- Format of mastered data

Unlike NIS clients, which do not require any authentication, NIS+ clients must present credentials to gain access to the service. These credentials are stored in the client's home domain. NIS+ can be initialized with one of three methods:

- Broadcast
- Specified Server
- Cold Start File

The Broadcast and Specified Server methods are similar to what NIS clients do. The Cold Start File method provides a file to a client that contains information about how to locate directory objects and also provides a set of credentials. This is the preferred method since it provides additional security. Only a trusted server can provide a Cold Start File.

Instead of pushing entire maps no matter how many changes are made, NIS+ masters only push out incremental changes. These changes are batched, then pushed out. The result is that the replicas are more likely to be in sync. Also, a transaction log keeps track of changes in case of a system failure before they can be pushed out.

Unlike NIS where the mastered data is kept in text files, NIS+ keeps mastered data in a binary format. This means that not only do these files need to be backed up, they also need to be checked periodically for corruption.

Solaris DNS Architecture Overview

The Domain Name System was created to solve the problem of locating computers on ARPANET, the forerunner of the Internet. As more and more systems were added, resolving hosts names to IP addresses by means of text files became unworkable. Large `hosts` files had to be maintained and propagated to every system in the network. Today, DNS is a requirement for access to the Internet.

DNS Client Architecture

Solaris system utilities that access DNS do so by using the resolver on the client. The resolver is actually a set of library routines that perform various types of queries. These queries get information about the location of the DNS servers by looking in the `/etc/resolv.conf` file. The following shows the format of this file:

```
domainname mydomain.com
nameserver IPaddr1
nameserver IPaddr2
nameserver IPaddr3
```

As you can see, more than one DNS server can be specified. In normal operation the resolver tries to contact the first server in the list. If contact cannot be established, the second server is tried, then the third. The current limit in the Solaris operating environment is three.

DNS Server Architecture

DNS supports a hierarchal namespace and replica or caching servers. The namespace is separated into zones that can have primary and secondary servers. Primary servers act as masters from which information is updated and then pushed out to the secondary servers.

The Berkeley Internet Name Domain (BIND) is the name server (`named`) that runs on a designated host in your organization. Since there are different features that are available in different versions, it is helpful to know what version you are running. TABLE 2-4 correlates the BIND version with the Solaris operating environment that it appears in.

TABLE 2-4   Solaris Versions of BIND

Solaris OE Version	BIND Version
SunOS 4.x	4.8.1
SunOS 2.0-2.5	4.8.3
SunOS 2.6	4.9.4-P1
SunOS 5.7	8.1.2
SunOS 5.8	8.1.2

DNS High Availability Features

DNS provides features for making itself more available and also features for making applications more available. Caching servers, which contain the same information and are synchronized, can be configured. Multiple IP addresses can be listed for a specific host name in a DNS record. Each time a request is made for that host, the next IP address in the list is handed out. This technique is often referred to as round robin; it is useful when a DNS client is provided with the address of an application server that is not operational because, with the round robin technique, the client will try again and get a different address.

DNS servers can be clustered to provide automatic failover of master servers, although this feature is not part of the architecture. With this technology, updates to DNS records can still be performed in case the master DNS server fails.

LDAP Architecture Overview

The Lightweight Directory Access Protocol (LDAP) is the newest addition to the list of Solaris naming services. Although included in the Solaris 8 release, it is an optional naming service that can coexist with legacy Solaris naming services. LDAP shares some characteristics with NIS and NIS+, but it is more sophisticated in the way data is structured and the methods used to access data.

LDAP's complex architecture is easier to explain if we divide it into the four models it supports and describe each model separately, as we do in the following sections. The four models are:

1. Information Model

2. Naming Model

3. Functional Model

4. Security Model

Each of these models are discussed in the following sections.

LDAP Information Model

The LDAP information model defines how entries in the directory are organized in the directory. Entries are arranged in a tree-like structure called the Directory Information Tree (DIT). At the top of the DIT is the directory root, which is identified by the server name and port number on which the directory service is running. Multiple instances of the directory service can be running on the same server with each instance having its own DIT.

Below the directory root is the directory suffix, of which there may be several per DIT. Suffixes can be expressed as an organization (o=) or as an Internet style domain component (dc=). The LDAP predecessor, X.500, dictated a specific format which included a country, locality, and organization. These names were registered to avoid duplication. Since LDAP does not enforce the same stringent naming rules as X.500 any organization name can be specified. The domain-based format typically mirrors a company's DNS domain address and is expressed as domain component (dc) entries. Since most companies have a registered DNS name which ensures uniqueness, this format essentially replaces the old X.500 style format.

FIGURE 2-8 is an example of a DIT:

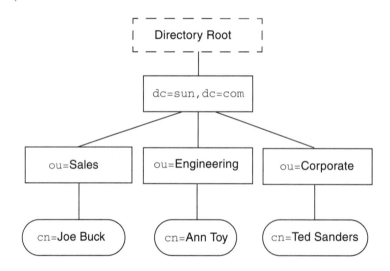

FIGURE 2-8   Sample Directory Information Tree

Located below the suffix are organization unit (ou) entries. These entries can nested, so an ou can contain other organization units. The name chosen for an ou only needs to be unique at the level at which it resides. You can use the same ou in a different portion of the DIT without creating a conflict. An ou entry called ou=People is created during the default iPlanet Directory Server installation; this entry is the default location for storing user account information, but any ou can be used for that purpose.

If you have multiple directory servers in a network, they can be linked by LDAP *referrals*. A referral is a mechanism that instructs an LDAP client searching the directory to continue the search on another directory server. The referral accomplishes this instruction by passing a uniform resource locator (URL) back to the client. Once the client receives the URL, it can access the specified directory server.

Overall, the topology of the directory resembles that of a Solaris file system. It is a hierarchal structure which has containers (ou entries) where directory entries reside. Referrals are similar to NFS mount points in concept, though implemented differently. Unlike the naming convention of a file system, that of an LDAP directory is quite different and the entries stored are much more complex than those in Solaris files.

LDAP Naming Model

Understanding the LDAP naming model is key to knowing how to configure and administer native Solaris LDAP. Most Solaris administrators are unfamiliar with this model and often are tripped up by some of the naming conventions. While the LDAP naming model may seem cryptic at first, keep in mind the goals of LDAP. It is designed to be flexible, but at the same time to provide a structure so that LDAP clients can access data in any LDAP-compliant directory.

Before a client can access data in a directory it must know how to locate that data. Unlike a Solaris file system where a search can always be initiated from the root file system (/), LDAP begins a search by specifying one specific entry, such as dc=blueprints, dc=com, as a search base. The entry name is specified as a distinguished name (DN) which is a series of relative distinguished names (RDNs). Each directory server contains a single root directory specific entry (DSE) which contains basic information about the LDAP server. The DSE is specified during base level searches on a directory when you do not know the name of a particular suffix.

As previously mentioned, each entry is identified by its DN. The DN is similar to a Solaris file system pathname, but is specified in the reverse order. However, for directory entries, unlike files, it is the value of their attributes which make each entry unique. To understand the role of attributes, a discussion on the structure of directory entries is useful.

Directory Objects and Attributes

The structure of a directory entry is defined by the object class to which it belongs. An object class defines a set of attributes that can be stored in a directory entry. LDAP object classes are extensible by creation of a new class that is a child of an existing one. All the attributes defined in the parent class are inherited by the child. The name of an object class must be unique within the directory server and can be registered as a standard LDAP object. These objects are assigned a numeric object identifier (OID) to ensure they will not conflict with another object class.

Attribute names are unique within the directory server and can be contained in more than one object class. The type of data that can be stored in an attribute is well-defined, as is the way LDAP searches treat the data. For example, data stored in a string can either be case sensitive or not. If the data is not case sensitive any combination of upper and lowercase characters in a string results in a match. If the data is case sensitive, an exact match is required. Attributes can also contain more than one value and can have aliases.

To promote interoperation, a set of standard LDAP object classes and attributes have been defined. Definitions of these ship with most LDAP servers in the form of *schema* configuration files. If they do not exist on a server, you can add the content of these schema files to your LDAP configuration files. For example, to use native LDAP, you need to add extra object classes and attributes to the iPlanet Directory Server configuration files, as discussed in Chapter 5, "Solaris 8 Native LDAP Configuration."

Directory Schema

The information specified in a directory schema includes the object class name, required and allowed attributes, an optional OID number, and the allowable syntax. TABLE 2-5 shows the schema definition for the `posixAccount` object class attributes that stores Solaris user account information.

TABLE 2-5   `posixAccount` Attributes

Attribute	Description	Syntax
cn(commonName)	Common Name of the POSIX account	cis (1-many)
gidNumber	Unique integer identifying group membership	int (single)
homePhone	The entry's home phone number	tel
uid(userID)	The user's login name	cis, 1
uidNumber	An integer uniquely identifying a user	int
description	A human-readable description of the object.	cis
gecos	GECOS comment field	cis
loginShell	Path to the login shell	ces (single)
userPassword	Entry's password and encryption method	bin, 1

In this example, cn is a case-insensitive string that can contain multiple values. The gidNumber and uidNumber are integers, and homePhone is represented by a special data type used for telephone numbers. Note that the LDAP uid, which is a string, is not the same as the numeric Solaris UID, which is represented by the LDAP attribute `uidNumber`. A complete description of all iPlanet Directory Server schema definitions can be found under documentation on the iPlanet Web site: `iplanet.com`.

Distinguished Names

Recall that a directory entry is identified by its DN, which is similar to a file system path name. However, entries are composed of many attributes, some of which are the same as other entries. To distinguish between entries that may have the same values for some attributes, one attribute is usually singled out as being unique. For user account entries defined in the `posixAccount` object class, that attribute is `uid`. To prevent duplicate values being used, the iPlanet Directory Server is configured by default to enforce `uid` attribute uniqueness. Entries that do not have a `uid` attribute are typically identified by the `commonName` (`cn`) attribute, which is available in most object classes, but is not required by all object classes such as organization (`o`) and organization unit (`ou`).

The form of a DN is:

attribute=value,container,suffix

where there may be multiple containers depending on the DIT topology. An example of a DN for an user account is:

`cn=Cathy Miller,ou=People,dc=blueprints,dc=com`

The RDN specifies the left-most portion of the DN, which uniquely identifies the entry relative to its parent. For example:

`cn=Cathy Miller`

In this case, `cn=Cathy Miller` has to be unique within the `ou=People` container.

LDAP Functional Model

Clients needing to access data on an LDAP server must begin by performing a bind operation. The bind operation requires, at a minimum, the DN of the user account entry the client wishes to bind as. If the entry has a password, then it is passed along with the DN. Alternatively, the client can perform an anonymous bind, which does not require a particular user name or password.

The type of authentication the directory server requires is specified as part of the bind request. The default is simple authentication, which compares the password sent with the password stored for the specified DN. Other authentication methods such as secure socket layer (SSL), CRAM-MD5, or Kerberos can be invoked instead by addition of another parameter to the bind operation call.

If the bind operation is successful, the client is considered authenticated. All subsequent client requests made on the connection established as a result of the bind are performed as the authenticated user. After the LDAP client requests are complete, an unbind operation is performed to release the connection. Chapter 5, "Solaris 8 Native LDAP Configuration" describes how the Solaris LDAP client binds to an LDAP server.

Note – If an LDAP bind operation is made with a DN, with no password, the bind is successful, but is considered an anonymous bind.

LDAP Security Model

Access to LDAP entries on the server is protected by the rights established for the authenticated user. The rights can be assigned at the container, object, or attribute level. A portion of the DIT can be assigned stricter (or looser) control than other parts of the DIT. All entries of the same object class type can be assigned the same control. Control can also be established at the attribute level to protect certain information. For example, an employee's password might have restricted access, while other information is available to everyone.

The mechanism used to assign access rights is called the access control instruction (ACI). A single ACI can protect the entire DIT, or several can be used to provide finer-grained protection. When multiple ACIs are created, the ACIs specifying deny access takes precedence. For example, if access is granted to everyone at the top level of the DIT but denied access to ou=Contractors, then the permissions set for ou=Contractors is enforced.

Note – ACIs are not defined in the LDAP v3 standard. Currently, each LDAP directory implementation has its own representation of ACIs.

Chapter 9, "Preventive Maintenance" discusses how ACIs are created and provides a more in-depth explanation of how they work. Establishing the correct ACI is critical to configuring the iPlanet Directory Server to support native Solaris LDAP, so Chapter 5, "Solaris 8 Native LDAP Configuration" provides examples. Note that the ACI syntax is not part of the LDAP specification, so the examples are specific to the iPlanet Directory Server implementation.

LDAP Replication

Replication is the mechanism by which directory data is automatically copied from one directory server to another. Using replication, you can copy anything from entire directory trees to individual directory entries between servers. Beside providing high data availability, some additional benefits include:

- Higher performance — By replicating directory entries to a location close to your users, you can vastly improve directory response times.
- Load balancing — By replicating your directory tree across multiple servers, you can reduce the access time load on any given machine, thereby improving server response time.
- Local data management — Replication allows you to own data locally and share it with other directory servers across your company.

To understand how replication works, you must first understand the roles LDAP servers play. To begin, every directory object must be mastered by one and *only* one directory server. The mastering directory server is called the *Supplier* server because it supplies the objects to other servers. Servers that receive directory objects from supplier servers are called *Consumer* servers.

Note – Any given directory server can be both a supplier of directory objects as well as a consumer of objects supplied to it from other servers. In future releases of iPlanet Directory Server, multi-master replication is supported which allows directory data to be updated by more than one server.

A Supplier server is responsible for the following:

- Managing any requests for changes to the replicated directory data. That is, whenever a request to add, delete, or change an entry in a replicated tree is received by a Consumer server, the request is referred to the Supplier server where the request is actually performed.
- Tracking the changes to the objects that it masters so that those changes can be replicated to Consumer servers.

You can configure the Supplier server to initiate replication, or you can configure your Consumer server(s) to initiate the replication process.

Consumer servers contain at least one directory entry that has been copied to it by a supplier server. Consumer servers can contain the following:

- The Supplier server's entire tree.
- A subsection, or subtree, of the Supplier server's directory tree.

Only read operations occur on the Consumer server. All other operations are handled on the Supplier server. Whenever an LDAP client tries to modify entries in a replicated tree, the Consumer server automatically refers the LDAP client's request to the supplying server.

FIGURE 2-9 and FIGURE 2-10 are examples of replication configurations:

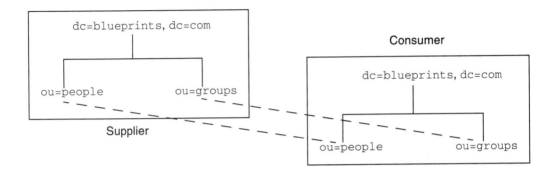

FIGURE 2-9 Full Tree Replication

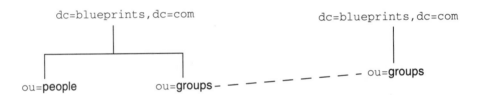

FIGURE 2-10 Subtree Replication

You choose which form of synchronization is used for each replication agreement. Replication synchronization can be initiated by either the Supplier or the Consumer server. A replication agreement indicates which directory entries will be replicated, which servers are participating in the replication, and when the replication can occur.

To decide on a synchronization method, follow these guidelines:

- If you want your consumer servers to be updated instantly, use Supplier-initiated replication.
- If you are using a dial-up connection to update your Consumer servers, use Consumer-initiated replication.

Comparison with Legacy Naming Services

Naming, or directory, services technology has evolved with the rise of network computing as the central concept of information technology. Host-based naming services, such as DNS, are widely deployed and have provided a key component of the network infrastructure in place today. Desktop LAN-based naming services like NIS have enjoyed much success in Solaris and UNIX environments but have not been widely accepted outside of these environments. Standards-based LDAP directories are starting to gain wide acceptance and look to be the backbone of corporate directory infrastructures in the future.

With so many Solaris naming services available, it is not always easy to keep the differences straight. To help you out, TABLE 2-6 summarizes the key features found in each of the naming services discussed in this chapter.

TABLE 2-6 Naming Service Feature Comparison

Naming Service	Hierarchal DIB	Dynamic Updates	Distributed DIB	Dynamic Replication	Extensible DIB
NIS					
NIS+	X	X	X	X	
DNS	X	X	X	X	
LDAP	X	X	X	X	X

Hierarchal Directory Information Base (DIB) — The ability to organize the name space in a layered, tree-like structure.

Dynamic Updates — The ability to add, modify, and delete information in the name space and have those changes be immediately visible to users of the service.

Distributed Directory Information Base (DIB) — The ability to service the namespace from multiple nodes on the network.

Dynamic Replication — The ability to dynamically propagate changes made to the DIB to other nodes that serve the DIB.

Extensible Directory Information Base — The ability to dynamically expand the type of information stored as part of the namespace.

## CHAPTER 3

Security Models

Computer resources can be protected by a variety of security methods. Some, methods, like firewalls, are designed to keep unwanted users out, and others are designed to verify the identity of anyone attempting to access a resource. The act of identity verification is commonly called *authentication*. The methods used to authenticate users vary, depending on the security model that you choose to implement.

Directories play an important role in the authentication process. The information, such as user credentials, required by an authentication service is usually stored in a directory. The directory service itself provides an authentication service that identifies users who attempt to access directory data. LDAP-enabled applications can take advantage of this authentication service to verify the identity of its clients by using the client's credentials to attempt directory service access.

This chapter begins by looking at traditional Solaris authentication and security models and at the role directories play. Since there is not a *one size fits all* authentication scheme, we discuss alternative authentication mechanisms including the Solaris and iPlanet Directory Server infrastructure designed to cope with multiple authentication methods.

Authentication versus Authorization

The terms authentication and authorization sound similar, but in the context of computer security each has a distinct meaning and has different implementation requirements. The security models discussed in this chapter deal primarily with authentication and not authorization, so it is important to understand the difference.

In general terms, authentication is the verification of someone's identity. This verification can be as simple as entry of a user name and password, or an alternative form can involve the use of digital certificates. In either case, the password or digital certificate needs to be stored in a secure manner. The format in which this information is stored and how it is retrieved without compromising security are the key distinguishing features of authentication methods.

Authorization is the granting of access to controlled system resources. In other words, once a user's identity is established, authorization grants only the access rights that the user is entitled to. The Solaris UFS file system uses octets of owner, group, and other permissions to determine whether the user can read, write, create, or delete files and folders. The user's identity is determined by the user ID (UID) and group ID (GID) of the login shell, which are established when the user is first authenticated.

The directory server controls access through access control instructions (ACIs) that are assigned to directory objects. The directory user identities are determined by the distinguished name (DN) they bind with. The act of binding is really an authentication process. As discussed in the following sections, LDAP users or clients can use several authentication methods to perform the binding.

Traditional Solaris Authentication

Traditional Solaris authentication is based on the method developed for early UNIX implementations. This method employs an one-way encryption hashing algorithm called *crypt(3)*. The encrypted password is stored either in a file or in a Solaris naming service, from which it is retrieved during the user login process. The traditional UNIX method of Solaris authentication, using crypt(3), is very popular and has been enhanced to use an LDAP directory as its data store.

Before we discuss authentication in more detail, you should understand what crypt(3) is. There is some confusion because of a naming conflict with an *application* named "crypt"; the latter is a standard tool that ships with Solaris and is a program for encrypting and decrypting the contents of a file, this program can be found in /usr/bin/crypt.

However, when the term "crypt" is referred to in authentication, it is normally cited as crypt(3) and refers to the standard UNIX password hashing algorithm "crypt(3)", as available to C-programmers in the libcrypt.a library.

A more sophisticated authentication method based on public key technology was introduced with the NIS+ naming service. This method does not replace crypt(3), but rather provides an additional security layer by introducing the concept of a network password. When users access network services through the secure RPC mechanism, the network password is required.

Realizing that new authentication models are likely to be developed, Sun created the pluggable authentication module (PAM) architecture which allows additional methods to be added without disturbing existing ones. The PAM architecture and alternatives to traditional Solaris authentication are presented starting in "Solaris PAM Framework" on page 52.

How UNIX Passwords Work

Passwords are created with the Solaris `passwd` command. The `passwd` command prompts the user for a (new) password, which the user enters as a text string. This text string is then *hashed*—or *one-way encrypted*—using the crypt(3) algorithm, and the result is stored either in `/etc/shadow`, or in the `passwd.byname` and `passwd.byuid` NIS maps. If you are using the NIS+ Naming Service, the results are stored in the `Passwd` and `Cred` table type. The crypt(3) algorithm is provided with a random seed, known technically as a "salt string," so that the result will be different each time the `passwd` command is run, even if the same text string is used.

When a user logs in, the Solaris `login` program challenges that user to provide a password. This password is hashed in the same manner as the `passwd` command. If the output from this process matches the output that is stored in the password database, the user is considered to have been authenticated.

FIGURE 3-1 Shows how the UNIX password process works.

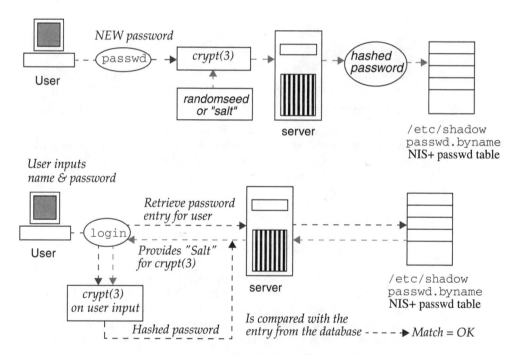

FIGURE 3-1 `Login` Program Text String Converting to a Hashed String

Benefits and Drawbacks of Crypt(3)

The major benefit of crypt(3) is that it is easy to implement in a closed environment. Authentication takes place on the system you are logging in to, so an authentication server is not required. Since clear-text passwords are never stored or sent over the network, you do not have to be concerned about eavesdroppers intercepting the password.

Since crypt(3) uses a one-way encryption algorithm, the passwords stored on the server cannot be decrypted. Only the user knows what the password actually is. This means that there is no way to convert passwords stored in crypt to another format required by a different authentication method.

NIS+ Credentials

The Solaris *crypt* method only checks to see if the text string the user types in matches the stored string for that particular login ID. There is no check to see if the user is logging in from a legitimate workstation or domain, since that information is not stored anywhere. NIS+ addresses this problem by issuing credentials to users.

Credentials were introduced in NIS+ as a means to identify legitimate users within a *domain* of workstations by maintaining more information than a simple user name. NIS+ establishes two sets of credentials: workstation and user.

The workstation credentials are created when a Solaris system becomes a member of an NIS+ domain. These credentials are then required when a workstation attempts to access the NIS+ directory service. In the NIS+ environment, users and machines are referred to as principals.

User credentials are created for users within a given NIS+ domain. These are in the form of unix.*userid@domainname* and stored in the NIS+ *cred* table. When users log into an NIS+ client workstation, the credentials are retrieved from the cred table. The cred table contains the user's *network* password and NIS+ uses this to check the password of the user. This cred table actually contains the public and private keys of the principals. The user's password is not stored in the cred table but the private key is encrypted by the user's secure RPC or network password. By default, the user's password and network password will be the same, so the user only needs to enter it once. In most cases, the two passwords are the same, but if they are not, the user will have to perform a *keylogin*, using the secure RPC password and then use chkey -p to make the two passwords the same.

The directory plays an important role in NIS+ authentication since credentials are based on public key technology. The public and private keys required are maintained in a directory so they can be universally accessed. For non-NIS+ clients requiring public key authentication, the key may be maintained in NIS maps.

Alternative Authentication Mechanisms

The Solaris crypt(3) and NIS+ credential mechanisms are fine for authenticating Solaris clients, but they are not the only methods used by applications and services running in the Solaris environment. In this section, alternative authentication methods are discussed. Some of these are available in the iPlanet Directory Server, others can be plugged into it through the extensible authentication mechanism called the Simple Authentication Security Layer (SASL). This facility is analogous to the Solaris PAM architecture. The presence of an authentication method in the directory server does not mean that method can be used for Solaris client authentication, and vice versa.

LDAP Authentication (Simple Authentication)

Before any form of authentication takes place in the LDAP directory you must first perform some form of authentication. This authentication enables the directory server to determine what level of access you have and what you can do in terms of operations in the directory server.

The most basic form of authentication is the simple authentication. Here you supply to the directory server the distinguished name (DN) and password; if you do not supply a password, that is, NULL password is supplied to the directory server you automatically obtain the credentials of the anonymous authenticated user.

Note – When you use simple authentication, you will be sending your password over the wire in clear text! To avoid this security breach choose an alternative mechanism such as SSL or SASL.

Authenticating to the directory as the anonymous user gives you only the most basic ability to perform operations. It is likely that you will enable users to make specific changes only to their own directory entry. If this is the case and you want to control what types of access your users have, then you should implement access control lists.

When access control lists are implemented, LDAP clients will authenticate to the directory server and be dependent on the access control instructions (ACIs) that have been set. The directory server will determine if that particular client is allowed to modify the directory—adding, modifying, or deleting entries.

When referring to ACIs in relation to entries, be aware that entries do not have to contain ACIs. The basic principle of an ACI is to grant or deny permissions to entries in the directory server. This works when the directory server processes the incoming requests from the LDAP client. The server then uses the ACIs for the particular entry to establish whether the LDAP client has the relevant permissions to perform the requested operation.

It is important to understand that at present, implementing access controls in LDAP is not yet covered by any form of standards document. What this lack of standardization leads to is proprietary access control mechanisms implemented by each LDAP software vendor. This situation is, of course, not desirable; having deployments of different LDAP servers from different vendors can be problematic. The good news is that the Internet Engineering Task Force (IETF) working group is developing a standard syntax for access control, and, in addition, a protocol for querying the access rights that are applicable to a particular directory entry is also being developed. The short-term downside is this: do not expect this functionality from any of the LDAP vendors.

CRAM-MD5

CRAM-MD5 is a SASL authentication mechanism described in the IETF Informational RFC 2195 (see Appendix B for additional information on RFCs). CRAM stands for Challenge Response Authentication Mechanism, it uses the Mechanism Digest 5 (MD5) hash algorithm developed by Ron Rivest for generating a message digest, which is used for authentication. The advantage of CRAM-MD5 is that a password is never sent in clear text to the server, as with a traditional crypt-based UNIX login, and this restraint prevents 'snoop attacks' while the password is being sent across the wire.

In this method of authentication, the server issues a challenge to the client in the form of an arbitrary string of random digits, a timestamp, and the fully qualified primary host name of the server. The client responds with the user name, a space, and an MD5 digest or hash of the challenge plus the password. The server then computes its own MD5 hash and compares the client response with its hash; if they match, the client is authenticated. If they do not match, an error is returned to the client. FIGURE 3-2 illustrates how this scheme works.

CLIENT   SERVER

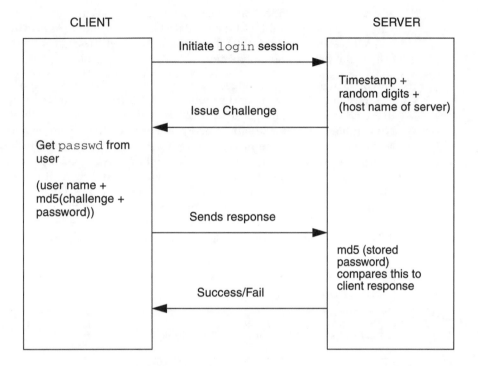

FIGURE 3-2 CRAM-MD5 Authentication

The disadvantage of CRAM-MD5 is that the password must be accessible to the server in a clear-text format. However, most servers store the password in some sort of encrypted format that can be retrieved when necessary.

In the case of LDAP, some servers support CRAM-MD5, which at one point was proposed as a required mechanism for LDAP v3 servers. CRAM-MD5 has since been replaced by DIGEST-MD5. Since the use of SASL is part of the LDAP v3 protocol, the LDAP v2 servers do not support CRAM-MD5. CRAM-MD5 authentication can be achieved by use of pam_ldap against a server that supports it.

MD5 is used in two areas of the Solaris operating environment today: the Kernel (TCP and IPsec) and the User (SLP and PPP). Ronald Rivest, who was at the time working at the Laboratory for Computer Science at the Massachusetts Institute of Technology, published MD5 as a RFC (RFC 1321) in April 1992. To better understand what CRAM-MD5 is, you should understand what MD5 is all about.

In your organization, when you send data over the wire, you will be concerned with three general issues: security, authenticity, and integrity. The security of your data ensures that no one else can read your data. This issue is important in many organizations that have information that can not be exposed to external sources. Authenticity guarantees knowledge of the originator of the data, in other words, where the data source is from. This issue is important in areas such as the legal world, where authentication issues (like digital signatures) are of great importance. Lastly, integrity guarantees that the data has not been tampered with in any way when it was transmitted, thus determining whether the data you received was the same data that was actually sent.

The MD5 algorithm guarantees the integrity of your data by taking a bit pattern of arbitrary but finite length and producing a 128-bit fingerprinter or message digest of that pattern. This pattern is always 128-bit, regardless of the length of the bit pattern. No two files produce the same fingerprint, and the fingerprint is not reversible. The MD5 algorithm is not complex and does not require large substitution tables. Security experts estimate that the difficulty of finding two bit patterns having the same digest is 2^{64} operations and the difficulty of finding a bit pattern having predetermined digest is 2^{128} operations. As mentioned earlier, it is not computationally possible to determine a file based on its fingerprint. This means that it is not possible for someone to figure out your data based on its MD5 fingerprint. Take a look at an example of the output produced by MD5 on the binary file /usr/bin/ls.

```
blueprints# md5 /usr/bin/ls
```

You should see output similar to the following:

```
4ec63a89e72c59c6dcf7d0d291f06134          /usr/bin/ls
```

What you see here is the fingerprint of /usr/bin/ls for example:

```
4ec63a89e72c59c6dcf7d0d291f06134
```

MD5 applied a mathematical algorithm to the binary ls and so produced the fingerprint. Now, what you see is that you will get the exact same fingerprint; if you do not, then you know that the binary has been altered in some way. Finally, since MD5 does not encrypt data, it is not restricted by any exportation laws, so you can distribute this tool freely anywhere in the world.

For the mathematical details of this process, refer to RFC 1321 (for detailed information on RFCs see Appendix B).

Note – Solaris 8 introduces libmd5, an implementation of MD5 (the same source that appears in /kernel/misc/{sparcv9/,}md5, or /platform/sun4u/ kernel/misc/{sparcv9/,}md5). It is tuned for UltraSPARC and exports the standard MD5 calls to a user program.

Kerberos

Kerberos is a network authentication protocol that provides strong authentication for client-server applications by means of secret-key cryptography. A free implementation of this protocol is available from the Massachusetts Institute of Technology (MIT).

The Internet is an insecure place. Many of the protocols used in the Internet do not provide security. Tools to "sniff" passwords on the network are in common use by systems crackers. Thus, applications that send an unencrypted password over the network are extremely vulnerable. Worse yet, other client-server applications rely on the client program to be "honest" about the identity of the user who is using it. Other applications rely on the client to restrict its activities to those for which it has permission, with no other enforcement by the server.

Some sites attempt to use firewalls to solve their network security problems. Unfortunately, firewalls assume that the bad guys are on the outside, which is often a faulty assumption. Most of the really damaging incidents of computer crime are carried out by insiders. Firewalls also have a significant disadvantage in that they restrict how your users can use the Internet. Firewalls are simply a less extreme example of the dictum that there is nothing more secure than a computer that is not connected to the network and that is turned off. In many places, these restrictions are simply unrealistic and unacceptable.

Kerberos was created at MIT as a solution to these network security problems. The Kerberos protocol uses strong cryptography so that a client can prove its identity to a server (and vice versa) across an insecure network connection. After a client and server have used Kerberos to prove their identity, they can also encrypt all of their communications to assure privacy and data integrity as they go about their business.

Kerberos is a solution to your network security problems. It provides the tools of authentication and strong cryptography over the network to help you secure your information systems across your entire company.

Kerberos as an Authentication Service

Kerberos is a distributed authentication service that allows a process (a client) running on behalf of a principal (a user) to prove its identity to a verifier (an application server, or just a server) without sending data across the network that might allow an attacker or the verifier to subsequently impersonate the principal. Kerberos optionally provides integrity and confidentiality for data sent between the client and server. Kerberos was developed in the mid-80s as part of MIT's Project Athena. As Kerberos spread to other environments, changes were needed to support new policies and patterns of use. To address these needs, design of Version 5 of Kerberos (V5) began in 1989. Though V4 still runs at many sites, V5 is considered to be standard Kerberos.

How Kerberos Works

The Kerberos Authentication System uses a series of encrypted messages to prove to a verifier that a client is running on behalf of a particular user. The Kerberos protocol is based in part on the Needham and Schroeder authentication protocol, but with changes to support the needs of the environment for which it was developed. Among these changes are the use of timestamps to reduce the number of messages needed for basic authentication, the addition of a "ticket-granting" service to support subsequent authentication without reentry of a principal's password, and a different approach to cross-realm authentication (authentication of a principal registered with a different authentication server than the verifier).

Kerberos Encryption

Though, conceptually, Kerberos authentication proves that a client is running on behalf of a particular user, a more precise statement is that the client has knowledge of an encryption key that is known by only the user and the authentication server. In Kerberos, the user's encryption key is derived from and should be referred to as a password; we will refer to it as such in this discussion. Similarly, each application server shares an encryption key with the authentication server; this key is referred to as the server key.

Encryption in the current version of Kerberos uses the data encryption standard (DES). It is a property of DES that if ciphertext (encrypted data) is decrypted with the same key used to encrypt it, the plaintext (original data) appears. If different encryption keys are used for encryption and decryption, or if the ciphertext is modified, the result will be unintelligible, and the checksum in the Kerberos message will not match the data. This combination of encryption and the checksum provides integrity and confidentiality for encrypted Kerberos messages.

Kerberos Ticket

The client and server do not initially share an encryption key. Whenever a client authenticates itself to a new verifier, it relies on the authentication server to generate a new encryption key and distribute it securely to both parties. This new encryption key is called a session key, and the Kerberos ticket distributes it to the verifier.

The Kerberos ticket is a certificate issued by an authentication server, encrypted by the server key. Among other information, the ticket contains the random session key that will be used for authentication of the principal to the verifier, the name of the principal to whom the session key was issued, and an expiration time after which the session key is no longer valid. The ticket is not sent directly to the verifier, but is instead sent to the client who forwards it to the verifier as part of the application request. Because the ticket is encrypted in the server key, known only by the authentication server and intended verifier, the client cannot modify the ticket without detection.

Basic Kerberos Authentication Protocol (Simplified)

Upon receipt of the application request, the verifier decrypts the ticket, extracts the session key, and uses the session key to decrypt the authenticator. If the same key was used to encrypt the authenticator as was used to decrypt it, the checksum will match and the verifier can assume the authenticator was generated by the principal named in the ticket and to whom the session key was issued. This is not by itself sufficient for authentication since an attacker can intercept an authenticator and replay it later to impersonate the user. For this reason, the verifier additionally checks the timestamp to make sure that the authenticator is fresh. If the timestamp is within a specified window (typically 5 minutes) centered around the current time on the verifier, and if the timestamp has not been seen on other requests within that window, the verifier accepts the request as authentic.

At this point the identity of the client has been verified by the server. For some applications, the client also wants to be sure of the server's identity. If such mutual authentication is required, the server generates an application response by extracting the client's time from the authenticator and returns it to the client together with other information, all encrypted with the session key.

Authentication Request and Response

The client requires a separate ticket and session key for each verifier with which it communicates. When a client wishes to create an association with a particular verifier, the client uses the authentication request and response messages to obtain a ticket and session key from the authentication server. In the request, the client sends the authentication server its claimed identity, the name of the verifier, a requested expiration time for the ticket, and a random number that will be used to match the authentication response with the request.

In its response, the authentication server returns:

- Session key
- Assigned expiration time
- Random number from the request
- Name of the verifier
- Other information from the ticket

and these are all encrypted with the user's password registered with the authentication server, together with a ticket containing similar information, that is forwarded to the verifier as part of the application request. Together, the authentication request and response and the application request and response constitute the basic Kerberos authentication protocol.

Additional Tickets

The basic Kerberos authentication protocol allows a client with knowledge of the user's password to obtain a ticket and session key and to prove its identity to any verifier registered with the authentication server. The user's password must be presented each time the user performs authentication with a new verifier. This procedure can be cumbersome; instead, a system should support single sign-on, whereby the user logs into the system once and provides the password at that time, and then subsequent authentication occurs automatically. The obvious way to support this scheme—caching the user's password on the workstation—is dangerous. Though a Kerberos ticket and the session key associated with it are valid for only a short time, the user's password can be used to obtain tickets, and to impersonate the user until the password is changed. The better approach used by Kerberos is to cache only tickets and encryption keys (collectively called credentials) that will work for a limited period of time.

When the user first logs in, an authentication request is issued and a ticket and session key for the ticket-granting service is returned by the authentication server. This ticket, called a ticket-granting ticket, has a relatively short life (typically, 8 hours). The response is decrypted, the ticket and session key saved, and the user's password forgotten.

Subsequently, when the user wishes to prove its identity to a new verifier, a new ticket is requested from the authentication server through the ticket-granting exchange. The ticket-granting exchange is identical to the authentication exchange with two exceptions: 1) the ticket-granting request has embedded within it an application request, authenticating the client to the authentication server, and 2) the ticket-granting response is encrypted with the session key from the ticket-granting ticket, rather than with the user's password.

The description of Kerberos just presented was greatly simplified. Additional fields are present in the ticket, authenticator, and messages to support bookkeeping and additional functionality. Some of the features present in Version 5 include renewable and forwardable tickets, support for higher-level authorization mechanisms, and support for multiple-hop cross-realm authentication.

Secure Socket Layer Authentication

Secure Socket Layer (SSL) authentication was developed by Netscape as a method for creating a secure connection between a web client and a web server. It can also be used to verify the identity of a client. This method of authentication is based on the issuance of signed digital certificates from trusted authorities. There are two types of certificates: server side and client side.

Server-Side Certificates

Server-side certificates are the most common type used with SSL. The client trusts the server, but the server will grant access to any client, such as a web browser that supports SSL. A typical example would be a credit card transaction over the Internet. Here's how it works.

1. The browser attaches to a secure port on a web server, usually done automatically, by following a link.

2. The server presents its signed digital certificate to the client.

3. The client deciphers the certificate to determine which third-party certificate authority issued it.

4. If the browser contains a list of trusted certificate authorities, it checks to see if the signed certificate is listed. If the browser does not contain such a list, then it displays a dialog box.

5. Once the certificate is accepted, a secret key is exchanged and used to encrypt the data during the remainder of the transaction.

Only server-side certificates are needed because the sharing of confidential information is in one direction *only*. The client sends its credit card information, but nothing the server sends back to the client is privileged information.

Client-Side Certificates

If the server contains confidential or privileged information, clients may be required to identify themselves before any information is transferred. The sequence of events for client-side certificates is this:

1. The server issues the client a certificate. In this situation, the server acts as the certificate authority.

2. The client stores the certificate in a secure location. The certificate contains a password the user must supply before the certificate can be used.

3. The client presents the certificate to the server when a connection is attempted.

4. The server examines the certificate to see if it is valid, then grants access to the client if it is.

The server might additionally check to see if the client certificate has been revoked. In this case, a list of certificates is kept in an LDAP directory and checked when a client attempts to establish a connection.

LDAP Over SSL

Creating a secure LDAP connection is accomplished through a client-side SSL. In normal operation, LDAP requests are made over an insecure connection with transmission performed in clear text. For public information, this may be acceptable, but clear-text transmissions of sensitive information are not.

To set up LDAP over SSL, you perform the following steps:

1. **Establish a Certificate Authority.**

2. **Configure a secure port for the LDAP server.**

3. **Issue the certificates to trusted clients.**

Detailed steps to set up a secure iPlanet Directory Server can be found in Chapter 4, "iPlanet Directory Server Installation and Configuration." Optionally, an LDAP directory could be set up to store information about issued certificates and make note if they are revoked.

Security Infrastructure

This section details the following security infrastructures:

- iPlanet Directory Server SASL
- Solaris PAM Framework
- PAM Module Types
- PAM Configuration File
- PAM LDAP Module

iPlanet Directory Server SASL

The Simple Authentication and Security Layer (SASL) is a proposed standard for pluggable authentication methods that will be used for adding authentication support to connection-based protocols such as LDAP. Of all the security mechanisms that are available for clear-text password authentication, the IETF's SASL framework is probably the best solution. With SASL, you negotiate between a client and a server from a list of multiple authentication schemes. SASL is beneficial as a modular security layer.

The default behavior of SASL specifies the clear-text authentication method, but most of the SASL implementations will use the CRAM-MD5 authentication mechanism. This mechanism uses a challenge-and-response protocol but can also be applied to multiple Internet protocols.

Note – The iPlanet Directory Server does not support CRAM-MD5 at this time; however, the Solaris 8 LDAP Client (Solaris native LDAP) allows the use of the CRAM-MD5 mechanism under SASL, which enables you to bind to the directory server without sending the password over the wire in clear text.

Currently, SASL is not a commonly known or supported protocol, but is the most likely candidate to succeed as the standard authentication layer among the Internet protocols.

You might find CRAM-MD5 SASL implementations in the Sun Directory Services product. These implementations are rare, but you will start to see that SASL will most likely support stronger authentications schemes because of such factors as the LDAP v3 protocol.

Using the SASL mechanism, you will find that the LDAP v3 protocol supports a command that will identify, then authenticate, a particular user to the directory server. This command works when you specify the name of the authentication mechanism that you are going to use, for example, CRAM-MD5. If this authentication is successful, then the client and server agree on a security layer, that provides the session protection. Currently, the iPlanet Directory Server supports the SASL mechanism that uses plug-in technology, so you can write your own plug-ins that use the SASL mechanism. If you want to write your own SASL mechanism, then you are required to register it with the Internet Assigned Numbers Authority (IANA). Some of the currently registered SASL mechanisms are KERBEROS_V4, GSSAPI, and CRAM-MD5.

To determine the SASL mechanisms that your LDAP v3 server supports (a requirement of LDAP v3 servers), issue the following command in the root DSE entry.

```
blueprints# ldapsearch -b "" -s base "objectclass=*"
supportedsaslmechanisms

dn:
supportedsaslmechanisms: EXTERNAL
blueprints#
```

Notice in the preceding response that the mechanism referred to as EXTERNAL, is used to determine that authentication has been agreed to by another source. This source could be, for example, Transport Layer Security (TLS) which is the new standard for SSL.

To obtain additional information about SASL refer to the RFC 2222 which you can find at the following Web site:
http://www.ietf.org/rfc/rfc8222.txt.

Solaris PAM Framework

The Pluggable Authentication Module (PAM) framework enables new authentication technologies to be "plugged-in" without the need to change commands such as login, ftp, and telnet. Use PAM to integrate UNIX login with other security mechanisms, such as Kerberos and LDAP authentication. Mechanisms for account, session, and password management can also be plugged-in through this framework.

PAM allows the system administrator to choose any combination of services to provide authentication. These include:

- Flexible configuration policy
  - Per application authentication policy
  - Choice of a default authentication mechanism for non-specified applications
  - Multiple passwords on high-security systems
- Ease of use for the end user
  - No retyping of passwords if they are the same
  - Password mapping, whereby a single password can be used, even if the password associated with separate authentication methods is different
  - Optional parameters passed to the services

PAM Module Types

PAM employs runtime-pluggable module types to provide authentication-related services. These modules are categorized into four types, based on the function they perform:

- Authentication
- Account management
- Session management
- Password management

The authentication modules provide authentication for the users and enables credentials to be set, refreshed, or destroyed. These modules also identify the user.

The account management modules check for password aging, account expiration, and access hour restrictions. Once the user is identified by the authentication modules, the account management modules determine whether the user can be given access.

The session management modules primarily manage the opening and closing of an authentication session. The modules can log activity, or clean up after the session is over.

The password management modules enable changes to the password and the password-related attributes.

PAM enables authentication by multiple methods through *stacking*. When a user is authenticated through PAM, multiple methods can be selected to fully identify the user. Depending on the configuration, the user can be prompted for passwords for each authentication method. This means the user need not execute another command to be fully authenticated. The order in which the methods are used is determined through the configuration file, /etc/pam.conf.

Stacking can require that a user remember several passwords. Password mapping, if supported by the underlying module, allows the primary password to be used to decrypt the other passwords, so the user does not need to remember multiple passwords. The other option is to synchronize the password across each authentication mechanism.

Note – Stacking may increase the security risk, because the security of each mechanism would be limited by the least secure password method used in the stack.

How PAM Works

The PAM software consists of a library, several modules, and a configuration file. The PAM library, /usr/lib/libpam, provides the framework to load the appropriate modules and manage stacking. It provides a generic structure for all of the modules to plug into.

FIGURE 3-3 illustrates the relationship between the applications, the library, and the modules. The applications ftp, telnet, and login use the PAM library to access the appropriate module. The pam.conf file defines which modules are to be used with each application. Responses from the modules are passed back through the library to the application.

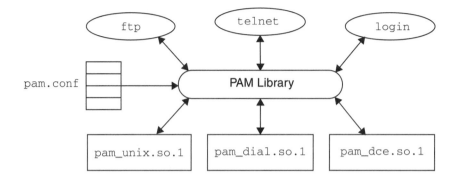

FIGURE 3-3 PAM and the Relationship Between Applications, Library, and Modules

PAM Modules

Each module provides the implementation of a specific mechanism. More than one module type (auth, account, session, or password) can be associated with each module, but each module needs to manage at least one module type. The following is a description of the modules.

- **pam_unix** — Supports authentication, account management, session management, and password management. The module uses UNIX passwords for authentication.
- **dial_auth** — Can only be used for authentication. The module uses data stored in the /etc/dialups and /etc/d_passwd files for authentication. It is mainly used by login.
- **rhosts_auth** — Can be used for authentication. The module uses data stored in the ~/.rhosts and /etc/host.equiv files and is mainly used by rlogin and rsh.
- **pam_dce** — Supports authentication, account management, and password management. Any of these three module type definitions are used with this module. The module uses DCE Registry for authentication.

For security, these files are required to be owned by root and to have their permissions set so that the files are *not* writable through group or other permissions. If the file is not owned by root, then PAM will not load the module.

PAM Configuration File

The PAM configuration file, /etc/pam.conf, determines what authentication services are used and in what order. Edit this file to select authentication mechanisms for each system-entry application.

Configuration File Syntax

The PAM configuration file consists of entries with the following syntax:

service_name module_type control_flag module_path module_options

where:

service_name is the name of the service (for example, ftp, login, telnet);

module_type is the module type for the service;

control_flag determines the continuation or failure semantics for the module;

module_path is the path to the library object that implements the service functionality;

module_options are the specific options passed to the service modules.

You can add comments to the pam.conf file by starting the line with a # (pound sign). Use white space to delimit the fields.

Note – An entry in the PAM configuration file is ignored if one of the following conditions exists: the line has fewer than four fields, an invalid value is given for *module_type* or *control_flag*, or the named module is not found.

TABLE 3-1 summarizes PAM configurations.

TABLE 3-1   PAM Configurations

Service Name	Daemon or Command	Module Type
dtlogin	/usr/dt/bin/dtlogin	auth, account, session
ftp	/usr/sbin/in.ftpd	auth, account, session
init	/usr/sbin/init	session
login	/usr/bin/login	auth, account, session
passwd	/usr/bin/passwd	password
rexd	/usr/sbin/rpc.rexd	auth
rlogin	/usr/sbin/in.rlogind	auth, account, session
rsh	/usr/sbin/in.rshd	auth, account, session
sac	/usr/lib/saf/sac	session
su	/usr/bin/su	auth, account, session

TABLE 3-1   PAM Configurations *(Continued)*

Service Name	Daemon or Command	Module Type
telnet	/usr/sbin/in.telnetd	auth, account, session
ttymon	/usr/lib/saf/ttymon	session
uucp	/usr/sbin/in.uucpd	auth, account, session

Control Flags

To determine continuation or failure behavior from a module during the authentication process, you must select one of four control flags for each entry. The control flags indicate how a successful or a failed attempt through each module is handled. Even though these flags apply to all module types, the following explanation assumes that the flags are being used for authentication modules. The control flags are as follows:

required — This module must return success in order for the overall result to be successful. If all of the modules are labeled as required, then authentication through all modules must succeed for the user to be authenticated. If some of the modules fail, then an error value from the first failed module is reported. If a failure occurs for a module flagged as required, all modules in the stack are still tried but failure is returned. If none of the modules are flagged as required, then at least one of the entries for that service must succeed for the user to be authenticated.

requisite — This module must return success for additional authentication to occur. If a failure occurs for a module flagged as requisite, an error is immediately returned to the application and no additional authentication is done. If the stack does not include prior modules labeled as required that failed, then the error from this module is returned. If an earlier module labeled as required has failed, the error message from the required module is returned.

optional — If this module fails, the overall result can be successful if another module in this stack returns success. The optional flag should be used when one success in the stack is enough for a user to be authenticated. This flag should only be used if it is not important for this particular mechanism to succeed. If your users need to have permission associated with a specific mechanism to get their work done, then you should not label it as optional.

sufficient — If this module is successful, skip the remaining modules in the stack, even if they are labeled as required. The sufficient flag indicates that one successful authentication will be enough for the user to be granted access.

Generic `pam.conf` File

The following is an example of a generic `pam.conf` file:

```
# PAM configuration
# Authentication management
#
login auth required /usr/lib/security/pam_unix.so.1
login auth required /usr/lib/security/pam_dial_auth.so.1
rlogin auth sufficient /usr/lib/security/pam_rhost_auth.so.1
rlogin auth required /usr/lib/security/pam_unix.so.1
dtlogin auth required /usr/lib/security/pam_unix.so.1
telnet auth required /usr/lib/security/pam_unix.so.1
su auth required /usr/lib/security/pam_unix.so.1
ftp auth required /usr/lib/security/pam_unix.so.1
uucp auth required /usr/lib/security/pam_unix.so.1
rsh auth required /usr/lib/security/pam_rhost_auth.so.1
OTHER auth required /usr/lib/security/pam_unix.so.1
#
# Account management
#
login account required /usr/lib/security/pam_unix.so.1
rlogin account required /usr/lib/security/pam_unix.so.1
dtlogin account required /usr/lib/security/pam_unix.so.1
telnet account required /usr/lib/security/pam_unix.so.1
ftp account required /usr/lib/security/pam_unix.so.1
OTHER account required /usr/lib/security/pam_unix.so.1
#
# Session management
#
login session required /usr/lib/security/pam_unix.so.1
rlogin session required /usr/lib/security/pam_unix.so.1
dtlogin session required /usr/lib/security/pam_unix.so.1
telnet session required /usr/lib/security/pam_unix.so.1
#
# Password management
#
passwd password required /usr/lib/security/pam_unix.so.1
OTHER password required /usr/lib/security/pam_unix.so.1
```

This generic `pam.conf` file specifies the following behavior:

1. When running `login`, authentication must succeed for both the `pam_unix` and the `pam_dial_auth` modules.

2. For `rlogin`, authentication through the `pam_unix` module must succeed if authentication through `pam_rhost_auth` fails.

3. The `sufficient` control flag indicates that for `rlogin` the successful authentication provided by the `pam_rhost_auth` module is sufficient; then, the next entry will be ignored.

4. Most of the other commands requiring authentication require successful authentication through the `pam_unix` module.

5. Authentication for `rsh` must succeed through the `pam_rhost_auth` module.

The OTHER service name allows a default to be set for any other commands requiring authentication that are not included in the file. The OTHER option makes it easier to administer the file, since many commands that use the same module can be covered by only one entry. Also, the OTHER service name, when used as a catchall, can ensure that each access is covered by one module. By convention, the OTHER entry is included at the bottom of the section for each module type. The rest of the entries in the file control account management, session management, and password management. With the use of the default service name, OTHER, the generic PAM configuration file is simplified as follows:

```
# PAM configuration
#
# Authentication management
#
login auth required /usr/lib/security/pam_unix.so.1
login auth required /usr/lib/scurty/pam_dial_auth.so.1
rlogin auth sufficient /usr/lib/security/pam_unix.so.1
rsh auth required /usr/lib/security/pam_rhost_auth.so.1
OTHER auth required /usr/lib/security/pam_unix.so.1
#
# Account management
#
OTHER account required /usr/lib/security/pam_unix.so.1
#
# Session management
#
OTHER session required /usr/lib/security/pam_unix.so.1
#
# Password management
#
OTHER password required /usr/lib/security/pam_unix.so.1
```

Normally, the entry for the `module_path` is *root-relative*. If the file name you enter for `module_path` does not begin with a slash (/), the path `/usr/lib/security/` is prepended to the file name. A full path name must be used for modules located in other directories. The values for the `module_options` can be found in the man pages for the module (for example, `pam_unix`(5)).

The `use_first_pass` and `try_first_pass` options, which are supported by the `pam_unix` module, lets users reuse the same password for authentication without retyping it.

If `login` specifies authentication through both `pam_local` and `pam_unix`, then the user is prompted to enter a password for each module. In situations where the passwords are the same, the `use_first_pass` module option prompts for only one password and uses that password to authenticate the user for both modules. If the passwords are different, the authentication fails. In general, this option should be used with an `optional` control flag, as shown below, to make sure that the user can still log in.

```
# Authentication management
#
login auth required /usr/lib/security/pam_unix.so.1
login auth optional /usr/lib/security/pam_local.so.1
use_first_pass
```

If the `try_first_pass module` option is used instead, the local module prompts for a second password if the passwords do not match or if an error is made. If both methods of authentication are necessary for users to gain access to all the tools they need, use of this option could cause some confusion for users since they could get access with only one type of authentication.

How to Add a PAM Module

1. Become superuser.

2. Determine the control flags and other options that should be used.

3. Copy the new module to `/usr/lib/security`.

4. Set the permissions so that the module file is owned by `root` and permissions are 555.

5. Edit the PAM configuration file, `/etc/pam.conf`, and add this module to the appropriate services.

Verification

It is essential to do some testing before the system is rebooted in case the configuration file is misconfigured. Run rlogin, su, and telnet before rebooting the system. If the service is a daemon spawned only once when the system is booted, it may be necessary to reboot the system before you can verify that the module has been added.

How to Prevent Unauthorized Access with PAM from Remote Systems

Remove the rlogin auth rhosts_auth.so.1 entry from the PAM configuration file. This action prevents someone from reading the ~/.rhosts files during a rlogin session and therefore prevents unauthenticated access to the local system from remote systems. All rlogin access requires a password, regardless of the presence or contents of any ~/.rhosts or /etc/hosts.equiv files.

Note – To prevent other unauthenticated access to the ~/.rhosts files, remember to disable the rsh service. The best way to disable a service is to remove the service entry from /etc/inetd.conf. Changing the PAM configuration file does not prevent the service from being started.

How to Initiate PAM Error Reporting

1. Edit the /etc/syslog.conf to add any of the following PAM error reporting entries:

   auth.alert – Messages about conditions that should be fixed immediately

   auth.crit – Critical messages

   auth.err – Error messages

   auth.info – Informational messages

   auth.debug – Debugging messages

2. Restart the syslog daemon or send a SIGHUP signal to it to activate the PAM error reporting.

Example: Initiating PAM Error Reporting

The example below displays all alert messages on the console. Critical messages are mailed to `root`. Informational and debug messages are added to the `/var/log/pamlog` file.

```
auth.alert /dev/console
auth.crit 'root'
auth.info;auth.debug /var/log/pamlog
```

Each line in the log contains a timestamp, the name of the system that generated the message, and the message itself. The `pamlog` file is capable of logging a large amount of information.

PAM LDAP Module

The PAM LDAP module (`pam_ldap`) was introduced in Solaris 8 for use in conjunction with `pam_unix` for authentication and password management with an LDAP server. This module was written to support stronger authentication methods such as CRAM-MD5, in addition to the UNIX authentication provided by `pam_unix`. Use the PAM LDAP module in Solaris native LDAP clients only. At the present time, `pam_ldap` provides support only for the authentication and password management. Support for account management is expected to be provided in the future.

The `pam_ldap` module should be stacked directly below the `pam_unix` module in the `/etc/pam.conf` configuration file. If there are other modules that are designed to be stacked in this manner, they could be stacked *under* the `pam_ldap` module. This design must be followed in order for authentication and password management to work when `pam_ldap` is used. A sample `/etc/pam.conf` with `pam_ldap` stacked under `pam_unix` follows:

```
# Authentication management for login service is stacked.
# If pam_unix succeeds, pam_ldap is not invoked.
login    auth sufficient /usr/lib/security/pam_unix.so.1
login    auth required /usr/lib/security/pam_ldap.so.1
try_first_pass
# Password management
other    password sufficient /usr/lib/security/pam_unix.so.1
other    password required /usr/lib/security/pam_ldap.so.1
```

It is important to note that the control flag for pam_unix is sufficient. This flag means that if authentication through pam_unix succeeds, then pam_ldap is not invoked. Also, other service types, such as dtlogin, su, telnet, etc. can substitute for login. See FIGURE 3-4.

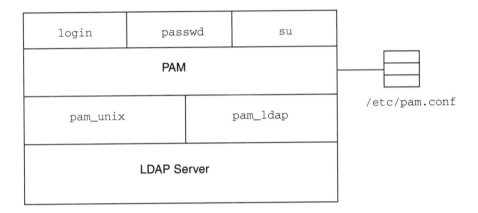

FIGURE 3-4 pam_ldap Structure

The options supported by the pam_ldap are described here:

- debug
  If this option is used with pam_ldap, then debugging information is output to the syslog(3C) files.

- nowarn
  This option turns off warning messages.

- use_first_pass
  For authentication, this option compares the password in the password database with the password entered when the user authenticated to the first auth module in the stack. If these do not match (or no password was entered), pam_ldap quits and does not prompt the user for a password.

  In the case of password management, the use_first_pass option compares the password in the password database with the user's old password entered to the first module in the stack. If these do not match (or no password was entered), then pam_ldap quits and does not prompt the user for the old password. It also attempts to use the new password entered to the first module in the stack as the new password for this module. If this attempt also fails, pam_ldap quits and does not prompt the user for a new password.

- try_first_pass
  This option does the same thing as the use_first_option in comparing the password in the database with the password entered to the first module in the stack. But unlike the use_first_pass option, it prompts the user for a password if the passwords do not match.

For password management, `try_first_pass` compares the password in the database with the old password entered to the first module in the stack; if they do not match, the user is prompted for the old password. `try_first_pass` also attempts to use the new password entered to the previous module; if that fails, `try_first_pass` prompts the user for a new password.

If the `/var/ldap/ldap_client_cache` file (which contains a list of LDAP servers, their transport addresses, and the authentication mechanisms used to access them) contains multiple authentication mechanisms specified for the `NS_LDAP_AUTH` parameter, then `pam_ldap` first attempts to authenticate with the first mechanism; if this fails, then `pam_ldap` goes to the next one and so forth until it succeeds or runs out of mechanisms.

How PAM and LDAP Work

The authentication mechanism currently used in Solaris native LDAP is SIMPLE authentication. SIMPLE authentication requires the client to pass a distinguished name (DN) and password to the server in clear text. Currently, the iPlanet Directory Server 4.12 does not support authentication mechanisms, such as CRAM-MD5, which sends only the digest over the wire. The matrixes explain when the clear-text password is sent across the wire.

TABLE 3-2 lists abbreviations we use in this discussion.

TABLE 3-2   PAM Abbreviations

Abbreviation	Description
UP	User password
PP	Proxy agent password
NP	New password
*	Not applicable (at least not yet)

The matrixes are easier to understand when you distinguish between how the password is stored and how the authentication mechanism is used to authenticate to the LDAP server. The password can be stored in a variety of formats, such as SHA, crypt, clear text, etc. The authentication mechanisms are SIMPLE or CRAM-MD5 (future authentication types includes DIGEST, etc.).

pam_unix Authentication

In authentication with `pam_unix`, the client retrieves the password that is stored in the server by making a call to the `getspnam` function. This function binds to the LDAP server with the proxy agent account (which is why the proxy `passwd` is sent across the wire in clear text). It is also worth mentioning that the ACIs of the proxy agent allow this account to have read access to all user passwords, which is how this account can retrieve a user's password. The encrypted password is retrieved to the client side and is compared with the crypted password supplied by the user at the password prompt. If there is a match, `pam_unix` returns success (see TABLE 3-3).

For updating passwords in `pam_unix`, the same comparison as for authentication takes place (since the user has to bind as the dn); then, the new password is passed over the wire in clear text (see TABLE 3-4).

TABLE 3-3   PAM Authentication

Authentication Mechanisms	pam_unix		pam_ldap	
SIMPLE	UP-No	PP-Yes	UP-Yes	PP-Yes
CRAM-MD5	UP-*	PP-No	UP-No	UP-No

TABLE 3-4   PAM Update of Password

Authentication Mechanisms	pam_unix		pam_ldap	
SIMPLE	UP-Yes(NP)	PP-*	UP-Yes	PP-*
CRAM MD5	UP-*	PP-*	UP-No	PP-*

pam_ldap Authentication

In authentication that uses `pam_ldap`, the user password is passed to the server in an `Auth` structure in clear-text, since you are only trying to authenticate with the user dn and password. If you are using SIMPLE authentication and the password matches, then success is returned. At present, using `pam_ldap` does not serve much purpose since `pam_unix` is sufficient for basic LDAP authentication. The reason is twofold; first, `pam_ldap` is required for stronger authentication mechanisms such as CRAM-MD5; and second, `pam_ldap` was designed to be extended for future authentication mechanisms and newer mechanisms to be supported in future releases. For additional information, see the `pam_ldap` man page (if you are using `pam_ldap`) for the correct way to stack in `/etc/pam.conf`.

When the CRAM-MD5 authentication mechanism is used, a digest is created and sent across the wire to authenticate to the server. The server compares the sent digest with the digest created by itself with the stored password and returns success if it matches. In this mechanism, the password is *not* sent in clear-text.

When passwords are updated in `pam_ldap`, the new password is sent across in clear-text (see TABLE 3-4).

iPlanet Directory Server Installation and Configuration

As part of the Solaris 8 media kit, Sun ships the iPlanet Directory Server software on one of the Bonus Software CDs. Since this software is not part of the Solaris installation mechanism, it needs to be installed separately after the operating system is installed.

Even though the iPlanet Directory Server can be installed on Solaris releases prior to version 8, the software is only licensed to run with the Solaris 8 operating environment. Therefore, this chapter assumes a Solaris 8 installation, even though the installation procedure is similar when installing software on earlier Solaris releases.

Copackaged with the iPlanet Directory Server is an administration framework with a GUI-based management tool that you can use to configure the server and perform routine administration functions. Although you can administer the iPlanet Directory Server without this set of tools, you will appreciate having the tools if you are an inexperienced LDAP administrator, so we discuss their installation.

Once you complete the initial installation, you must perform a number of postinstallation procedures. This chapter presents the most common of these procedures.

Product Architecture

Before starting the iPlanet Directory Server installation, you should understand the product's architecture so that the installation options will be more meaningful. Besides the Directory Server, two other components are available for installation. These are:

- Administration Server Console
- Netscape (iPlanet) Console

The Administration Server Console is actually a daemon, called ns-admin, that runs on the same system as the Directory Server Console and acts as a controller. It can also be the control point for servers other than the directory server, but this chapter focuses only on its use with the directory server.

The Netscape Console connects to the administration server when it starts. Once connected, the Console GUI is used to issue commands to the directory server, for example, stopping and starting the server.

Note – The iPlanet Directory Server is derived from the Netscape Directory Server, so many references to Netscape exist in the software and product documentation. For the purposes of this chapter, think of Netscape Directory Server and iPlanet Directory Server as interchangeable terms.

Administration Domains

One of the installation options is the creation of or the joining of an administrative domain. An administration domain allows a common login to work across several servers. If this is the only server you are setting up or if you do not wish to manage several servers as a group, then a domain of one is established. The procedures in this chapter assume that a new administration domain is being established.

Configuration Data

Configuration data for both the administration server and directory server is maintained in the directory database under the o=NetscapeRoot suffix, which is automatically created during the installation process. Information about administration domains and preferences used by the administration server is kept here. An interesting feature is that critical configuration data for the administration server, such as the admin login account, is kept in the directory database. This means that the directory server must be running before the administration server starts. During the installation, the directory server is already running when the administration server is started, so this requirement is not an issue. However, the directory server is not automatically started when the system is rebooted unless a startup script is added manually. A script to generate a custom startup script is included in "Postinstallation Procedures" on page 83, which starts the directory and the administration servers in the correct order. A sample startup script is also included in the Solaris Extensions package.

FIGURE 4-1 shows the layout of the NetscapeRoot portion of the directory tree as viewed from the Directory Server Console.

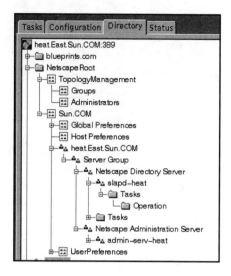

FIGURE 4-1 Layout of the `NetscapeRoot` Portion of the Directory Tree

Login Accounts

Two accounts are created during the installation: `admin` and `Directory Manager`.
The `admin` account is the account generally used to log into the Netscape Console.
This account can do most of the configuration and administration functions required
to maintain the directory server. The `Directory Manager` account is akin to the
superuser in the Solaris environment and can perform special functions such as
establishing directory-wide access control policies. Functions that require
`Directory Manager` authority are noted throughout this chapter, otherwise assume
the `admin` login.

Netscape Console

The Netscape Console is a Java application invoked with the `startconsole`
command. FIGURE 4-2 shows how the components interact.

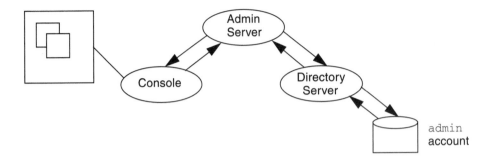

FIGURE 4-2 Diagram of Component Interactions

As you can see in FIGURE 4-2, both the administration server and the directory server need to be running for the Netscape Console to work. This is why there are several questions regarding the administration server and the choice of the directory server that will store the configuration data.

Planning the Installation

Before beginning the installation, have at hand the following information:

- **Installation directory** — This is where the installation files are placed. The actual directory server software is installed in the target directory. The installation directory should have approximately 100 Mbytes of free space.

- **Path name to target directory** — This is where the iPlanet Directory Server software will be initially installed. About 100 Mbytes should be available here. After the installation, we recommend that you move the directory database to a separate partition before you load your data, so the disk space consumed here should not get larger. The operation for relocating the directory database is discussed in "Postinstallation Procedures" on page 83.

- **Directory suffix** — This is the top node of the directory tree. You can use any name, but it is customary to name this the same as the DNS name of the system (which is the default). During the typical installation, two empty containers, ou=People and ou=Administrators, are created under this suffix. If you change your mind about the suffix, you can easily add a new suffix after the installation and remove the one specified during installation. The procedure for adding a new suffix is explained in Chapter 9, "Preventive Maintenance."

- Directory Manager **and** admin **account passwords** — Two separate accounts are set up during the installation, each requiring a password. The admin password can be any length, but the Directory Manager password must be at least 8 characters. Both of these can be easily changed.

- **Host name of server** — This can be the host name, without the trailing `domain` name, but the fully qualified DNS name is recommended. You must be able to `ping` the host name specified here from other systems in the network.

- **Administration domain name** — This can be any name and is only meaningful if you are setting up multiple servers and want one administrator to administer all of them. The default here is the trailing part of the DNS domain name, for example, `sun.com`.

- **Directory Server port number** — The default LDAP port number is 389. Unless the multiple directory servers are run on the same system, or you want to change the port number for security reasons, the default is recommended.

- **Administration server port number** — During the installation, a random unused port number is chosen as the default. To make this port number easier to remember, you can choose a number like 20000.

- **User to run the Directory Server as** — For security reasons, the default here is `nobody`. However, if you plan to run the NIS Extensions, the Directory Server must have `root` privileges. The user can be changed later, but the ownership of several files that are created during installation will also have to be changed. For example, if you initially install the server as `root`, then change it to `nobody`, the permissions on any writable files must be changed to grant `nobody` write permission. Changing the owner from `nobody` to `root` is not an issue, since `root` always has write permission on all files.

Disk Storage Partitioning/Layout

The directory database can grow to be quite large, and for performance reasons it should reside on its own file system. During the installation, the database is created in the file system specified for installation, for example, the default is `/usr/netscape`. After the installation, the database should be relocated to another partition. Guidelines for sizing the directory database are contained in Chapter 7, "Capacity Planning and Performance Tuning."

Installation Procedure

The iPlanet Directory Server can be found on the `www.iplanet.com` Web site and is packaged as a single `tar` file called:

```
directory-4.12-export-us.sparc-sun-solaris2.6.tar
```

Note – This software can also be found on the Solaris 8 Bonus Software CD in an extracted format, so the following step can be omitted. However, the older 4.11 is contained on the CD instead of the maintenance release 4.12 (available on the Web site). The same installation procedures apply to 4.12. Also, the reference of Solaris 2.5.1 is misleading since both the Solaris 2.6 and Solaris 8 operating environments are supported.

---

1. **Place this file into the installation directory.**

   This directory should not be in the same place as the target directory. To extract the installation files, run the `tar` command:

   ```
   # tar xf directory-4.12-export-us.sparc-sun-solaris2.6.tar
   # ls -l
   -rwxr-xr-x   1 root     other         1589 May 23  1999 LICENSE.txt
   -rwxr-xr-x   1 root     other          470 May 23  1999 README.txt
   drwxr-xr-x   2 root     other          512 Sep 19  1999 admin
   drwxr-xr-x   2 root     other          512 Sep 19  1999 base
   -rw-r--r--   1 root     other     44912640 Mar 22 10:40 directory-
   4.12-export-us.sparc-sun-solaris2.5.1.tar
   -rwxr-xr-x   1 root     other      1399904 Apr 15  1999 setup
   -rw-r--r--   1 root     other         1213 Sep 19  1999 setup.inf
   -rwxr-xr-x   1 root     other         5295 Apr 15  1999 silent.inf
   drwxr-xr-x   2 root     other          512 Sep 19  1999 slapd
   drwxr-xr-x   2 root     other          512 Sep 19  1999 svrcore
   ```

2. From the installation directory, run the setup **command:**

```
# ./setup

                    Netscape Communications Corp.
             Netscape Server Products Installation/Uninstallation
------------------------------------------------------------------

Welcome to the Netscape Server Products installation program.
This program will install Netscape Server products and the
Netscape Console on your computer.

It is recommended that you have "root" privilege to install the
software.

Tips for using the installation program:
  - Press "Enter" to choose the default and go to the next screen
  - Type "Control-B" to go back to the previous screen
  - Type "Control-C" to cancel the installation program
  - You can enter multiple items using commas to separate them.
    For example: 1, 2, 3


Would you like to continue with installation? [Yes]:
```

3. Choose the items to install:

```
Select the items you would like to install:

1. Netscape Servers
   Installs Netscape Servers with the integrated Netscape Console
   onto your computer.

2. Netscape Console
   Installs Netscape Console as a stand-alone Java application on
   your computer.

To accept the default shown in brackets, press the Enter key.

Select the component you want to install [1]:
```

In most cases, choose 1. Since the Netscape Console is X-windows-based, it can run on any graphical display, so it does not need to be loaded separately on another system.

4. Choose an installation type:

```
Choose an installation type:

   1. Express installation
        Allows you to quickly install the servers using the most
        common options and pre-defined defaults. Useful for quick
        evaluation of the products.

   2. Typical installation
        Allows you to specify common defaults and options.

   3. Custom installation
        Allows you to specify more advanced options. This is
        recommended for experienced server administrators only.

To accept the default shown in brackets, press the Enter key.

Choose an installation type [2]: 2
```

For most installations, the second option is recommended. The difference between the three options is the number of questions asked. The Typical installation uses a subset of the questions asked in the Custom installation and the Express installation uses a subset of the Typical installation questions. The next section shows all of the installation defaults and identifies what questions each type of installation asks. Default values are used where the installation script does not prompt you to enter an option.

Note – The same files are installed for each of the installation types. The only difference is which configuration parameters get set; all can be changed later.

Performing a Typical Installation

The following text shows the dialog for the Typical installation option. The system prompt is shown in **boldface** with comments and recommendations below the prompt.

Install location [/usr/netscape/server4]: /opt/netscape

Comment: This is where the directory server programs and database will be placed. Allow about 100 Mbytes for the installation. You probably do not want to install the directory under /usr, which is typically reserved for Solaris programs and libraries, so specify another directory. If the specified directory does not exist, it will be created.

Netscape Server Products components:

1. Netscape Server Products Core Components (3)

2. Netscape Directory Suite (2)

3. Administration Services (2)

Specify the components you wish to install [All]:

Comment: Selecting **All** is recommended. If you decide not to run the Administration Services, you can disable them later.

Netscape Server Products Core Components:

1. Netscape Server Products Core Components

2. Netscape Core Java classes

3. Java Runtime Environment

Specify the components you wish to install [1, 2, 3]:

Comment: Selecting the default will assure you have the correct Java environment to run the Netscape Console.

Netscape Directory Suite components:

1. Netscape Directory Server

2. Netscape Directory Server Console

Specify the components you wish to install [1, 2]:

Comment: This option enables installation of the Directory Server Console without the need to install the directory server. It assumes you are setting up the admin server on a separate server. The additional overhead of running the admin and directory servers on the same system is negligible. Unless you have some good reason for separating the two, choose the default.

Administration Services components:

1. Netscape Administration Server

2. Administration Server Console

Specify the components you wish to install [1, 2]:

Comment: Again, unless you do not want to run the administration server on the same server, choose the default.

Computer name [blueprints.sun.com]:

Comment: This is the fully qualified name of the server. It should equate to the host name + DNS domain name. The name has to be resolvable to this host or the directory server will generate a "no such host" error when it is started by the installation script.

Caution – The installation script finds the system's domain name by executing the `domainname` command, which returns your NIS domain name. If your NIS domain name is different from your DNS domain name, the wrong domain will appear as the default. If this is the case, you should change the NIS domain name to match the DNS fully qualified name.

System User [nobody]:

System Group [nobody]:

Comment: The directory server process, `ns-slapd`, runs as this user and group. The specified user and group must already exist, so choosing `nobody` is convenient because `user` and `group` are created automatically during the Solaris operating environment installation. Running this process as a non-superuser is recommended for security reasons, but not mandatory. If you plan to run the NIS extensions on this system, you must run the directory server as user `root` and group `other`. If you want to change the user and group after the installation, see "Changing the `ns-slapd` Process Owner" on page 87.

Do you want to register this software with an existing

Netscape configuration directory server? [No]:

Comment: The iPlanet Directory Server stores configuration data about itself in the directory under `o=NetscapeRoot`. If you have multiple directory servers, you could store all configuration data in one place, however this choice creates another point of failure. By accepting the default, you ensure that the data will be maintained by the directory server you are installing, as is recommended in most cases.

Do you want to use another directory to store your data? [No]:

Comment: This question relates to the previous question. An example of the data that could be stored on another directory server is the `admin` user account information. If you have multiple administration servers, maintaining all their account data on one directory server may simplify administration, but doing so introduces another point of failure. Again, in most cases accept the default.

Directory server network port [389]:

Comment: The default port for an LDAP server is 389. You can change this port assignment, but LDAP clients will have to be aware of what the port number is. If an LDAP server is already running on this port, the default will appear as a random number instead of 389.

Caution – If you are reinstalling the iPlanet Directory Server, an instance of `ns-slapd` may already be running. In this case, the installation script will not display port 389 as the default and will not accept that port number. Also, if you are not running the installation script as `root`, you will not be allowed to make a port assignment below 1024.

Directory server identifier [blueprints]:

Comment: This identifier distinguishes between multiple instances of the directory server running on the same system. A separate subdirectory, called `slapd`-*identifier*, is created for each instance. In most cases, only a single instance of the directory server will be running, so accepting the default (host name) is quite acceptable.

administrator ID [admin]:

Password:

Comment: These are the account and password used to log into the administration server. The account is maintained under the `o=NetscapeRoot` suffix instead of where other user accounts are stored. Additional `admin` accounts can be set up after the software is installed. The passwords can be any length and can be easily changed.

Note – This is only a directory account and not a Solaris account. It will not appear in `/etc/passwd`, NIS+, or NIS.

Suffix [o=sun.com]:

Comment: The default here is to use the DNS domain name as the directory suffix, but it could be any string. It simply acts as an identifier for a top node in the directory information tree (DIT), for example: `o=sun.com`. You can add suffixes later.

Directory Manager DN [cn=Directory Manager]:

Password:

Comment: The Directory Manager is a special account that has authority similar to that of `root` in the Solaris operating environment. It has higher authority than does the `admin` account and must be used to perform certain operations such as setting directory-wide access control policies. The password must contain at least 8 characters and can be easily changed later.

Administration Domain [sun.com]:

Comment: Every administration server belongs to an administration domain. The domain can consist of a single server, in which case the name is insignificant. If multiple administration servers are grouped for more flexible administration control, then all those servers would belong to the same domain. The DNS domain name is used as the default, but any string can be entered here.

Administration port [24087]:

Comment: The installation script chooses a random port to start the administration server. You may want to change this to a port number that is easier to remember, such as **20000**. If you forget this number you can look at the `startconsole` script to which the number is written during the installation.

Run Administration Server as [root]:

Comment: Although not required, running the administration server as `root` virtually eliminates potential access problems. This user can be changed after the software is installed.

Installation Defaults

The following shows the complete list of installation questions asked during the Custom installation along with defaults. Questions asked during the Express installation are shown in *bold italic* type with **bold** type used to denote the Typical installation option.

Install location [/usr/netscape/server4]:

Netscape Server Products components:

1. Netscape Server Products Core Components (3)

2. Netscape Directory Suite (2)

3. Administration Services (2)

Specify the components you wish to install [All]:

Netscape Server Products Core Components components:

1. Netscape Server Products Core Components

2. Netscape Core Java classes

3. Java Runtime Environment

Specify the components you wish to install [1, 2, 3]:

Netscape Directory Suite components:

1. Netscape Directory Server

2. Netscape Directory Server Console

Specify the components you wish to install [1, 2]:

Administration Services components:

1. Netscape Administration Server

2. Administration Server Console

Specify the components you wish to install [1, 2]:

Computer name [blueprints.east.sun.com]:

System User [nobody]:

System Group [nobody]:

Do you want to register this software with an existing

Netscape configuration directory server? [No]:

Do you want to use another directory to store your data? [No]:

Directory server network port [389]:

Directory server identifier [blueprints]:

administrator ID [admin]:

Password:

Suffix [o=sun.com]:

Directory Manager DN [cn=Directory Manager]:

Password:

Administration Domain [sun.com]:

Do you want to configure this directory server

to use replication? [No]:

Do you want to install the sample entries? [No]:

You may wish to populate your new directory instance with some data.

Type the full path and filename, the word suggest, or the word none

[suggest]:

Do you want to disable schema checking? [No]:

Administration port [24087]:

IP address:

Server Administrator ID [admin]:

Password:

Run Administration Server Console as [root]:

Differences between the Installations

As you can see from the listing, only a few additional questions are asked during the Custom installation. Most of them concern the initial population of the directory database and replication setup. Both of these operations can be performed after the software is installed.

Starting the Netscape Console

Once the installation is complete, you start the **Netscape Console** by executing the startconsole command. If the server where the software was installed does not have a monitor, you can X-display it on a remote system as shown in the following example.

```
blueprints# setenv DISPLAY mysys:0
blueprints# cd install_dir
blueprints# ./startconsole&
```

After the command executes, the following login screen is displayed. You can then enter the admin password to bring up the **Netscape Console**; see FIGURE 4-3.

FIGURE 4-3 Netscape Console

Note – The Administration URL, which is displayed, assumes your NIS and DNS domain names are the same. If they are not, you will have to edit this box, since the NIS domain name is displayed instead of the DNS domain name.

Verifying the Installation

The first indication of a successful installation is that the **Netscape Console** is started without errors. From the main Console you should be able to summon the Directory Server Console; click the **Directory Server** icon under **Server Group**. A separate window is then displayed, from which you can view the directory content. The installation can also be verified from the command line as follows.

```
blueprints# cd install_dir/shared/bin
blueprints# ./ldapsearch -b "" -s base "objectclass=*"
dn:
objectclass: top
namingcontexts: dc=blueprints,dc=sun,dc=com
namingcontexts: o=NetscapeRoot
subschemasubentry: cn=schema
supportedldapversion: 2
supportedldapversion: 3
changelog: cn=changelog
firstchangenumber: 1
lastchangenumber: 110
dataversion: blueprints.sun.com:389 020000314150203
netscapemdsuffix: cn=ldap://:389,dc=blueprints,dc=sun,dc=com
blueprints#
```

If either of these methods fail, try restarting both the administration and the directory server as explained in the next section.

Restarting the Administration and Directory Servers

If the **Netscape Console** fails to start properly, try to restart both the administration and directory servers by executing the commands shown below.

```
blueprints# cd install_dir/slapd-instance
blueprints# ./restart-slapd
blueprints# cd install_dir
blueprints# ./restart-admin
blueprints# ps -e | grep ns-
  2429 ?          0:02 ns-slapd
  2434 ?          0:00 ns-admin
blueprints# ./startconsole&
```

If the servers do not restart properly refer to "Installation Troubleshooting Tips" on page 92.

Installation File Navigation

Before explaining how configuration options are set, we look at the location of the important files. FIGURE 4-4 shows the layout diagram starting at the target installation directory.

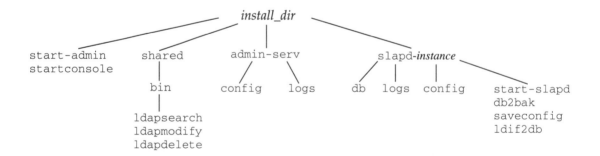

FIGURE 4-4 Layout Diagram

Commands like start-admin and startconsole, which do not pertain to a particular directory instance, appear directly under the installation directory. Most of the configuration files that we discuss in the next section reside under the slapd-instance subdirectory. In most cases, you will have only one instance of the directory server running on a server, so this will be the primary directory for performing configuration changes.

Postinstallation Procedures

The following postinstallation procedures have to be considered:

- Saving the configuration
- Changing the DB files location
- Changing the transaction log location
- Changing the DB backing files location

▼ Saving the Configuration

After a successful installation, one of the first tasks you should perform is a backup of the directory configuration data stored in the directory database. This data resides under the o=NetscapeRoot container.

It is wise to back up this portion of the DIT because if it is accidently deleted, the **Netscape Console** will not function. To perform this backup, run the saveconfig script as described below.

```
blueprints# cd install_dir/slapd-instance
blueprints# ./stop-slapd
blueprints# ./saveconfig
```

See Chapter 9, "Preventive Maintenance" for information of how to restore the configuration and for other maintenance procedures.

▼ Changing the DB Files Location

The directory database and associated index files are stored in the *install_dir*/slapd-*instance* directory by default. Since this is where all your directory data will be kept, you will want to move it to its own volume for better performance. See Chapter 7, "Capacity Planning and Performance Tuning" on what type of volumes are best.

To relocate the database files, perform the following steps.

```
blueprints# cd install_dir/slapd-instance
blueprints# ./stop-slapd
blueprints# cd config
blueprints# cp slapd.ldbm.conf slapd.ldbm.conf.bak
blueprints# vi slapd.ldbm.conf
...
suffix   "dc=blueprints, dc=com"
suffix   "o=NetscapeRoot"
directory        "/db_fs/db" <--- add this line
cachesize        100000
dbcachesize      125000000
...
blueprints# mkdir /db_fs/db
blueprints# cp db/*.db2 /db_fs/db
blueprints# chown -R nobody /db_fs/db
blueprints# chgrp -R nobody /db_fs/db
blueprints# ./start-slapd
```

Note – The above procedure assumes the target volume is mounted on the file system /db_fs and the directory server is running as nobody. The subdirectory db should be empty before you copy the *.log files there.

▼ Changing the Transaction Log Location

Every operation performed on the directory is recorded in a transaction log, so the directory can be rolled back to a known good state in the event of a server crash. Data is being continuously written to the log, even during search operations. Therefore, it is important for performance reasons to locate this log on a separate volume. Chapter 7, "Capacity Planning and Performance Tuning" provides additional details on the performance hit caused by leaving the transaction log on the same volume as the database files.

The following procedure explains how to move the transaction log.

```
blueprints# cd install_dir/slapd-instance
blueprints# ./stop-slapd
blueprints# cd config
blueprints# cp slapd.ldbm.conf slapd.ldbm.conf.bak
blueprints# vi slapd.ldbm.conf
...
suffix   "dc=blueprints, dc=com"
suffix   "o=NetscapeRoot"
directory         "/db_fs/db"
db_logdirectory          "/log_fs/logs" <--- add this line
cachesize       100000
dbcachesize     125000000
...
blueprints# mkdir -p /log_fs/logs
blueprints# chown nobody /log_fs/logs
blueprints# chgrp nobody /log_fs/logs
blueprints# ./start-slapd
```

Note – The above procedure assumes the target volume is mounted on the file system /log_fs and the directory server is running as nobody.

▼ Changing the DB Backing Files Location

If your system is experiencing excessive paging, you can improve performance by moving __db_lock.share, __db_mpool.share, and __db_txn.share to a tmpfs file system. If the amount of free memory is exhausted on a heavily loaded system, the Solaris operating environment will flush pages from memory. To increase performance, the directory database cache will flush the pages to the *.share files. If this paging condition occurs, performance will suffer because of the increased writes to disk. To eliminate this bottleneck, move the *.share files to a tmpfs file system shown in the following example.

```
blueprints# cd install_dir/slapd-instance
blueprints# ./stop-slapd
blueprints# cd config
blueprints# cp slapd.ldbm.conf slapd.ldbm.conf.bak
blueprints# vi slapd.ldbm.conf
...
suffix    "dc=blueprints, dc=com"
suffix    "o=NetscapeRoot"
directory          "/db_fs/db"
db_logdirectory            "/log_fs/logs"
db_home_directory          /tmp/dir_home     <-- add this line
cachesize          100000
dbcachesize        125000000
...
blueprints# mkdir -p /tmp/dir_home
blueprints# cd install_dir/slapd-instance/db
blueprints# mv *.share /tmp/dir_home
blueprints# chown <server-owner>/tmp/dir_home
blueprints# ./start-slapd
```

To complete this procedure, modify the slapd-start script to automatically create /tmp/dir_home when the server starts, as shown below. If this modification is not done, the dir_home directory will not be re-created after a reboot.

```
blueprints# vi install_dir/slapd-instance/slapd-start
...
if [ ! -d /tmp/dir_home ]
        then
        mkdir /tmp/dir_home
        chown <server-owner>/tmp/dir_home
fi
...
blueprints#
```

Changing Common Installation Configuration Parameters

When changing common installation configuration parameters, you should consider the following:

- Changing the ns-slapd process owner
- Changing the directory manager password
- Changing the admin password

▼ Changing the ns-slapd Process Owner

The directory server process, ns-slapd, assumes the identity of the user specified during the installation. The default is nobody, but in some cases, such as when the NIS extensions are running, it needs to run as root. If the server was installed with the default nobody, you can change it by editing the slapd.conf file.

```
blueprints# cd install_dir/slapd-instance
blueprints# ./stop-slapd
blueprints# cd config
blueprints# cp slapd.conf slapd.conf.bak
blueprints# vi slapd.conf
. . .
schemacheck       on
enquote_sup_oc    on
security          off
localuser         nobody  <----- change this to the new user
userat  "/files/netscape/slapd-iplanet/config/
slapd.user_at.conf"
useroc  "/files/netscape/slapd-iplanet/config/
slapd.user_oc.conf"
. . .
blueprints# install_dir/slapd-instance/start-slapd
```

Note – If the new user specified is not root, then the ownership on the *.db, log, and config files need to be changed.

▼ Changing the Directory Manager Password

The easiest way to change the Directory Manager password is through the Directory Server Console. If you started the console with the default admin account, you will need to login as Directory Manager (see FIGURE 4-5).

FIGURE 4-5 **Login to Directory** Window

Go to the **Configuration —> Manager** tab and input the new password as shown in FIGURE 4-6.

FIGURE 4-6 **Manager** Tab

Note – Any encryption method can be chosen. This method affects only the Directory Manager account.

If you forget the Directory Manager password you can reset it by editing the slapd.conf file for the instance of the directory server you are running.

▼ Changing the admin Password

You change the admin account password from the Directory Server Console by going to the **Configuration Administrator** screen, under the **Directory** tab:

NetscapeRoot —> Topology Management —> Administrators —> Configuration Administrator

Use this screen to change the admin password.

Importing Directory Data

Once you have installed the directory server, you can populate the directory with data. You can input data one entry at a time through the Directory Server Console or you can import it as a batch process by running an import script. Import scripts usually take data entered in LDAP Data Interchange Format (LDIF) and then use one of two methods:

1. Initialize complete database

2. Append to current database

Initializing the Database

The quickest way to import data is to initialize the whole database. That is, remove all the current data and replace it with data from an LDIF file. This operation is performed while the directory server is offline. The command for initializing a database is `ns-slapd` with the `ldif2db` argument.

One problem with performing a database initialization is that the configuration data that was placed there during the installation is lost. To preserve this data, you must back it up, then restore it. The easiest way to do this is to run the `ldif2db` script or run **Import** from the Directory Server Console.

Note – `ldif2db` is a script that runs the `ns-slapd` command with the `ldif2db` argument. There is no `ldif2db` executable.

The following is an example of running the ldif2db script.

```
blueprints# cd install_dir/slapd-instance
blueprints# ./stop-slapd
blueprints# ./ldif2db -i LDIF_file
saving configuration ...
[25/Mar/2000:10:20:56 -0500] - Processed 109 entries.
Importing configuration and data
[25/Mar/2000:10:20:57 -0500] - ldif2db: Index buffering enabled
with buffer size 7
[25/Mar/2000:10:20:59 -0500] - ldif2db: Beginning import job...
[25/Mar/2000:10:20:59 -0500] - ldif2db: Processing file /files/
netscape/slapd-blueprints/confbak/2000_03_25_102053.ldif
-------Index Task-------State--Entry----Rate-
Processed 0 entries, Average rate 0.0, Recent rate 0.0, Hit Ratio
0%
[25/Mar/2000:10:21:00 -0500] - ldif2db: Processing file /home/
tom/LDIF/100.ldif
Done...
Waiting for workers to stop...Done.

Indexing complete...Postprocessing...Flushing caches...Closing
files...
[25/Mar/2000:10:21:05 -0500] - ldif2db: Import complete.
Processed 213 entries in 8 seconds at a rate of 26.62 entries per
second
blueprints# ./start-slapd
```

As part of the import process, indexes are automatically created as shown in the output of ldif2db. Refer to Chapter 7, "Capacity Planning and Performance Tuning" for information on the purpose and modification of indexes.

An alternative to running the ldif2db command is to use the **Import** feature of the Directory Server Console. To invoke this screen, click the **Configuration** tab, click the **Console** icon on the top tool bar, then choose **Import**. Once invoked, the **Import Database** screen (see FIGURE 4-7) is displayed.

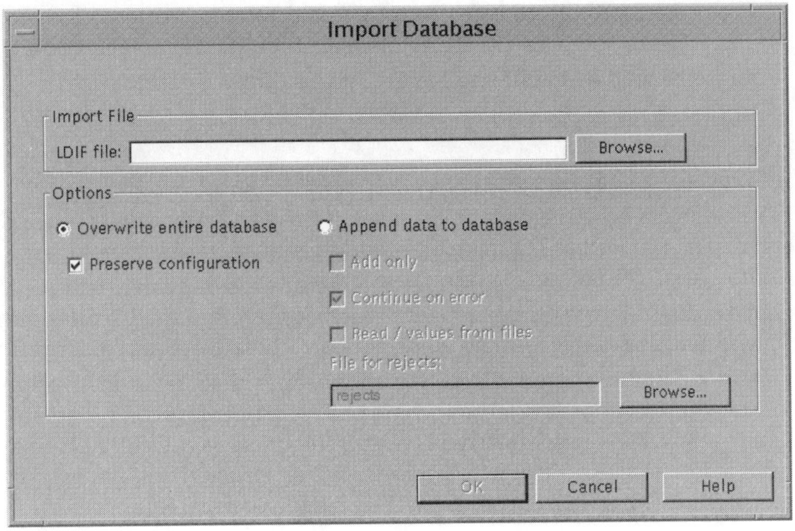

FIGURE 4-7   **Import Database** Window

In FIGURE 4-7, the **Overwrite entire database** and **Preserve configuration** items are selected. With these options, the database can be initialized with the configuration data stored in it, saved, and then restored. While the import is performed the directory server is automatically shut down and then restarted.

Appending to the Database

You can append data to an existing database by running the `ldapmodify` command. Use this command to add a single entry or to read from an LDIF file to update a large number of files. Unlike the command that initializes a database, this command can be invoked while the directory server is online. Since `ldapmodify` uses the LDAP protocol, it must *bind* to the directory server before it can add any data. To avoid permission problems during large imports by `ldapmodify`, it is wise to bind to the server as `Directory Manager`.

Since `ldapmodify` is used in various ways, several options can be specified when it is invoked. To simplify imports, a script called `ldif2ldap` is provided. The following is an example of the use of this script.

```
blueprints# cd install_dir/slapd-instance
blueprints# ./ldif2ldap "Directory Manager" password LDIFfile
```

From the Directory Server Console, you do the equivalent of running the ldif2ldap script by using the procedure in the previous section and specifying the **Append data to database** option.

Reinstalling iPlanet Directory Server

To reinstall the iPlanet Directory Server software, you should first run the uninstall program located in the server root directory, which halts the processes associated with the directory server. Once the uninstall procedure has completed, you will still need to remove all the files in the installation directory to do a clean installation. These steps are necessary since if the server processes are still running during the new installation, you will not be able to assign the same port numbers specified during the previous installation.

The following steps are recommended before you perform another installation.

```
blueprints# install_dir/uninstall
blueprints# rm -r install_dir/*
```

Installation Troubleshooting Tips

A number of factors can cause the installation to fail. Usually the first indication of a failed installation is the failure of the ns-slapd process to start. If you suspect this is the case, check to see if the process is running, then check for errors in the error log.

```
blueprints# ps -e | grep ns-slapd
blueprints#
blueprints# tail install_dir/slapd-instance/logs/error
...
[09/Mar/2000:11:30:00 -0500] - start: Failed to start ns-slapd,
err=22 Invalid host name: blueprints.Eng.East.Sun.COM
...
blueprints#
```

Three common causes of a failed installation are:

1. The domain name suffix created by the installation program is wrong (the NIS domain is different than the DNS domain).

2. The server port is already in use (perhaps there is a hung ns-slapd process).

3. The fully qualified domain name must resolve to this host.

If the `ns-slapd` process starts correctly (no errors), but the Netscape Console fails to start, make sure the `ns-admin` process is running, then check to see if the configuration data appears in the database.

```
blueprints# ps -e | grep ns-admin
  1984 ?        0:00 ns-admin
blueprints# ldapsearch -b "o=NetscapeRoot" "objectclass=*"
o=NetscapeRoot
objectclass=top
objectclass=organization
o=NetscapeRoot
aci=(targetattr="*")(version 3.0; acl "Enable Configuration
Administrator Group modification"; allow (all) groupdn = "ldap:/
//cn=Configuration Administrators, ou=Groups,
ou=TopologyManagement, o=NetscapeRoot";)
aci=(targetattr="*")(targetfilter=(o=NetscapeRoot))(version
3.0; acl "Default anonymous access"; allow (read, search)
userdn="ldap:///anyone";)
aci=(targetattr="*")(version 3.0; acl "Enable Group Expansion";
allow (read, search, compare) groupdnattr="ldap:///
o=NetscapeRoot?uniquemember?sub";)
. . .
```

If no configuration data is found, then you must run the `restoreconfig` command, assuming you have run `saveconfig` earlier.

Directory Replication

Once the primary directory server is installed and configured the next step is to set up a replica server. The role of a replica server is explained in Chapter 2, "Solaris Naming Services Architecture." You set up replica servers directly from the installation program by choosing the Custom installation option, or you can set them up after the directory server software is installed. This section discusses how a replica is set up after the initial installation.

Planning Directory Replication

Before setting up a replica server you need the following required information:

- How the replication will be initiated — by the Consumer or by the Supplier

- Replication account name and password
- Portion of DIT to be replicated
- Frequency of replication
- Location of the `changelog`

Replication can be initiated either in a pull or push mode. The pull mode is referred to as Consumer initiated and the push mode is called Supplier initiated. Consumer-initiated replication is rare these days and is only useful if you have unreliable WAN connections. For most cases choose Supplier.

The Supplier logs in as (binds to) a special account that is required to be on the Consumer system. The default account name is `Replication Manager`. An alternative method to binding is the use of client certificates, as discussed in the next section.

You can replicate the entire DIT or only a portion of it. In some cases, you may choose to replicate only a portion of the DIT since it is the only part relevant to the clients accessing the replica.

The Supplier maintains a list of all changes that take place in the directory. The changes are then propagated to the Consumer at specified intervals. You can choose to have the changes propagated immediately or only during a specified time. The changes are maintained in the `changelog`. If many modifications are taking place there could be a lot of write activity to this file. To avoid a potential bottleneck, this file should not reside on the same disk as the directory database.

For information on replication strategies and architecture, refer to Chapter 8, "Deploying Highly Available LDAP Data Services."

▼ Setting up Replication

Perform the following steps to set up replication.

1. **On the Consumer: In the Directory Server Console, go to the Configuration —> Database —> Replication Agreements tab and choose Consumer Settings.**

   Enter the DN (see FIGURE 4-8) that the Supplier will use and assign it a password.

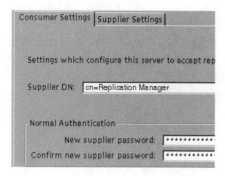

FIGURE 4-8 **Consumer Settings** Tab

2. **On the Supplier: In the Directory Server Console, go to**

   Configuration —>Database —>Replication Agreements tab and choose Supplier Settings.

   Enter the location (FIGURE 4-9) where you want the changelog to be stored, along with a maximum age or number of records to prevent the log from getting too large.

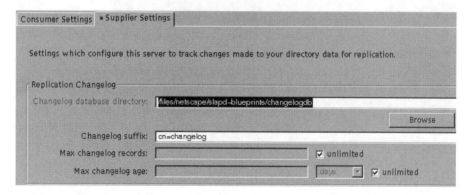

FIGURE 4-9 **Supplier Settings** Tab

3. **Log in as Directory Manager, then right-click Replication Agreements and choose New Replication Agreement.**

   In the form shown in FIGURE 4-10, enter the Consumer server's host name and port number along with the account information that was set up on the Consumer server. Then enter, or use the browse list to choose, the portion of the DIT you want to replicate.

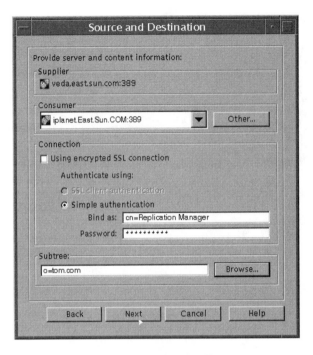

FIGURE 4-10 Source and Destination Form

4. Choose either to keep the directories in sync or to synchronize only on specified days and time of day.

Option 1: Always keep directories in sync

Option 2: Sync on the following days:

Replication will take place between:

Note – To use bandwidth efficiently, choose the second option.

---

5. Specify how you want to initialize the Consumer.

When a replica server first comes online, it needs to be populated with directory data contained on the Supplier. You populate the directory either through the LDAP protocol or by importing an LDIF file. The LDAP protocol method is very slow and is only recommended if you have a limited number of directory entries.

Note – If the suffix being replicated does not exist on the Consumer, it must be created before the **Initialize consumer now** option is invoked. The LDIF file is generated on the Supplier and automatically creates any required suffixes when it is imported on the Consumer.

Importing an LDIF file through the command line is the preferred and most commonly used method, since the GUI method will take considerably longer. You create an LDIF file on the Supplier then import it on the Consumer. FIGURE 4-11 shows the available options.

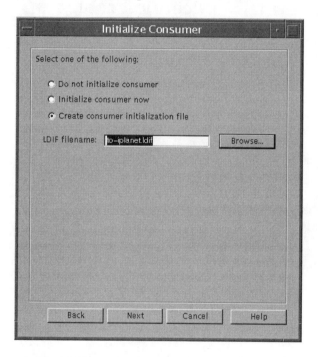

FIGURE 4-11 Creating an LDIF File

Alternatively, run the `ldapmodify` command to import the LDIF file.

6. Import the LDIF file on the Consumer

In the Directory Server Console, log in as `Directory Manager`, go to the **Configuration** tab, click the **Console** icon in the top tool bar, then choose **Import**.

Note – Make sure you *append* to the existing database, not reinitialize it.

Verifying Replication

To verify that replication is working properly, check the status on the **Supplier Replication Agreement**. On the Directory Server Console:

1. **Go to the Status tab**
2. **Click Replication Status and observe the status which should read: (in sync)**

Troubleshooting Replication Problems

One common problem is that the Supplier fails to bind to the Consumer. To see if this is happening, check the error log on the Supplier and the access log on the Consumer. Chapter 8, "Deploying Highly Available LDAP Data Services" discusses how to view these log files.

Another problem that you can spot by checking the error log is whether the suffix could not be created. This problem can occur if the **Initialize consumer now** option is chosen.

Modifying the Supplier Initiated Agreement

You can change the parameters used to establish the agreement by going to **Replication Agreements —> Supplier Initiated** under the **Configuration** tab and clicking the agreement name.

You disable replication by deleting the agreement.

Setting up a Secure System Using SSL and Certificates

By default, data transfer to and from the directory server is performed in clear text. Also, by default, authentication is performed by use of a simple `login name/ password` pair. Since most of the data maintained in the directory may not be proprietary in nature and data transfer is behind the corporate firewall, clear-text and simple authentication is quite acceptable.

However, there may be some sensitive data or situations where tighter security access control is required. This section details how to make the directory server more secure by setting up the Secure Socket Layer (SSL) protocol, which uses digital certificates.

Note – The iPlanet Directory Server can function in a secure and insecure mode simultaneously. By following the procedure in this section, you are adding a secure access point and not necessarily replacing the insecure access point.

Planning a Secure Server Configuration

Two aspects of security are discussed in this section: authentication and data encryption. Authentication can take place by the server identifying itself to the client, the client identifying itself to the server, or both. Data encryption takes place once authentication has taken place and a secret key is passed between the server and client.

The mechanism used for identity identification is the digital certificate. For server identification the server side certificate is used. For client side identification, client side certificates are used. These certificates are created by a trusted Certificate Authority (CA). This section focuses on installing server side certificates.

Before configuring SSL you must either have access to a CA, or create your own. Trusted CAs such as Verisign, are useful for doing secure transactions over the Internet. They act as a trusted third-party. For use within a corporate intranet, setting up your own CA makes the most sense.

These steps are required to obtain and install a server side certificate:

1. Fill out a request form

2. Send the request to a CA

3. Receive and install the certificate

Running the Certificate Setup Wizard

You use the **Certificate Setup Wizard** to generate requests for server certificates and to install server certificates. The following procedure shows how to generate a request for a certificate.

Generating a Certificate Request

Perform the following steps to generate a certificate request:

1. **In the Directory Server Console, invoke the Certificate Setup Wizard, which is located under the Task tab.**

2. **Specify use internal as the Cryptographic Device and check no to the Is server certificate ready to install? question.**

3. **Specify a password containing at least eight characters and at least one non-alphabetic character.**

   Since this is the first time you will be adding a certificate to this server, a trust database is created. A password is assigned to the trust database and must be supplied when the database is accessed. The password is required to start the directory server in a secure mode.

Note – The actual database is created in the *install_dir*/alias directory and maintained in the slapd-*instance*-cert7.db and slapd-*instance*-key3.db files. These files are stored as binary data and cannot be edited directly.

---

4. **Supply the information requested in** FIGURE 4-12.

FIGURE 4-12 Certificate Setup Wizard Generating a Certificate Request

After the form is complete, an encrypted certificate request, which looks like the following, is created:

-----BEGIN NEW CERTIFICATE REQUEST-----

MIIBLDCB1wIBADByMQswCQYDVQQGEwJVczEWMBQGA1UECBMNTUFTU0F
DSFVTRVRUUzETMBEGA1UEBxMKQnVybGluZ3RvbjEMMAoGA1UEChMDQ1FB
MQswCQYDVQQLEwJFRTEbMBkGA1UEAxMSYmx1ZXByaW50cy5zdW4uY29tMF
wwDQYJKoZIhvcNAQEBBQADSwAwSAJBAK04VWg+fnGSE5PJegmxCMeuCO7kb
EqTDucJd8aj3oc1hMNxthwRh+2HXmIG9i6beBTWfmrsfZ+1Mjsmd4EDJXcCAwEAA
aAAMA0GCSqGSIb3DQEBBAUAA0EAaAV8aWoqBRgWZNt5Q1LP6aOXZsrQxw1m
KvvAlXIeWXsftoQ5rNyC/OTWtjOl8sVaK9fdjar53DjUHTjJB6ZRdw==

-----END NEW CERTIFICATE REQUEST-----

The request can either be sent via email to the CA or cut and pasted into a CA enrollment tool. Make sure you include the BEGIN and END lines when performing this operation.

5. **Receive the certificate from the CA.**

A certificate which looks like the one below will either be sent by email, stored in a file, or displayed on a web page for cutting and pasting, depending on what CA is being used.

-----BEGIN CERTIFICATE-----

MIIDhjCCAzCgAwIBAgIIYf8KzQAAABswDQYJKoZIhvcNAQEEBQAwdjELMAkG
A1UEBhMCVVMxCzAJBgNVBAgTAkRDMRMwEQYDVQQHEwpXYXNoaW5ndG9
uMRYwFAYDVQQKEw1VUyBHb3Zlcm5tZW50MRIwEAYDVQQLEwlQcmVzaWRl
bnQxGTAXBgNVBAMTEFJpaXhvbi5jcnQwDQYJKoZIhvcNAQEEBQADQQAJzQaM
esR5sFom9hBLPGRYhFq6hDT2gaWAp6Fc3SccXSeZ8kXkTijn2KN4KTsO0WYbr5Rqo
uC7OU8QDrHUsqjd.. . .

-----END CERTIFICATE-----

Installing the Server Certificate

Once a server certificate is received from a CA, it can be installed in the directory server. The same tool, **Certificate Setup Wizard**, used to generate a certificate request is also used to install the certificate. After the wizard is started, choose the Yes option for Question 2, then follow these steps:

1. **Enter the password that was assigned during the creation of the trust database.**

2. **When the screen shown in** FIGURE 4-13 **is displayed, either specify the file containing the certificate or paste in the certificate.**

FIGURE 4-13 Certificate Setup Wizard to Install a Certificate

Enabling SSL on the Server

Once the certificate is installed, SSL is activated through the **Configuration** tab of the Directory Server Console.

1. **Inside the Configuration tab, click the top line, which is the name of the directory server. Click Settings and make a note of the Encrypted port number (the well known LDAPS port is 636). Change this number if you do not want to use this particular port number.**

2. **Click the Encryption tab and select Enable SSL (see** FIGURE 4-14**).**

   You should also check **RSA** for the cipher and **Allow Client Authentication**.

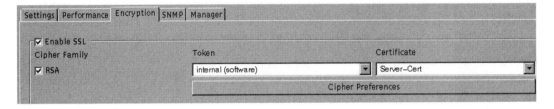

FIGURE 4-14 Encryption Tab

Once the changes are saved, the server is running SSL on the encrypted port. To verify that it is running, try to telnet to the encrypted port:

```
blueprints# telnet blueprints 636
Trying 129.148.181.130...
Connected to blueprints.
Escape character is '^]'.
```

Rebooting the Secure Server

To restart the directory server once SSL has been enabled, enter the password for the trust database, as shown below.

```
# ./restart-slapd
Enter PIN for Internal (Software) Token:
```

If you want the server to start without prompting for a PIN, then create a text file called: *install_dir*/alias/slapd-*instance*-pin.txt. This file must contain the directive: Internal (Software) Token=*password*. Refer to the documentation on http:www.iplanet.com.

Changing the Trust Database Password or PIN

From the **Task** tab in the Directory Server Console, choose **Change Key Password** from the **Console** menu (see FIGURE 4-15).

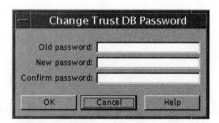

FIGURE 4-15 Change Key Password

Using SSL for Replication

One of the uses of SSL is to create a secure channel between the Supplier and the Consumer during replication. The following steps are required to accomplish this.

1. **Install a server certificate on the Consumer and Supplier.**

2. **Trust the certificate on the Supplier.**

3. **Enable the SSL connection.**

   Both the Supplier and Consumer need to be set up for SSL. This setup requires installation of a server certificate on both servers. In addition, the Consumer's trust database must include a certificate from the Supplier's CA. Instructions for using the iPlanet Certificate Server as a CA can be found on the iPlanet Web site at `http://www.iplanet.com`.

4. **Specify SSL in the Supplier's replication agreement as shown in** FIGURE 4-16.

FIGURE 4-16 Specification of SSL

This example uses the same bind operation as before, but, alternatively, SSL client authentication could be used. Instructions for using the iPlanet Certificate Server to generate and maintain client certificates can be found on the iPlanet Web site at `http://www.iplanet.com`.

iPlanet Directory Server Startup Files

The iPlanet Directory Server installation does not automatically create startup or run command (`rc`) scripts. Unless these scripts are added to the Solaris `rc` directory, you have to manually start up the directory and administration servers. Find sample startup files in the Solaris Extension `Samples` directory. Alternatively, as described in this section, you can run an interactive script that generates a start script (`S72ns-slapd`) and a kill script (`K72ns-slapd`). Once generated, these scripts should be placed in the `/etc/rc2.d` directory with a hard link created to `/etc/init.d`.

Script Generation Program

The following is an interactive script that creates the proper rc files for your environment.

```
#!/bin/sh

PATH=/sbin:/bin:/usr/bin:$PATH
export PATH

# takes two arguments, a PROMPT and the default value (Y | N).
# Returns 0 if the user specified "Y", nonzero otherwise.
yes_or_no()
{
        OK=n
        while [ "$OK" = n ]
        do
                echo >/dev/tty
                echo "$1 [$2]: \c" >/dev/tty
                read ans
                if [ "$ans" = "" ]
                then
                        ans=$2
                else
                        if [ "$2" = "y" -o "$2" = "n" ]
                        then
                                case $ans in
                                "Y"|"y"|"YES"|"yes"|"Yes") ans=y;;
                                "N"|"n"|"NO"|"no"|"No") ans=n;;
                                esac
                        fi
                fi
                if [ "$ans" = y -o "$ans" = n ]
                then
                        OK=y
                else
                        echo $ans >/dev/tty
                echo "Is this correct (y/n) [y] \c" >/dev/tty
                        read OK
                        case $OK in
                        ""|"Y"|"y"|"YES"|"yes"|"Yes") OK=y;;
                        "N"|"n"|"NO"|"no"|"No") OK=n;; esac
                fi
        done
        echo $ans
```

```
}

echo ""
echo CURRDATE='date'
echo HOST='hostname'
echo DOMAIN='domainname'

echo ""
echo "i-Planet Directory Server for Solaris rc* configuration program"

OK='yes_or_no "Would you like to continue with installation?" "y"'
if [ "$OK" != "y" ]
then
  exit 0
fi

BASEDIR=/usr/netscape/server4
SLAPDINSTANCENAME='/usr/bin/hostname'

echo ""
echo "Specify the server root location. This is where the server programs,
the Administration Server, and the server configuration files are located."
echo ""
echo "To accept the default shown in brackets, press the Enter key."

BASEDIR='yes_or_no "Installation Location is" $BASEDIR'

echo""
echo "Creating iPlanet rc startup scripts..."

echo "Setting permissions on iPlanet rc startup scripts..."

echo "Creating link to the iPlanet rc startup scripts..."
echo""

#
# installation is now complete
# set the rc scripts to start slapd and admin server automatically at boot
time
#
cat <<% > /etc/init.d/ns-slapd
```

```
#!/sbin/sh
#
#
# Copyright(c) 1997, by Sun Microsystems, Inc.
# All rights reserved.
#
#ident    "@(#)ns-slapd       1.0     200/02/17 SMI"
#
# This script will automatically start/stop/restart the
# i-Planet Directory Server 4.12
#
SLAPDDIR=$BASEDIR/slapd-$SLAPDINSTANCENAME
BASEDIR=$SLAPDDIR$BASEDIR

case "\$1" in
'start')
        rm -f \$SLAPDDIR/logs/pid
        \$SLAPDDIR/start-slapd > /dev/null 2>&1
        \$BASEDIR/start-admin > /dev/null 2>&1
        echo "Directory Services Started."
        ;;

'stop')
        \$SLAPDDIR/stop-slapd
        \$BASEDIR/stop-admin
        echo "Directory Services Stopped"
        ;;

'restart')
        \$SLAPDDIR/restart-slapd
        \$BASEDIR/restart-admin
        echo "Directory Services Restarted"
        ;;

*)
        echo "Usage: /etc/init.d/ns-slapd { start | stop | restart }"
        exit 1
        ;;
esac
exit 0
%

#
# Set the correct file permissions
#
```

```
/usr/bin/chmod 744 /etc/init.d/ns-slapd

#
# Set the correct group permissions
#
/usr/bin/chgrp sys /etc/init.d/ns-slapd

# Check for the existance of the hard link
# if it exists, remove it, then create the new
# links.

    /usr/bin/rm -f /etc/rc2.d/S72ns-slapd
    /usr/bin/ln /etc/init.d/ns-slapd /etc/rc2.d/S72ns-slapd
    /usr/bin/rm -f /etc/rc0.d/K72ns-slapd
    /usr/bin/ln /etc/init.d/ns-slapd /etc/rc0.d/K72ns-slapd
```

Installing the NIS Extensions

Chapter 8, "Deploying Highly Available LDAP Data Services" covers in great detail
the installation of NIS extensions. Installation of the extensions is performed after
the directory installation. Before the extensions are installed, the server should be
configured as either an NIS master or NIS slave.

```
# cd /cdrom/cd_4.1_ext/Solaris_Extension
# pkgadd -d .
The following packages are available:
  SUNWdsnis    Solaris Extensions for Netscape Directory Server
- NIS (sparc) 4.1

2 SUNWdsrad    Solaris Extensions for Netscape Directory Server
- RADIUS (sparc) 4.1

3 SUNWdsutl    Solaris Extensions for Netscape Directory Server
- Utilities (sparc) 4.1

Select package(s) you wish to process (or 'all' to process all
packages). (default: all) [?,??,q]:
```

Next, run dsypinstall.

```
blueprints#  ./dsypinstall
```

Additional information on NIS configuration is presented in Chapter 6, "NIS Extensions Configuration."

## CHAPTER 5

Solaris 8 Native LDAP Configuration

After you install the iPlanet Directory Server as detailed in Chapter 4, "iPlanet Directory Server Installation and Configuration," several configuration changes need to be made to it before Solaris LDAP clients can be supported. This chapter explains what these configuration changes are, why they are necessary, and the steps required to make them. So you can gain a better understanding of the nature of these changes, the first part of the chapter presents some architectural concepts and implementation details. The second part of the chapter contains the actual procedures for setting up the LDAP server and LDAP clients.

Both a graphical user interface (GUI) and a command-line interface provided with the iPlanet Directory Server can be used to make the necessary configuration changes. Some can be made either by editing the configuration files, running the LDAP commands like `ldapmodify`, importing LDIF files, or through the Directory Console. The method you choose depends on the type of changes required and your proficiency at using LDAP tools. Since a lot of hand editing is required and commands can be quite lengthy, you can download the example text from:

`www.sun.com/blueprints`

After downloading the text, cut and paste it into the configuration files, the LDIF files, and the command lines.

Definition of Native LDAP

As discussed in Chapter 2, "Solaris Naming Services Architecture," the Solaris 8 operating environment introduces a new naming service based on LDAP technology. This is referred to as a *native* implementation because it is built into the Solaris naming service infrastructure as a core component. Technically, native LDAP is a client implementation only and not tied to any particular LDAP directory server. However, for Solaris LDAP clients to work, a properly configured LDAP server must exist on the network.

Solaris LDAP clients have been available for some time in the form of web browsers, like Netscape Communicator, and LDAP-enabled applications like messaging servers. These implementations were designed to perform a specific function, such as searching an address book, and provided their own LDAP libraries. Since core network services, such as accessing a naming service, are not available through those LDAP clients, a native Solaris LDAP client is required.

An alternative to deploying native LDAP is presented in Chapter 6, "NIS Extensions Configuration," which discusses the NIS extension implementation. Although they address the same issue as native LDAP, the extensions are a server-only implementation. Solaris clients that access an iPlanet Directory Server running the NIS extensions use the NIS protocol, not LDAP.

Implementing LDAP as a Solaris naming service requires information to be stored in an LDAP directory. The directory schema needs to be extended to accommodate it and you need to set proper access rights, so that some of the information can be read by everyone but some, like passwords, can only be modified by the Solaris user who owns it. Changes to the Solaris security model are required so that users can be authenticated by LDAP methods. Clients need a way of locating available LDAP servers and knowing where in the directory information tree (DIT) to begin searching for information.

The next section presents a closer examination of the components, which constitute the native LDAP implementation. Understanding how these components work is helpful to an understanding of the nature of changes required on the LDAP server and how Solaris LDAP clients are configured. If you already know how Solaris LDAP was implemented, you can skip this section and proceed directly to "Server Configuration Procedure" on page 119 and "Client Configuration" on page 140.

Native Solaris LDAP Implementation

In general, the goal of this implementation is to store in an LDAP directory all the information formerly stored in NIS maps and NIS+ tables and enable Solaris clients to access that information through LDAP rather than the NIS/NIS+ protocol. As discussed in Chapter 2, "Solaris Naming Services Architecture," LDAP uses different naming, information, security, and access models than those of NIS/NIS+, a number of changes are required. The Solaris LDAP client must first *bind* to the directory before information can be accessed, and the stored information has to be returned in a format that Solaris utilities can use.

When a Solaris LDAP client boots, a couple of configuration files are read. One file contains the client's credentials and describes how authentication is to take place, and the other one locates LDAP servers and sets various configuration parameters.

These files are dynamic and refreshed from information stored in the LDAP directory as client *profiles*. Enough information to bind to an LDAP server and retrieve an initial profile is supplied during the LDAP client initialization.

After the client successfully binds to the server, Solaris utilities that access data through the Solaris Naming Switch can now access LDAP data, provided the `ldap` tag is included in the name switch configuration file. The Solaris `login` utility can also authenticate users through the enhanced Solaris 8 PAM mechanism. Since the directory binding takes place before a user logs in, an account that is independent of any user must be set up on the server for the client machine. Since creating a separate account for each client can be tedious, you can a special account which by default is called `cn=proxyagent` to perform the binding for all clients within a domain.

Similar to the NIS and NIS+ naming services, LDAP clients are grouped into domains that all share a common namespace. On the LDAP server, an entry in the DIT identifies the domain it services. To support this, a new object class, called `nisDomainObject,` that contains the `nisdomain` attribute is created. The client checks this attribute to make sure it binds to a server in the same domain it belongs to.

Since information is stored in LDAP entries rather than in NIS maps or NIS+ tables, an LDAP definition, or schema, needs to be established along with LDAP containers to hold the entries. The standard RFC 2307 schema, which is discussed in Chapter 2, "Solaris Naming Services Architecture," defines most of what is required, but some changes are needed to support the native Solaris LDAP implementation. Therefore, the NIS object classes and attributes that ship with the iPlanet Directory Server require modification since they are based on RFC 2307.

Solaris LDAP Client Profiles

To simplify Solaris LDAP client configuration, a client profile entry is created on the directory server. A separate client profile can be created for each client, or several clients can share the same one. The following is a list of client profile attributes and their description.

- **SolarisLDAPServers** — A comma-separated list of LDAP servers that can be used by the client. This is a mandatory attribute that must contain at least one server name. If multiple servers are listed, the first server is tried first, and if after a specified timeout period it doesn't respond, then the next server in the list is tried.
- **SolarisSearchBaseDN** — LDAP naming context where the Solaris naming information will be stored.
- **SolarisBindDN** — `bindDN` used by the clients. Usually this is the `proxyagent` DN. The default is a `NULL` string that is used with anonymous authentication.

- **SolarisBindPassword** — The password when SIMPLE or CRAM_MD5 authentication is used. The default is a NULL string.
- **SolarisAuthMethod** — Authentication method to be used by the clients: NONE, SIMPLE, or CRAM_MD5. If multiple methods are specified, the first one is tried, and if it fails, the next method listed is tried. The default is NONE.
- **SolarisTransportSecurity** — Secured transport to be used by the client when updating information on the server. Currently, NONE is the only option supported.
- **SolarisDataSearchDN** — Alternate baseDN when searching for naming information. This attribute allows you to override one or more of the default containers established on the server.
- **SolarisSearchScope** — Search scope to be used to look up naming information. Base, One level, and Subtree are possible values. The default is One level.
- **SolarisSearchTimeLimit** — Time limit in seconds when searching for naming information. The default is 30 seconds.
- **SolarisCacheTTL** — Time-To-Live (TTL) value for clients to refresh their profile information from the server. If 0 (zero) is specified then automatic refreshes are disabled.
- **SolarisSearchReferral** — Referral option to be used to look up naming information. Default is to always follow referrals.

The ldap_gen_profile(1M) command is used to create client profiles. Its usage is described in "Client Configuration" on page 140.

NIS Domain

Although native LDAP does not use NIS, the concept of an NIS domain is carried over. Solaris clients find a server for a specific domain by checking the value of the nisDomain attribute in the nisDomainObject object class as defined in the root DN entry of the DIT representing the desired domain. The client uses this information when initializing the system and refreshing the client profile. During the initialization, the client searches for an entry on the LDAP server that has a value in nisDomain matching the desired domain. The DN of the entry found is used as the BaseDN for the naming information.

When refreshing the client profile, the program ldap_cachemgr, which performs the refresh, verifies that nisDomain defined in the root DN entry matches the domain desired before refreshing its profile.

This is an example entry, in LDIF format, setting nisdomain to the domain
mydomain.blueprints.com.

```
dn: dc=mydomain,dc=blueprints,dc=com
dc: mydomain
objectclass: top
objectclass: domain
objectclass: domainRelatedObject
objectclass: nisDomainObject
nisdomain: mydomain.blueprints.com
```

Authentication Method

When a Solaris LDAP client binds to a directory server, LDAP authentication is
performed. That is, the authentication takes place on the directory server, not on the
client. Currently, the supported mechanisms by Solaris 8 clients are SIMPLE, CRAM-
MD5, and NONE. A password and DN are passed to the server during SIMPLE
authentication. CRAM-MD5, as described in Chapter 3, "Security Models," uses a
challenge-response mechanism that provides a higher degree of security. However,
the iPlanet Directory Server 4.12 does not support CRAM-MD5, so SIMPLE
authentication is the only viable option. If NONE is specified, then anonymous
authentication is used.

Solaris applications that run on an LDAP client are authenticated through the
Pluggable Authentication Module (PAM) mechanism as described in Chapter 3,
"Security Models." Here, the client can choose from pam_unix or pam_ldap
authentication.

pam_unix

The pam_unix module has been enhanced in the Solaris 8 operating environment to
be LDAP aware. It uses the traditional model of UNIX authentication, which means
the following steps take place:

1. The encrypted password of the user is retrieved from the directory and passed to
   the local machine.

2. Users are prompted for their passwords.

3. The user's password is encrypted on the local machine.

4. The system compares the two encrypted passwords locally to decide if the user should be authenticated or not.

If clients using LDAP are configured with this module, the userPassword attribute must be readable by the identity that the client is using (anonymous or the configured cn=proxyagent). Additionally, there are two more restrictions to pam_unix:

- The password must be stored in an attribute called userPassword.

- The password must be stored in UNIX crypt format (not clear text or SHA-1).

pam_ldap

Since the traditional method of authentication used by pam_unix is not necessarily the best option when you are deploying LDAP directories, a new PAM mechanism, pam_ldap, was added in the Solaris 8 operating environment to authenticate users directly to the directory. This module allows Solaris clients to work with newer and more advanced authentication methods that the directory server might support in the future. Solaris clients using pam_unix do not require read access to the password attribute, and they do not need the password to be stored in any specific format in the directory.

As an added benefit, because pam_unix authenticates users directly to the directory server, user level access controls can be put in place to control an individual's authentication by means of ACIs.

Note – SIMPLE authentication, which passes passwords in clear text, is the only method currently supported by the iPlanet Directory Server through pam_ldap. Therefore pam_unix is recommended.

Proxy Agent

Unless anonymous authentication is used, all naming information lookups from a Solaris LDAP client are performed as a proxy agent. The proxy agent entry can be created anywhere in the DIT but must contain a userPassword attribute. The recommended entry location is under the *ou=profile* container and uses the person object class as shown below.

```
dn: cn=proxyagent,ou=Profile,dc=blueprints, dc=com
sn: proxyagent
objectclass: top
objectclass: person
cn: proxyagent
userpassword: {crypt}xxxxxxxxxxxxxx
```

The userpassword type specifies the format used to store the password (here it is crypt). Any entry containing the userPassword attribute can be used, but for easy identification, cn=proxyagent is commonly used.

Directory Information Tree

Solaris LDAP clients use the information in a predefined Directory Information Tree (DIT). The DIT is divided into containers that are subtrees containing entries for a specific information type. TABLE 5-1 lists the container and information type stored in the DIT.

TABLE 5-1   Directory Information Tree

Container	Information Type
ou=Ethers	bootparams, ethers
ou=Group	group
ou=Hosts	hosts, ipnodes
ou=Aliases	aliases
ou=Netgroup	netgroup
ou=Networks	networks, netmasks
ou=People	passwd, shadow, user_attr, audit_user, publickey for users
ou=Protocols	protocols
ou=Rpc	rpc
ou=Services	services
ou=Profile	Solaris client profile
ou=SolarisAuthAttr	auth_attr

TABLE 5-1   Directory Information Tree *(Continued)*

Container	Information Type
`ou=SolarisProfAttr`	`prof_attr, exec_attr`
`ou=projects`	`project`
`nismapname=auto_*`	`auto_*`

Loading Data

To facilitate loading of legacy naming service data into an LDAP directory, Solaris 8 provides a tool called `dsimport` included on the Solaris 8 companion CD containing the NIS extensions. With `dsimport`, you can load data in `/etc` file format into the iPlanet Directory Server. To import data from NIS maps, use the source files for those maps.

A definition of how the `/etc` formatted data should be converted to an LDAP format is contained in a mapping file. The rules defined in the file can be modified, but unless you have a specific reason for doing so, modification is not recommended.

Caution – Early versions of `dsimport`, which shipped with Sun Directory Server, do not support conversion to the native Solaris LDAP format. You can verify you have the right version by checking to see if `dsimport` accepts the **-S** flag.

Naming Context

As discussed in Chapter 2, "Solaris Naming Services Architecture," the LDAP naming model supports two styles of naming the top node of the DIT, or naming context. One is the original X.500 style which defines a country code (`c=`) and organization (`o=`) and the other is domain naming, which defines domain component (`dc=`) entries. The iPlanet Directory Server supports both styles and uses the X.500 style (`o=`) as the default during installation.

The domain naming style has become popular because users can align the name of their `rootDN` with their DNS address. Since almost all companies have a registered DNS address, this alignment ensures uniqueness among other directory servers. The examples used here assume the fictitious domain of `blueprints.com` and use the `dc=` naming conventions.

Server Configuration Procedure

The procedure to set up the iPlanet Directory Server to support Solaris LDAP clients is far more complex than that for setting up the client. One reason is that the Solaris native LDAP implementation was designed to be independent of the LDAP directory server. Since Sun has decided to ship the iPlanet Directory Server with the Solaris 8 operating environment, it is likely a simplified procedure will be available in the future.

Many changes are required, so grouping them into separate categories makes the task of setting up a server less daunting. These categories are:

- **Changes to the directory schema**

New object classes and attributes need to be added. One minor tweak to an existing object class is also required.

- **Creation of the DIT structure and support entries**

The containers that will hold the Solaris naming information need to be created along with client profile entries and an entry to use as a proxy agent. Correct permissions need to be set on containers and attributes for proper operation. Also the server needs to be configured to store passwords in crypt format.

- **Performance optimization**

Attribute indexes need to be created to increase directory search performance. Native LDAP will work without these indexes, but performance will suffer. Virtual list views (VLV) need to be created so containers with a large number of entries can be viewed.

- **Population of the DIT**

Finally, your legacy naming service data needs to be loaded into the iPlanet Directory Server. A small amount of sample data can be loaded first for testing.

Tools and Techniques

There are four basic techniques for changing configuration data on the iPlanet Directory Server:

1. Using the Directory Console GUI.

2. Creating an LDIF file that defines the changes, then importing it.

3. From the command line, by running `ldapmodify` and `ldapadd` commands.

4. Modifying the server configuration files with an editor.

If you are unfamiliar with LDAP tools, the Directory Console is the easiest method to use when making small changes. Since a number of the examples assume the Directory Console is being used, procedures for bringing up the appropriate screens are presented next. Later, the procedural steps show the data fields that need to be modified and assumes you know where to find the input form.

Creating an LDIF file is a popular method, but is most efficient when you have a template or a script that generates it for you. Check the Web site www.sun.com/ blueprints for LDIF templates and scripts. Chapter 9, "Preventive Maintenance," presents an overview of how to import and export LDIF files.

The command-line method is the most difficult method because the command lines tend to be very complex. If you use LDAP commands, it is best to embed them in a script. Correct usage of these commands can be found in the iPlanet Directory Server documentation on the www.iplanet.com Web site.

Modifying the directory server configuration files is the most efficient way of adding new object classes and attributes. The text of these changes can be found on www.sun.com/blueprints and can easily be cut and pasted into the configuration files.

Using the Directory Console to Make Configuration Changes

The Directory Console is useful for creating new objects, such as containers, special entries such as the proxyagent entry, and setting permissions by creating ACIs.

▼ Adding an Object to the DIT

1. **Run the Directory Console and login as cn=Directory Manager.**

2. **Go to the Directory tab and highlight the portion of the tree in the left pane where you want to insert the new object.**

3. **Hold down the right mouse button and choose New from the pull-down menu.**

   Four choices are offered: **User, Group, Organizational Unit,** and **Other.** For the objects defined as ou entries choose Organizational Unit; for the other objects, such as the nisMap object, choose Other and choose the appropriate object from the list. FIGURE 5-1 shows what adding an nisMap object would look like.

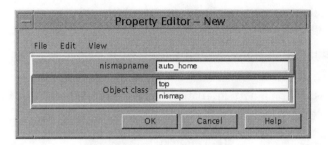

FIGURE 5-1 **Property Editor** View Window

4. **Click OK**

   If you accidently create the object in the wrong portion of the DIT, you can delete it by choosing **Delete** from the pull-down menu.

5. **To verify that the data entered is correct, choose Properties from the pull-down menu.**

Note – You can add attributes and change their values by invoking the **Property Editor** on an existing entry.

▼ Setting Permissions by Creating ACI Entries

1. **Run the Directory Console and login as cn=Directory Manager.**

2. **Go to the Directory tab and highlight the top node of the DIT where you want to place the object.**

3. **If an ACI already exists for that object it is displayed on the Multivalue ACI Selector screen. You can either modify an existing ACI by clicking it or create a new one by choosing New (see** FIGURE 5-2**).**

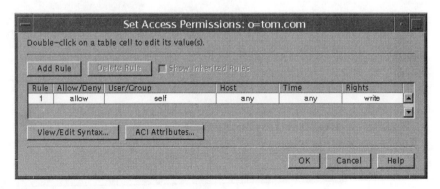

FIGURE 5-2 **Set Access Permissions** Window

4. **Double-click the User/Group box to specify which users and groups the access rights apply to.**

5. **Double-click the Rights box to specify read, write, search and compare access rights.**

6. **To set permissions on a particular attribute, click the ACI Attribute box and fill in the information in** FIGURE 5-3.

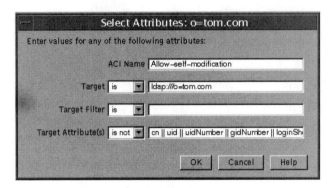

FIGURE 5-3   **Select Attributes** Window

Note – The value of an ACI can also be changed from the **Property Editor.**

▼ Importing LDIF Files from the Directory Console

1. **Run the Directory Console and login as cn=Directory Manager.**

2. **From the Configuration Tab, left click Console on the top bar and choose Import.**

   Use the defaults in the **Import** screen and browse to the location of the LDIF file you created.

Caution – Never choose the **Overwrite entire database** option because that option will wipe out any changes you made to the directory.

Importing LDIF Files from the Command Line

Usage:

`ldapmodify -a -D `*`bindDN`*` -w `*`password`*` -f `*`filename.ldif`*

where:

`-a` assumes the change type is add
`-D` DN of entry you are binding as, usually `cn=Directory Manager`
`-w` password associated with the DN specified

Example:

```
blueprints# ldapmodify -a -D "cn=Directory Manager" -w secret -f\
dit.ldif
```

Summary of Steps Required

The following list summarizes the changes required on the iPlanet Directory Server to support native LDAP clients. The changes are described in detail following the summary. Before you make these changes, the server should already be installed and configured as described in Chapter 4, "iPlanet Directory Server Installation and Configuration."

Directory Schema Update

1. **Modify the** `slapd.user.at.conf` **file to add new attributes.**

2. **Modify the** `slapd.oc.conf` **configuration file to change the definition of an existing object class.**

3. **Modify** `slapd.user_oc.conf` **configuration files to add new object classes.**

DIT and Support Entry Creation

4. **Configure the server to store passwords in the** `unix_crypt` **format.**

5. **Add new containers to the directory tree.**

6. **Modify the top-level access control permissions to restrict those attributes that can be changed by the entry owner for security reasons.**

7. **Enable anonymous viewing on VLV Control ACI.**

8. **Add the proxy agent entry.**

9. **Give** `cn=proxyagent` **password read permission.**

10. **Generate the client profile.**

Performance Optimization

11. **Create indexes for the native LDAP client specific attributes.**

12. **Create Virtual List View (VLV) indexes for containers with a large number of objects.**

Loading Data

13. **Create sample test entries.**

14. **Populate the directory by running the** `dsimport` **command.**

▼ Step 1. Modifying `slapd.user_at.conf`

The `slapd.user_at.conf` file adds new attributes that are not defined in the `slapd.at.conf` configuration file. If you are modifying the server after a fresh install, this file is empty.

1. **Stop the directory server (if it is running) and edit the** `slapd.user_at.conf` **file.**

```
blueprints# install_dir/slapd-instance/stop-slapd
bluebrints# vi install_dir/slapd-instance/config/slapd.at.conf
```

2. **Add the following entries:**

The `nisMapEntry` attribute.

```
# Sun nisMapEntry attributes
attribute nisPublickey 1.3.6.1.1.1.1.28 cis
attribute nisSecretkey 1.3.6.1.1.1.1.29 cis
attribute nisDomain 1.3.6.1.1.1.1.30 cis
```

The following lines for LDAP client profile.

```
# XXX attributes for LDAP client profile
attribute SolarisLDAPServers 1.3.6.1.4.1.42.2.27.5.1.15 cis
attribute SolarisSearchBaseDN 1.3.6.1.4.1.42.2.27.5.1.16 dn single
attribute SolarisCacheTTL 1.3.6.1.4.1.42.2.27.5.1.17 cis single
attribute SolarisBindDN 1.3.6.1.4.1.42.2.27.5.1.18 dn single
attribute SolarisBindPassword 1.3.6.1.4.1.42.2.27.5.1.19 ces single
attribute SolarisAuthMethod 1.3.6.1.4.1.42.2.27.5.1.20 cis
attribute SolarisTransportSecurity 1.3.6.1.4.1.42.2.27.5.1.21 cis
attribute SolarisCertificatePath 1.3.6.1.4.1.42.2.27.5.1.22   ces single
attribute SolarisCertificatePassword 1.3.6.1.4.1.42.2.27.5.1.23   ces single
attribute SolarisDataSearchDN 1.3.6.1.4.1.42.2.27.5.1.24 cis
attribute SolarisSearchScope 1.3.6.1.4.1.42.2.27.5.1.25 cis single
attribute SolarisSearchTimeLimit 1.3.6.1.4.1.42.2.27.5.1.26 int single
attribute SolarisPreferredServer 1.3.6.1.4.1.42.2.27.5.1.27 cis
attribute SolarisPreferredServerOnly 1.3.6.1.4.1.42.2.27.5.1.28 cis single
attribute SolarisSearchReferral 1.3.6.1.4.1.42.2.27.5.1.29 cis single
```

The `mailGroup` **attribute**.

```
# XXX Sun additional attributes to RFC2307 attributes (NIS)
attribute mgrpRFC822MailMember 2.16.840.1.113730.3.1.30 cis
attribute rfc822mailMember ces
attribute nisNetIdUser 1.3.6.1.4.1.42.2.27.1.1.12 ces
attribute nisNetIdGroup 1.3.6.1.4.1.42.2.27.1.1.13 ces
attribute nisNetIdHost 1.3.6.1.4.1.42.2.27.1.1.14 ces
```

▼ Step 2. Modifying `slapd.oc.conf`

The `slapd.oc.conf` configuration file defines LDAP standard object classes. Normally, it is not advisable to edit this file, but one small change is required. Back up the file before making the change.

1. **Stop the directory server and edit** `slapd.oc.conf`.

```
blueprints# install_dir/slapd-instance/stop-slapd
blueprints# vi install_dir/slapd-instance/config/slapd.oc.conf
```

2. **Modify the `ipNetwork` entry to change** cn **from** requires **to** allows.

Before changes:

```
objectclass ipNetwork
oid 1.3.6.1.1.1.2.7
requires objectClass, ipNetworkNumber, cn
allows ipNetmaskNumber, manager, l, description
```

After changes:

```
objectclass ipNetwork
oid 1.3.6.1.1.1.2.7
requires objectClass, ipNetworkNumber
allows cn, ipNetmaskNumber, manager, l, description
```

▼ Step 3. Modifying `slapd.user_oc.conf`

The `slapd.user_oc.conf` file adds new object classes that are not defined in the `slapd.oc.conf` configuration file. If you are modifying the server after a fresh install, this file is empty. To avoid having to edit these entries by hand, you can download a sample file from `www.sun.com/blueprints`.

Note – The object classes added here contain attributes that are defined in Step 3. You should perform both Steps 2 and 3 before restarting the directory server.

---

1. **Stop the directory server (if it is running) and edit the** `slapd.user_oc.conf` **file.**

```
blueprints# install_dir/slapd-instance/stop-slapd
blueprints# vi install_dir/slapd-instance/config/slapd.oc.conf
```

2. **Add the following entries:**

The `publickey objectclass`.

```
# NIS publickey objectclass
objectclass NisKeyObject
oid 1.3.6.1.1.1.2.14
superior top
requires cn, nisPublickey, nisSecretkey
allows uidNumber, description
```

The nisDomainObject objectclass.

```
# NIS domain objectclass
objectclass nisDomainObject
oid 1.3.6.1.1.1.2.15
superior top
requires nisDomain
```

The LDAP client profile objectclass.

```
# LDAP client profile objectclass
objectclass SolarisNamingProfile
oid 1.3.6.1.4.1.42.2.27.5.2.7
superior top
requires cn, SolarisLDAPservers, SolarisSearchBaseDN
allows SolarisBindDN, SolarisBindPassword,
SolarisAuthMethod,SolarisTransportSecurity,
SolarisCertificatePath,
SolarisCertificatePassword,SolarisDataSearchDN,
SolarisSearchScope,
SolarisSearchTimeLimit,SolarisPreferredServer,
SolarisPreferredServerOnly, SolarisCacheTTL,SolarisSearchReferral
```

The mailGroup objectclass.

```
# mailGroup objectclass
objectclass mailGroup
oid 2.16.840.1.113730.3.2.4
superior top
requires mail
allows cn, mgrpRFC822MailMember
```

The nisMailAlias objectclass.

```
# nisMailAlias objectclass
objectClass nisMailAlias
oid 1.3.6.1.4.1.42.2.27.1.2.5
superior top
requires cn
allows rfc822mailMember
```

The `nisNetId` objectclass.

```
# nisNetId objectclass
objectClass nisNetId
oid 1.3.6.1.4.1.42.2.27.1.2.6
superior top
requires cn
allows nisNetIdUser, nisNetIdGroup, nisNetIdHost
```

▼ Step 4. Changing Password Store to Crypt Format

By default, the iPlanet Directory Server stores passwords in the `SHA-1` format. Since the native LDAP client does not support this format, the server needs to be configured to store passwords in another format: `unix_crypt`. Additional information on how crypt works can be found in Chapter 3, "Security Models."

The easiest method for changing the password store format is through the Directory Console. Note that changing the configuration does not affect how existing passwords are stored, but affects only new ones. Therefore, this change needs to take place before the directory is populated.

1. **Bring up the Directory Console and login as cn=Directory Manager.**

2. **Under the Configuration tab, highlight Database in the left pane.**

3. **Under the Password tab, use the Password encryption pull-down menu to change the format to UNIX crypt as shown in** FIGURE 5-4.

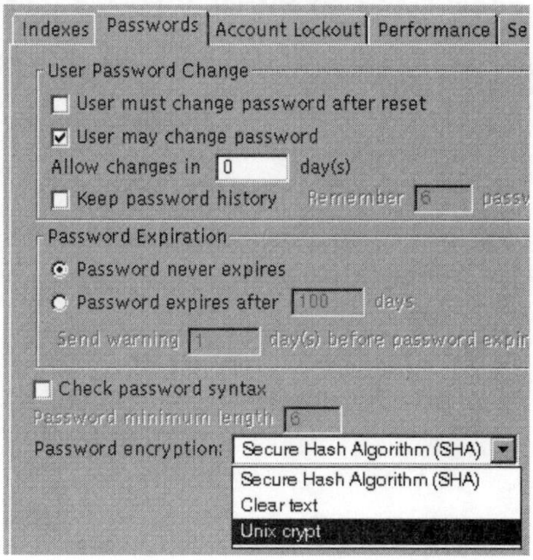

FIGURE 5-4 **Password** Tab

▼ Step 5. Adding New Containers

You create the containers required to hold LDAP entries either by importing an LDIF file or by using the Directory Console. To import the entries, you must first create an LDIF file that contains the entry information shown below, then run the `ldapmodify` command, as described earlier, or run **Import** from the Directory Console.

1. **Modify the top entry to add the `nisDomainObject` properties.**

   To import it, create the following LDIF file:

   ```
   dn: dc=blueprints,dc=com
   changetype: modify
   add: objectclass
   objectclass: nisDomainObject
   add: nisdomain
   nisdomain: mydomain.blueprints.com
   ```

2. **Add the following Organizational Unit (ou) entries at the top level of your DIT.**

   a. **Method 1: From the Create New Organizational Unit screen in the Directory Console, create entries with these Name fields:**

   - People
   - Group
   - Rpc
   - Protocols
   - Networks
   - Netgroup
   - Aliases
   - Hosts
   - Services
   - Ethers
   - Profile

   Note – These names are not case sensitive.

---

   b. **Method 2: Create the following LDIF file, then import it.**

   The example uses `dc=blueprints,dc=com` as the top DIT level and will need to be changed to reflect your environment.

   ```
   dn: ou=People,dc=blueprints,dc=com
   ou: People
   objectClass: top
   objectClass: organizationalUnit


   dn: ou=Group,dc=blueprints, dc=com
   ou: Group
   objectClass: top
   objectClass: organizationalUnit


   dn: ou=Rpc,dc=blueprints, dc=com
   ou: Rpc
   objectClass: top
   objectClass: organizationalUnit


   dn: ou=Protocols,dc=blueprints,dc=com
   ou: Protocols
   objectClass: top
   ```

```
objectClass: organizationalUnit

dn: ou=Networks,dc=blueprints,dc=com
ou: Networks
objectClass: top
objectClass: organizationalUnit

dn: ou=Netgroup,dc=blueprints,dc=com
ou: Netgroup
objectClass: top
objectClass: organizationalUnit

dn: ou=Aliases,dc=blueprints,dc=com
ou: Aliases
objectClass: top
objectClass: organizationalUnit

dn: ou=Hosts,dc=blueprints,dc=com
ou: Hosts
objectClass: top
objectClass: organizationalUnit

dn: ou=Services,dc=blueprints,dc=com
ou: Services
objectClass: top
objectClass: organizationalUnit

dn: ou=Ethers,dc=blueprints,dc=com
ou: Ethers
objectClass: top
objectClass: organizationalUnit

dn: ou=Profile,dc=blueprints,dc=com
ou: Profile
objectClass: top
objectClass: organizationalUnit
```

3. **Add the following NIS map objects by creating** `nisMap` **entries:**

   a. **Method 1: From the Directory Console, invoke the object editor with New —> Other and choose** `nisMap` **from the pick list.**

   Create the NIS map entries by filling in the **nismap** field with these names:

   - `auto_home`
   - `auto_direct`
   - `auto_master`
   - `auto_shared`

   b. **Method 2: Create and import a LDIF file that looks like this:**

```
dn: nismapname=auto_home,dc=blueprints,dc=com

nismapname: auto_home

objectClass: top

objectClass: nisMap


dn: nismapname=auto_direct,dc=blueprints,dc=com

nismapname: auto_direct

objectClass: top

objectClass: nisMap


dn: nismapname=auto_master,dc=blueprints,dc=com

nismapname: auto_master

objectClass: top

objectClass: nisMap


dn: nismapname=auto_ON,dc=blueprints,dc=com

nismapname: auto_ON

objectClass: top

objectClass: nisMap


dn: nismapname=auto_shared,dc=blueprints,dc=com

nismapname: auto_shared

objectClass: top

objectClass: nisMap
```

▼ Step 6. Modifying Self-Entry Modification

As discussed in Chapter 10, "Managing Directory Services," you set permissions on a directory object by creating an ACI. You set the ACI either by using the Directory Console or by creating an LDIF file that contains ACI statements.

1. **Method 1: Directory Console**

   a. Run the Directory Console and login as cn=Directory Manager.

   You can do this from the **Task** tab.

   b. Go to the Directory tab and highlight the top node of the DIT where the NIS objects reside.

   c. Right-click and choose Set Access Permissions on the pull-down menu. The Multivalue ACI Selector form is displayed.

   Set the **User/Group** field to `self` by double-clicking the field, then enter the text string `self`. Also, set the **Rights** to write by double-clicking the field and checking the **write** box.

   d. Click the ACI Attribute box and fill in the information in the following form:

   Target Attribute(s) **is not:**

   ```
   cn || uid || uidNumber || gidNumber || homeDirectory || loginShell
   || gecos || shadowLastChange || shadowMin || shadowMax ||
   shadowWarning || shadowInactive || shadowExpire || shadowFlag ||
   memberUid
   ```

2. **Method 2: Create a LDIF file that looks like this:**

   dn: dc=blueprints, dc=com

   changetype: modify

   add: aci

   aci: (target="ldap:///dc=blueprints,dc=com")(targetattr!="cn || uid
   || uidNumber || gidNumber || homeDirectory || shadowLastChange ||
   shadowMin || shadowMax || shadowWarning || shadowInactive ||
   shadowExpire || shadowFlag || memberUid")(version 3.0; acl "Allow
   self entry modification"; allow (write) userdn = "ldap:///self";)

▼ Step 7. Setting VLV Control ACI

The default behavior of iPlanet Directory Server is to grant permission for all valid users to access the directory by using Virtual List View (VLV) controls. Since the `ldapclient` program uses VLV control to access the directory and does this as an anonymous user, the default setting needs to be changed to allow anonymous access. The easiest way to change the VLV control ACI is through the Directory Console.

1. **In the left pane, click config, then features.**

   The **VLV Request Control** entry is displayed.

2. **Right-click the VLV Request Control entry and choose Properties.**

   Expand the window, so the `userdn=ldap:///all` portion of the ACI field shows.

3. **Change `all` to `anyone` and click OK.**

   After you modify the ACI, check it by running the `ldapsearch` command.

```
# ldapsearch -b cn=features,cn=config objectclass=*
dn: oid=2.16.840.1.113730.3.4.9,cn=features,cn=config
objectclass: top
objectclass: directoryServerFeature
oid: 2.16.840.1.113730.3.4.9
cn: VLV Request Control
aci: (targetattr !="aci")(version 3.0; acl "VLV Request Control";
allow (compare,read,search) userdn = "ldap:///anyone";)
```

▼ Step 8. Adding the Proxy Agent Entry

The `cn=proxyagent` and `userPassword` fields are used as input to the `ldap_gen_profile` command. This is the DN that Solaris LDAP clients use to bind to the directory.

1. **Add the proxy agent's entry in the LDAP server. You can create this entry from the Directory Console by using the new user form or by importing an LDIF file that looks like this:**

```
dn: cn=proxyagent,ou=profile,dc=blueprints,dc=com
cn: proxyagent
sn: proxyagent
objectclass: top
objectclass: person
userpassword: proxy_agent_password
```

▼ Step 9. Setting Password Read Permission for `proxyagent`

If `pam_unix` is used to authenticate Solaris users (as recommended) the `cn=proxyagent` DN, with which the Solaris LDAP client binds to the server, must be granted read permission for user account passwords. To perform this operation through the Directory Console, follow these steps:

1. **Click the right mouse button on the top-level object, then choose Set Access Permissions from the pull-down menu and add the following data:**
   - Allow/Deny – `allow`
   - User/Group – `cn=proxyagent, ou=profile` (use Add User to List)
   - Host – `any`
   - Time – `any`
   - Rights – `compare, read, search`

   Under ACI Attributes
   - ACI Name – allow-read-password (or any descriptive name)
   - Target Attribute(s) – `userPassword`

2. **When done click OK.**

   An LDIF file can also be used to change the ACI. For example:

   dn: `dc=blueprints, dc=com`

   changetype: `modify`

   add: `aci`

   aci: `(target="ldap:///dc=blueprints,dc=com")` `(targetattr="userPassword")`

   `(version 3.0; acl "password read"; allow (compare,read,search)`

   `userdn = "ldap:///cn=proxyagent,ou=profile,dc=blueprints,dc=com"; )`

▼ Step 10. Generating the Client Profile

1. **Now generate the client profile and then add it into the LDAP server. You should generate the profile on a 2.8 Solaris machine or higher because older OS levels won't have the** `ldap_gen_profile` **utility.**

   ```
   blueprints# ldap_gen_profile -P profile -b baseDN -D bindDN \
   -w bindDNpasswd ldapServer_IP_address(es)[:port#]
   ```

The `bindDN` used here is the bind DN of the proxy agent. You can specify more than one LDAP server's IP address if you want to failover to another LDAP server. Capture the above result in a file, like `profile.ldif`.

Example:

```
blueprints# ldap_gen_profile -P myProfile -b "dc=mydomain,dc=blueprints,
dc=com" \
-D cn=proxyagent,ou=profile,dc=mydomain,dc=blueprints,dc=com" \
-w proxy_agent_pswd -a simple xx.xx..xx.xx > profile.ldif
```

The following example shows the generated profile:

```
dn: cn=myprofile,ou=profile,dc=mydomain,dc=blueprints,dc=com
SolarisBindDN:cn=proxyagent,ou=profile,dc=mydomain,dc=blueprints,dc=com
SolarisBindPassword: {NS1}xxxxxxxxxxxxxx
SolarisLDAPServers: 192.146.85.197
SolarisSearchBaseDN: dc=mydomain,dc=blueprints,dc=com
SolarisAuthMethod: NS_LDAP_AUTH_SIMPLE
SolarisTransportSecurity: NS_LDAP_SEC_NONE
SolarisSearchReferral: NS_LDAP_FOLLOWREF
SolarisDataSearchDN:profile:(ou=other,dc=mydomain,dc=blueprints,dc=com)
SolarisSearchScope: NS_LDAP_SCOPE_ONELEVEL
SolarisSearchTimeLimit: 30
SolarisCacheTTL: 43200
cn: myprofile
ObjectClass: top
objectclass: SolarisNamingProfile
```

Note – There may be a problem with `ldap_gen_profile` inserting a leading tab in the second line onward. The leading tab, if present, needs to be deleted before you import the file.

2. **Import the LDIF file using the** `ldapmodify` **command.**

```
blueprints# ldapmodify -a -D "cn=Directory Manager" \
-w password -f profile.ldif
```

▼ Step 11. Creating Indexes

To optimize directory search performance, the creation of indexes is recommended. Indexes can be created through the Directory Console as described in Chapter 7, "Capacity Planning and Performance Tuning." The following attributes should be indexed along with the type of recommended indexing:

- `membernisnetgroup` pres,eq,sub
- `nisnetgrouptriple` pres,eq,sub
- `memberuid` pres,eq
- `macAddress` pres,eq
- `uid` pres,eq
- `uidNumber` pres,eq
- `gidNumber` pres,eq
- `ipHostNumber` pres,eq
- `ipNetworkNumber` pres,eq
- `ipProtocolNumber` pres,eq
- `oncRpcNumber` pres,eq
- `ipServiceProtocol` pres,eq
- `ipServicePort` pres,eq
- `nisDomain` pres,eq
- `nisMapName` pres,eq
- `mail` pres,eq

1. **Login into the Directory Console as** `Directory Manager`.

2. **Under the Configuration Tab, highlight Database and go to the Index Tab.**

3. **Click Add Attribute, choose one of the attributes listed above and check off the index types (Equality, Presence, Substring) shown as** `eq`, `pres`, **and** `sub` **above.**

▼ Step 12. Creating Virtual List View Indexes

In addition to the attribute indexes listed in **Step 11**, you should create Virtual List View (VLV) indexes (also referred to as browsing indexes) for any container, such as `password`, `group`, `host`, and `network`, that contains a large number of entries. If you do not create these indexes, search performance will suffer and the directory server will seem unresponsive.

You can create VLV indexes by using the Directory Console or the **Property Editor** to define new `vlvIndex` and `vlvSearch` objects or by importing an LDIF file. The **Property Editor** method is cumbersome since a lot of information needs to be entered manually and so is not recommended.

1. **For each attribute, create an LDIF file that looks like this:**

```
cn: cn=getpwent,cn=config,cn=ldbm
objectclass: top
objectclass: vlvSearch
cn: getpwent
vlvBase: ou=people,dc=blueprints,dc=com
vlvScope: 1
vlvFilter: (objectclass=posixAccount)
aci: (target="ldap:///
cn=getpwent,cn=config,cn=ldbm")(targetattr="*")
 (version 3.0; acl
"Config";allow(read,search,compare)userdn="ldap:///anyone";)

dn: cn=getpwent,cn=getpwent,cn=config,cn=ldbm
cn: getpwent
vlvSort: cn uid
objectclass: top
objectclass: vlvIndex
```

Repeat the above, substituting the following attributes and `objectclasses`:

- `getspent, objectclass=posixAccount`
- `getgrent, objectclass=posixGroup`
- `gethostent, objectclass=ipHost`
- `getnetent, objectclass=ipNetwork`

2. **Run the** `ldapmodify` **command to import the LDIF file.**

```
blueprints# ldapmodify -a -D "cn=Directory Manager" -w password -f vlv.ldif
```

3. **Build the index databases.**

```
blueprints# cd install_dir/instance/
blueprints# ./vlvindex getpwent
blueprints# ./vlvindex getgrent
blueprints# ./vlvindex gethostent
blueprints# ./vlvindex getspent
```

Note – Place the directory server in read-only mode when creating index database files. See Chapter 9, "Preventive Maintenance" for instructions.

▼ Step 13. Creating Sample Test Entries

For test purposes, you can create sample entries through the Directory Console. For example, you could add an `ipHost` entry in the **Hosts** container by invoking the **New Object** menu item.

▼ Step 14. Populating the LDAP data

Information from your current naming service can now be placed in the LDAP directory. For bulk-load of real production data use the `dsimport` command.

The `dsimport` command is included in the NIS Extensions software which is discussed in Chapter 6, "NIS Extensions Configuration." To load the `dsimport` command without installing the NIS extensions, load the Utilities package only. Example:

```
blueprints# cd install_dir/Solaris_Extension
blueprints# pkgadd -d SUNWdsutl
```

The command syntax for `dsimport` is:

```
blueprints# /opt/SUNWconn/ldap/sbin/dsimport [-n] [-r] [-s] [-c
dsserv_conf_file] [-d debuglevel] [-D binddn] [-f front_end] [-h
host] [-m mapping_file] [-M bindmethod] [-p port] [-S
schema_entry_dn] -t table [-T ldap-timeout] [-V variable=value]...
[-w passwd] [ file...]
```

Before you can create the LDIF file used to populate the directory, an NIS to LDAP mapping file must exist. A default one, called `nis.mapping`, is created in:

`/etc/opt/SUNWconn/ldap/current/mapping`

The `SUNWdsnis` package must be loaded before the file can be installed. It should be modified to match the topology of your DIT.

The `dsimport` command takes a text file in `/etc/files` format as input. Typically, you use the same files that are maintained to generate your NIS maps.

1. **To load password data (assuming** `passwd.nis` **as an input NIS data file):**

```
blueprints# cat passwd.nis | dsimport -n -m file.mapping -t passwd
\ -M SIMPLE -D "adminDN" -w "adminPasswd" > passwd.nis
```

2. **Now load this generated password data** (`passwd.ldif`) **into the LDAP server.**

```
blueprints# ldapmodify -a -c -D "cn=Directory Manager" -w password
-f passwd.ldif
```

3. **Repeat the process for all other NIS maps.**

Client Configuration

Solaris 8 LDAP clients need to be initialized after the operating system is installed. First, you will need to install the client specifying NIS, NIS+, or `files` as the naming service, then convert it to LDAP. You should also make sure the `SUNWldap` package is loaded or the LDAP utilities will not be installed.

How LDAP Clients Initialize

The following is an overview of the client initialization process.

1. The `domainname` is set on the client.

```
ldap_client# domainname mydomain.blueprints.com
```

2. The `ldapclient` command is run on the client to specify a directory server IP address and the name of a profile that resides on the server.

3. The `ldapclient` command performs an anonymous search of the server looking for the `nisDomainObject`, then checks the value of the `nisdomain` attribute.

   Since the client uses VLV control for this search, it is mandatory to have the VLV Control ACI set to `userdn=anyone` to permit anonymous access.

4. A check is made to see if the value of the `nisdomain` attribute matches the name of the domain the client is set to.

5. The profile entry specified on the command line is retrieved, and the information is used to create two local files: `/var/ldap/ldap_client_file` and `/var/ldap/ldap_client_cred`.

6. The `/etc/nsswitch.conf` file is modified to include `ldap` as a naming service.

7. When the client is rebooted, the `/usr/lib/ldap/ldap_cachemgr` program is run to read the two files and then caches the information.

8. When an LDAP naming service request is made, the client used the cached information to bind to the server and retrieve the data.

9. Periodically, `ldap_cachemgr` checks the server to see if the profile has changed and updates the cached information if it has.

Sample `/var/ldap/ldap_client_file`

```
#
# Do not edit this file manually; your changes will be lost.Please
use ldapclient (1M) instead.
#
NS_LDAP_FILE_VERSION= 1.0
NS_LDAP_SERVERS= 145.107.100.1
NS_LDAP_SERVERS= 147.217.200.1
NS_LDAP_SEARCH_BASEDN= dc=blueprints,dc=com
NS_LDAP_AUTH= NS_LDAP_AUTH_SIMPLE
NS_LDAP_TRANSPORT_SEC= NS_LDAP_SEC_NONE
NS_LDAP_SEARCH_REF= NS_LDAP_FOLLOWREF
NS_LDAP_DOMAIN= mydomain.blueprints.com
NS_LDAP_EXP= 957424982
NS_LDAP_SEARCH_SCOPE= NS_LDAP_SCOPE_ONELEVEL
NS_LDAP_SEARCH_TIME= 30
NS_LDAP_PROFILE= default
NS_LDAP_SEARCH_DN=passwd:(ou=people,dc=blueprints,dc=com)
```

This information in the sample file has the following meanings:

`NS_LDAP_SERVERS` — Server Information: Server's IP addresses [:port]

`NS_LDAP_SEARCH_BASEDN` — Search `basename`, `baseDN` name for LDAP operation.

`NS_LDAP_AUTH` — Authentication Mechanism, the security mechanism to be used.

`NS_LDAP_TRANSPORT_SEC` — Secure Transport, the transport service to be used.

`NS_LDAP_SEARCH_REF` — Search referral option, follow or don't follow referral.

`NS_LDAP_DOMAIN` — Domain name

`NS_LDAP_EXP` — Server Info Expiration Time, the time when the configuration stored in this file and the `ldap_client_cred` files become stale. Default is 12 hours from last refresh. The parameter is expressed in seconds.

NS_LDAP_SEARCH_DN — Alternate `baseDN`, for a specific database search. The default is defined internally (`multi_value`).

NS_LDAP_PROFILE — Name of the client profile

NS_LDAP_SEARCH_SCOPE — Scope of the LDAP search. Default is one level.

NS_LDAP_SEARCH_TIME — Search time out, maximum time after which, if a search operation doesn't get the result, it returns to timeout. Default is 30 seconds; can be increased or decreased depending upon the complexity of the network.

Note – Some of these parameters might not be present in the configuration file; their absence means they have a default value.

Sample `/var/ldap/ldap_client_cred` File

```
#
# Do not edit this file manually; your changes will be lost.Please
use ldapclient (1M) instead.
#
NS_LDAP_BINDDN= cn=proxyagent,ou=profile,dc=blueprints,dc=com
NS_LDAP_BINDPASSWD= {NS1}XXXXXXXXXXXXXXX
```

This information in the sample file has the following meanings:

NS_LDAP_BINDDN — Binding DN, the LDAP client name used for general naming information lookup.

NS_LDAP_BINDPASSWD — Bind DN Password, the LDAP client password for authentication.

`ldap_cachemgr` Daemon

The `ldap_cachemgr` is a daemon that runs on the LDAP client machines. It serves two purposes:

- Refreshes the information in the `/var/ldap/ldap_client_file` file from the LDAP server.
- Accesses the credential information from the `/var/ldap/ldap_client_cred` file which is readable only by `root`.

If this process is not running, then the refresh is done per process and the `/var/ldap/ldap_client_file` will not be updated. Also, only anonymous connections can be made to the directory server (unless permissions of `ldap_client_cred` are changed to allow read access to everyone).

Besides providing the update capability, the `ldap_cachemgr` also reduces the LDAP network traffic generated during the refresh and provides a robust parsing mechanism that can flag any invalid syntax in the configuration file. See the `ldap_cachemgr`(1M) man page for additional information.

`ldaplist` Command

`ldaplist` is an LDAP utility that lists the Naming information from the LDAP servers. It uses the simplified API to access the information, thus obeying all the security and options defined by the configuration files. See the `ldaplist`(1) man page for additional information.

```
blueprints# ldaplist hosts lizzy
dn:
cn=lizzy+ipHostNumber=181.232.103.177,ou=Hosts,dc=blueprints,dc=com
```

Without any argument, `ldaplist` returns all the containers in the current search baseDN.

```
ldapclient# ldaplist
dn: ou=Directory Administrators, dc=blueprints,dc=com
dn: ou=People, dc=blueprints,dc=com
dn: ou=Special Users,dc=blueprints,dc=com
dn: ou=Group,dc=blueprints,dc=com
dn: ou=rpc,dc=blueprints,dc=com
dn: ou=protocols,dc=blueprints,dc=com
dn: ou=networks,dc=blueprints,dc=com
dn: ou=Groups, dc=blueprints,dc=com
dn: ou=netgroup,dc=blueprints,dc=com
dn: ou=aliases,dc=blueprints,dc=com
dn: ou=Hosts,dc=blueprints,dc=com
dn: ou=services,dc=blueprints,dc=com
dn: ou=Ethers,dc=blueprints,dc=com
dn: ou=profile,dc=blueprints,dc=com
dn: nismapname=auto_home,dc=blueprints,dc=com
dn: nismapname=auto_direct,dc=blueprints,dc=com
dn: nismapname=auto_master,dc=blueprints,dc=com
```

LDAP Client Initialization Example

```
ldapclient# ldapclient -v -P default 129.148.181.130
parsing -P option
findDN: begins
findDN: calling __ns_ldap_default_config()
found 3 namingcontexts
findDN: __ns_ldap_list(NULL,
"(&(objectclass=nisDomainObject)(nisdomain=blueprints.com))"
rootDN[0] dc=blueprints,dc=com
found baseDN dc=blueprints,dc=com for domain blueprints.com
Servers addresses 129.148.181.130
About to configure machine by downloading a profile
...
```

Client Verification

To double-check that the LDAP client is set up properly, run the `ldaplist` command as described earlier. If the command fails, check the following:

- Check that `ldap` exists as a source in `/etc/nsswitch.conf`.
- Check that the files `/var/ldap/ldap_client_file` and `/var/ldap/ldap_client_cred` exist.
- Check that the `ldap_cachemgr` is running (`ps -ef |grep ldap` should show it running).
- Run `ldapclient -l` to check out the contents of the LDAP client cached files.

Caution – Do not try to read the `/var/ldap/*` files directly—there is no guarantee they are in ASCII readable format.

- Verify that the requested profile exists on the server.

Troubleshooting Tips

This section describes LDAP configuration problems and suggested solutions to the problems.

Unresolved Host Name

The Solaris LDAP client back end returns fully qualified host names for host lookups, such as host names returned by gethostbyname(3N) and getipnodebyname(3N). If the name stored is fully qualified (it contains at least one dot), then the client returns the name as is. For example, if the name stored is hostB.eng, the returned name is hostB.eng.

If the name stored in the LDAP directory is not fully qualified (it does *not* contain a dot), the client back end appends the domain part to the name. For example, if the name stored is hostA, the returned name is hostA.domainname.

Unable to Reach Systems in the LDAP Domain Remotely

If the DNS domainname is different from the LDAP domainname, change the nsswitch.conf file. In the host entry, specify dns or put dns before ldap.

Sendmail Fails to Deliver/Receive Mail To/From Remote Users

If your mail domain (commonly the DNS domain) is different from the LDAP domain, you might run into a mail delivering problem. sendmail(1M) derives the mail domain from the domain portion of the host name returned by gethostbyname(3N). This means the return address will be in the LDAP domain. Because the mail/DNS domain is different from the LDAP domain, external users cannot respond to the email to fix this problem, you should change the host entry in the nsswitch.conf file to dns or put dns before ldap.

Login Does Not Work

LDAP clients use the PAM(3) modules for user authentication during the logins. When the standard UNIX PAM module is used, the password is read from the server and checked on the client side.

Authentication can fail for the following reasons:

- Password on the server is not readable by the proxy agent. You need to allow at least the proxy agent to read the password because the proxy agent returns it to the client for comparison.

- The proxy agent is incorrectly configured.

Lookup Too Slow

The LDAP database relies on indexes to improve the performance. A major performance degradation occurs when indexes are not configured properly. As part of the documentation, a common set of attributes that should be indexed have been provided. You can also add your own indexes to improve performance at your site.

ldapclient Cannot Bind to Server

If ldapclient fails to initialize the client when using the -P profile option, there are several possible causes:

- nisDomain attribute is not set in the DIT to represent the entry point for the specified client domain (nisDomainObject NOT FOUND message).
- Virtual list view (VLV) indexing ACI does not allow anonymous access (nisDomainObject NOT FOUND message).
- ACI is not set up properly on the server, thus disallowing anonymous search in the LDAP database.
- Incorrect server IP address passed to the ldapclient command. Use ldapsearch(1) to verify the server address.
- Incorrect profile name passed to the ldapclient command. Use ldapsearch(1) to verify the profile name in the DIT.

## CHAPTER 6

NIS Extensions Configuration

Sun provides a two-way synchronization service between LDAP and NIS, as an extension to the iPlanet Directory Server. As described in Chapter 4, "iPlanet Directory Server Installation and Configuration," this extension is installed by the addition of optional software packages. However, once the packages are installed, the directory server needs to be configured to support the extensions. Once the server is configured, several deployment options that can be considered.

This chapter presents an overview of what the NIS extensions are, how they are integrated into the iPlanet Directory Server, what schema changes are necessary, and how they can be deployed to coexist with your current NIS environment. Since the directory server deployed to support the NIS extensions can be used to support other applications, we discuss how configuration changes might affect these applications.

Overview

The NIS Extensions for Netscape Directory Server were originally developed as part of the Sun Directory Server. Since Sun now ships the iPlanet Directory Server as part of the Solaris software distribution, the extensions were ported to that server. The motivation for providing NIS support is the same and the implementation is similar. If you have experience with the Sun Directory Server version, the content in this chapter will be very familiar to you.

Although you could configure and deploy the extensions without knowing the software architecture and implementation details, you will find some background to be helpful in determining when and how to deploy the extensions. There may also be some confusion as to the relationship between the NIS extensions and other LDAP features found in the Solaris 8 operating environment. We hope that reading this section will clear up that confusion.

Note – Due to a name change, for the purposes of this chapter think of NIS Extensions for Solaris and Solaris Directory Extensions as interchangeable terms.

What the Extensions Are

NIS extensions are an add-on software package to the iPlanet Directory Server which provides a service that allows NIS map data to be stored in an LDAP directory, then made available to NIS clients. The service is referred to as a synchronization service since data is maintained in more than one place, in NIS maps and as LDAP entries. The architecture of the extensions is such that an entire NIS server deployment can be replaced or deployed as an NIS slave server to complement an existing environment.

When the NIS extension software package is installed, a plug-in is added to the iPlanet Directory Server. The plug-in communicates with a Solaris process called `dsservd` that emulates an NIS server. NIS clients communicate with `dsservd` in the same manner they would with the native Solaris process `ypserv`. The NIS server emulator maintains a set of NIS maps just as a native NIS server would.

Besides being able to respond to NIS client requests, `dsservd` can update its NIS maps when NIS data changes in the LDAP directory and, conversely, can update the LDAP data when NIS maps are changed. This synchronization occurs through an interprocess communication channel between the iPlanet Directory Server plug-in and `dsservd`. The next section explains the flow of data in greater detail.

NIS Extensions Architecture

FIGURE 6-1 shows how NIS data is accessed by both NIS and LDAP clients.

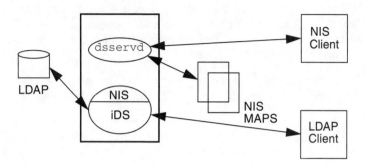

FIGURE 6-1 NIS Data Accessibility

The server shown in FIGURE 6-1 is running the iPlanet Directory Server with NIS extensions. As you can see, the server maintains both an LDAP directory and a set of NIS maps. The dsservd process shown looks like a ypserv process to the NIS client, which is bound to it. The binding occurs either by the Broadcast method or by a list of NIS servers specified at boot time (Specified Server method). NIS requests are serviced by consulting data in the NIS maps.

LDAP clients communicate directly with the directory server. Since the data is synchronized between the two data stores, each client sees the same view. FIGURE 6-2 shows how data is synchronized.

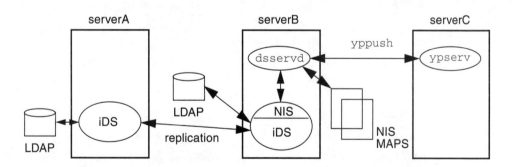

FIGURE 6-2 Data Synchronization

In FIGURE 6-2, serverB is running the iPlanet Directory Server with NIS extensions. serverA is running the directory server with the extensions, and serverC is running as a native NIS server. Two forms of data replication are being used. One is NIS-based and the other is LDAP-based.

serverB can run in either NIS master or NIS slave mode. In the master mode, the NIS maps on serverB are updated, then pushed to serverC. Changes to NIS data can occur by use of standard NIS methods, such as regeneration of an NIS map with makedbm, by updates to the LDAP directory, by LDAP methods such as ldapmodify, or by an imported LDIF file.

Synchronization occurs when either the NIS plug-in or dsservd process detects a change. The changes are then propagated from one data store to the other.

Note – When the NIS extensions are run in NIS slave server mode, you can only perform read operations on the NIS information in the LDAP directory.

Storing NIS Information in LDAP

Recall from Chapter 2, "Solaris Naming Services Architecture," that the model for storing data in LDAP directories is quite different from the one for storing data in NIS maps. To compensate for this mismatch, NIS information needs to be *mapped* to equivalent LDAP entries. Since new attributes that are not part of the standard LDAP are being introduced, a new schema definition is required. While this may not seem like a major issue, agreeing on exactly what goes into the new definition can be a lengthy process.

TABLE 6-1 lists the attributes required to support NIS information in an LDAP directory.

TABLE 6-1   NIS-Specific Attributes

Attribute	Description
uidNumber	Solaris UID
gidNumber	Solaris GID
gecos	/etc/passwd comment field
homeDirectory	User's home directory
loginShell	User's log in shell, for example, sh, ksh, or csh
shadowLastChange	Last time password was changed
shadowMin	Minimum length for password
shadowMax	Maximum length for password
shadowWarning	Time to change a password
shadowInactive	User account disabled
shadowExpire	Password no longer valid

TABLE 6-1   NIS-Specific Attributes *(Continued)*

Attribute	Description
shadowFlag	Type of account
memberNisNetgroup	Member of the netgroup
nisNetgroupTriple	hostname/username/domainname format
ipServicePort	Port on which service is running
ipServiceProtocol	Name of protocol
ipProtocolNumber	Number assigned to protocol
oncRpcNumber	RPC number of the RPC service
ipHostNumber	IP address in dotted decimal form
ipNetworkNumber	IP network number
ipNetmaskNumber	IP netmask
macAddress	Media Access Control (MAC) address
bootParameter	Parameters for remote booting
bootfile	Name of the file to boot
nisMapName	Name of an NIS map
nisMapEntry	Entry in an NIS map
nisPublicKey	Public key used by NIS
nisSecretKey	Secret key used by NIS
nisDomain	Name of the NIS Domain

To create a directory entry using these new attributes, you create object classes that contain them. These new object classes are listed in TABLE 6-2.

TABLE 6-2   New Object Classes

Object	Description
posixAccount	Adds Solaris attributes to account object
shadowAccount	Maps to /etc/shadow
posixGroup	Maps to /etc/group
ipService	Maps to /etc/services
ipProtocol	Maps to /etc/protocols
oncRpc	Maps to /etc/rpc
ipHost	Maps to /etc/hosts

TABLE 6-2 New Object Classes *(Continued)*

Object	Description
ipNetwork	Maps to /etc/networks
nisNetgroup	Maps to /etc/netgroup
nisMap	User-defined NIS map
nisObject	User-defined NIS object
ieee802Device	Maps to /etc/ethers
bootableDevice	Maps to /etc/bootparams
nisKeyObject	NIS public key
nisDomainObject	NIS domain

Directory Information Tree (DIT) Structure

For entries to be found in an LDAP directory, they must reside in well-defined containers, or organization units (ou), within the directory tree. The installation script which is run after installation of the NIS extension software package is installed, creates the proper directory tree structure for you. The components of this subtree represent standard NIS maps and any custom maps you may have created.

FIGURE 6-3 shows what a typical subtree might look like.

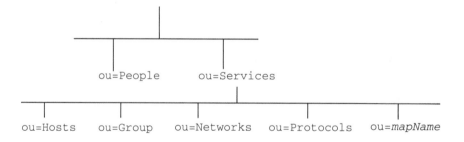

FIGURE 6-3 Typical Subtree

The container ou=People stores user account information. Information from /etc/passwd and /etc/shadow is used to create the entries found here. The ou=Services containers maintain the information stored in the rest of the NIS maps. A configuration file called nis.mapping contains the default mappings of standard NIS maps to containers in the subtree. This file also contains rules for how LDAP attributes are mapped.

Default NIS Mappings

The amount of information stored in the standard NIS maps varies from map to map. The `ethers` map contains a key with a single associated value, and the `passwd` map contains a key with a string representing multiple values associated with it. The rules defined in the `nis.mapping` file determine which values get stored in which attributes. The `group` map is a good example to illustrate this point. An entry in this map might look like this:

```
sales:*:1001:tom,linda,bill,cathy
```

When converted to an LDAP entry, the following attributes are defined.

cn: `sales`

userPassword: `*`

gidNumber: `1001`

memberUid: `tom`

memberUid: `linda`

memberUid: `bill`

memberUid: `cathy`

Generic Mappings

Containers and mapping rules are also generated for any custom NIS maps you may have created. The initialization script parses the NIS `Makefile` to discover any additional NIS maps. If any are found, a container with the same name as the NIS map is created with generic mapping rules applied to the contents of the NIS map. These rules are shown in TABLE 6-3.

TABLE 6-3   Generic Mapping Rules

LDAP Attribute	NIS Information
cn	nisKey (case ignored in LDAP searches)
sunNisKey	nisKey
nisMapEntry	nisValue
nisMapName	map name found in `Makefile`
objectClass	top, nisSunObject

This generic mapping is useful for representing custom NIS maps such as the ones commonly used to contain `automounter` information. For example, if you have an NIS map, called `auto.tools`, that contains mount points for software tools used in your organization, an LDAP entry representing an NIS map entry might look like this:

cn: `java`

sunNisKey: `java`

nisMapEntry: `javaserver:/export/javatools`

nisMapName: `auto.tools`

NIS Extensions Initialization

The previous section described the data should go into the LDAP directory to support the NIS extensions. This section describes how that data gets there. Most of the configuration is performed automatically by execution of the initialization script, but it is still helpful to know what the script is doing in case something goes wrong. Therefore, we present an overview of what is being configured.

Initialization Overview

The following steps summarize the configuration changes that must be made.

1. Update the directory schema.

2. Examine and modify the NIS Master's `Makefile`.

3. Create the subtree topology where the NIS information is stored.

4. Import NIS information.

5. Establish NIS server role.

6. Set up NIS replication policy.

Directory Schema Update

The additional object classes and attributes required to support the NIS extensions are added to the user-defined attribute and object class configuration files `slapd.user_at.conf` and `slapd.user_oc.conf`. View these changes as follows:

```
blueprints# more install-dir/instance/config/slapd.user_at.conf
# User defined attributes
# These attributes can be updated via LDAP by modifying the
# cn=schema schema entry. The attributes in slapd.at.conf can not
# be updated
attribute rfc822mailMember       rfc822mailMember-oid cis
attribute nisNetIdUser           1.3.6.1.4.1.42.2.27.1.1.12 ces
attribute nisNetIdGroup          1.3.6.1.4.1.42.2.27.1.1.13 ces
attribute nisNetIdHost           1.3.6.1.4.1.42.2.27.1.1.14 ces
attribute sunNisMapFullName      1.3.6.1.4.1.42.2.27.1.1.1 ces
attribute sunNisDomain 1.3.6.1.4.1.42.2.27.1.1.2 ces
. . .
blueprints#
```

```
blueprints# more install-dir/instance/config/slapd.user_oc.conf
# user defined objectclasses
# These ObjectClasses are read/writable over LDAP
# The ObjectClasses in slapd.oc.conf are read only and may not be
# updated
objectclass nismailalias
        oid 1.3.6.1.4.1.42.2.27.1.2.5
        superior top
        requires
                cn
        allows
                rfc822mailMember

objectclass nisnetid
        oid 1.3.6.1.4.1.42.2.27.1.2.6
        superior top
        requires
                cn
        allows
                nisNetIdUser,
                nisNetIdGroup,
                nisNetIdHost
. . .
blueprints#
```

`Makefile` Examination and Modification

The creation of NIS maps is determined by targets defined in `Makefile`, which by default resides in `/var/yp` on the NIS master server. The NIS extension software consults this file to determine which NIS maps are currently being used and then modifies it so a special `make` command is invoked instead of the standard `makedbm`.

The following lines in `Makefile` are modified.

```
YPDBDIR=/var/yp
MAKEDBM=$(SBINDIR)/makedbm
MKALIAS=$(YPDIR)/mkalias
```

These lines are changed to:

```
YPDBDIR=/var/yp/ldapsynch
MAKEDBM=/opt/SUNWconn/ldap/lib/dsmakedbm
MKALIAS=/opt/SUNWconn/ldap/lib/dsmakealias
```

This change results in a new version of `makedbm` and `mkalias` being executed when NIS maps are generated. This new version also updates the LDAP directory in addition to creating updated `dbm` files.

LDAP containers are created according to the targets listed in `Makefile`. For example, an `ou` will be created for each target map listed below:

```
all: passwd group hosts ipnodes ethers networks rpc
        services protocols \
         netgroup bootparams publickey \
         auto.master auto.home
```

Creating the Subtree

The initialization script automatically creates subtree components in the directory by issuing `ldapmodify` commands. The portion of the directory tree where these components are created is determined by the `NAMING_CONTEXT` variable. You can set the variable by uncommenting it in the `nis.mapping` file, as shown below. If the variable is not set, then the NIS domain name is used instead.

```
# The name of the NIS domain
    DOMAIN_NAME=blueprints.com

#
# NAMING_CONTEXT, if defined, gives the root of the naming tree
# if it is not defined, the naming tree root is derived from
# the DOMAIN_NAME variable using dc attributes for each
# element in the domain name (airius.com --> dc=airius,dc=com)
# NAMING_CONTEXT=O=XYZ,C=US
#
```

Importing NIS Maps

Once the system is initialized to be an NIS server, the data contained in the NIS maps needed to be imported into the LDAP directory. You import the data by reading the text files used to generate the NIS maps and then issuing `ldapmodify` commands to update the directory.

Initialization Checklist

Before running the `dsypinstall` script, have at hand the following information:

1. The name of the NIS domain managed by the server.

   This is also the default name in the directory subtree where NIS information is stored.

2. The installation directory for your iPlanet Directory Server.

3. The distinguished name (DN) and password of the directory manager. For example:

   `cn=Directory Manager`

4. The port number of the directory server. The default is 389.

5. The DN of the administrator for NIS information. Optional, if you do not want to use the directory manager as the administrator.

6. The location of the NIS source files. These files are used as the import source.

7. A list of other NIS servers in your domain.

▼ Initialization Procedure

To initialize an NIS server:

1. **Setup the system as an NIS server by running** `ypinit`**(1M).**

   Use the default `/var/yp` location for the `Makefile`.

2. **Run the** `/opt/SUNWconn/sbin/dsypinstall` **script.**

   The script prompts for the information mentioned in the checklist.

3. **Verify the installation.**

   The next section describes how to check to see if the installation was performed correctly.

Postinstallation Verification

Once the installation is successfully completed, the same NIS information is accessible from both NIS clients and LDAP clients. To verify this from the NIS side, make sure your client is bound to the server you just installed, then issue a `ypcat` command. For example:

```
nis_client# ypwhich
blueprints
nis_client# ypcat passwd
cmiller:IzBtd1LP0vCic:2848:20:Cathy Miller:/home/cmiller:/bin/sh
ludovic:Cxitd1LP0jkic:3808:20:Ludovic Poitou:/home/ludop:/bin/sh
mhaines:GHikZZxvFUxiM:1349:20:Michael Haines:/home/mh:/bin/sh
........
nis_client#
```

From an LDAP client, you should be able to access the NIS data by executing the `ldapsearch` command. For example:

```
ldap_client# ldapsearch -D "cn=Directory Manager" -w netscape -b\
"ou=Hosts,ou=Services,dc=blueprints,dc=com" objectclass=ipHost
"cn=*"
cn=localhost,ou=Hosts,ou=Services,dc=blueprints,dc=com
cn=heat,ou=Hosts,ou=Services,dc=blueprints,dc=com
cn=summer,ou=Hosts,ou=Services,dc=blueprints,dc=com
ldap_client#
```

In this example, all the entries in the `host` map are searched. This is equivalent to performing a `ypcat hosts` command.

Viewing NIS Data From the iPlanet Directory Console

FIGURE 6-4 shows what you will see under the **Directory** tab.

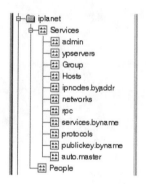

FIGURE 6-4   Directory Tab

To display NIS entries, click any of the containers shown.

Updating NIS Maps

Once the directory is populated, you can update NIS information in two ways:

1. From an LDAP client, like the iPlanet Directory Console.

2. By updating the NIS source files, then running `make` in the `/var/yp` directory.

You should be aware that the NIS source files are not automatically updated when changes are made through an LDAP client. You can resynchronize them by running the `dsexport` command.

Propagating NIS Maps

There are two methods of propagating NIS maps between master and slave servers. Between two iPlanet Directory Servers, choose LDAP replication. Between an iPlanet Directory Server and a native NIS server use standard NIS replication.

Capacity Planning and Performance Tuning

When directory servers become overloaded, they can no longer provide the level of service users have come to expect. Even though the server may still be considered *up*, response times can become so long that the directory service becomes unusable.

Preventing overload conditions requires identifying the proper hardware configuration to handle the load and the proper tuning of the directory server software to assure peak performance.

In this chapter, methodologies for correctly sizing your directory server are examined and some guidelines are offered. Additional tips for optimizing performance are presented so unnecessary bottlenecks can be removed.

Server Sizing

You must consider several factors before determining the optimum server configuration:

- Size of directory
- Frequency of directory access
- Type of directory access
- Security requirements
- Replication strategy
- Number of concurrent connections

Knowing the impact of these factors helps determine which hardware components are required to provide optimum performance. These hardware components include:

- Physical memory
- CPU
- Disk storage
- Network adapters

Failure to properly size any one of these components can cause a bottleneck that degrades the total system performance no matter how well the other components are sized. In general, you want enough memory to prevent swapping and you want fast disk storage devices that can handle the expected I/O throughput. Network adapters are rarely a factor because of the high data rates they can sustain, but you still must be aware of the network bandwidth consumption.

Eventually, some component, such as the CPU speed, will become a limiting factor. By carefully matching the components, you can push this limitation as far up the performance curve as practical.

Directory Considerations

Directory considerations include the following:

- Directory size
- Directory access
- Security requirements
- Replication strategy

Directory Size

The size of the directory affects both the amount of disk storage and physical memory required. It is important to choose sufficient disk storage to accommodate the current directory size along with space for expansion. Optimum directory performance is obtained when all the directory entries together with the directory indexes can fit into physical memory.

Calculating how much space is required for the directory entries is a straightforward process. The average size of an entry is determined, then it is multiplied by the number of entries. However, in addition to the directory entries are the index databases used to increase search performance. The size of these databases can vary depending on the number of attributes indexed and the type of indexing employed.

Directory Access

The way directory data is accessed has a profound effect on performance. The iPlanet Directory Server is optimized for search speeds and performs very well when the bulk of requests are searches. Assuming the directory data fits into physical memory, search performance is limited by the speed of the CPU and memory bandwidth.

Write performance is substantially less than read performance and will have a greater impact on performance. Additionally, there is a trade-off between tuning for read and write performance. Read or search performance is greatly enhanced by indexing the directory data based on what type of searches are likely to occur. However, as the number of indexes increases, so does the time it takes to update them.

Another factor affecting performance is how the LDAP client establishes a connection to the server. If the client is an LDAP-enabled application, then the same connection can be used for all client accesses, and this technique greatly increases performance. If a new connection is created each time a client, such as a web browser, accesses the directory server, a significant additional load is placed on the server. These two types of connections are commonly referred to as persistent and nonpersistent.

The more connections that a directory server has to maintain, the greater the load on the system resources.

Security Requirements

The level of security at which the directory server operates has a great effect on performance. The implementation of access control affects directory performance because more checking is required. Transmission to and from the directory server can be in clear or encrypted text. Encryption based on SSL, which the directory server supports, provides greater security at the expense of performance.

Authentication is another aspect of security that can be performed simply by entry of a name and password or by presentation of a client certificate via the SSL protocol. The public key exchange, which is an integral part of SSL and the encryption algorithms used to protect data, are CPU intensive and have a significant impact on performance.

Replication Strategy

Replication is a handy tool for increasing search performance by load distribution across more than one server. However, overhead is associated with replication. Changes to the directory database need to be recorded in a change log, then pushed out to replicas. Therefore, disk write speed and network bandwidth are important. In addition, CPU cycles are used during the transfer of data from the Supplier to the Consumer.

Capacity Planning Methodology

Sizing a directory server is not an exact science. As discussed earlier, there are many factors to consider. However, you can remove some uncertainty by employing the following techniques:

1. Calculating the size of your directory database

2. Determining what indexes are useful

3. Obtaining data from industry-standard benchmarks

4. Developing your own prototype/benchmarks

Once the directory server is placed into production, you can do additional fine-tuning by monitoring directory activity. This section discusses how to calculate the size of your directory database and provides some test results as guidelines.

Calculating Directory Database Size

The directory database consists of two components:
- Database entries
- Database indexes

Each database entry consists of a number of attributes and the values assigned to them. An entry varies in length depending on the number of attributes and size of values assigned to them. The value is an arbitrary string so its length will be different for different entries.

The database indexes contain only part of the entire entry, but they can still get quite large. In fact, if there are numerous indexes, the total size of these can be about the same as the entry size.

Directory Sizing Example

Here is an example of how the directory database grows in size.

For each person in the company, you have an entry that looks like this:

cn: Laura Weng

givenName: Yanna Laura Weng

sn: Weng

uid: lweng

description: NYC Financial SE

telephoneNumber: 555-566-7133

homePhone: 555-274-6401

mobile: 555-964-9769

pager: 888-856-1234

userpassword: ********

ou: people

mail: lweng@blueprints.com

departmentNumber: 777-100-1234

facsimileTelephoneNumber: 555-235-3232

initials: ylw

title: Systems Engineer

If the database is populated with 10,000 entries, the corresponding size of the entries and indexes grows, as shown below:

```
iplanet# cd database_dir/db
iplanet# ls -l
total 26530
-rw-------   1 root     other          18 Apr  5 10:42 DBVERSION
-rw-------   1 root     other       16384 Apr  5 10:35 aci.db2
-rw-------   1 root     other      729088 Apr  5 10:41 cn.db2
-rw-------   1 root     other       16384 Apr  5 10:40 copiedfrom.db2
-rw-------   1 root     other       16384 Apr  5 10:40 default.db2
-rw-------   1 root     other      811008 Apr  5 10:41 dncomp.db2
-rw-------   1 root     other     1310720 Apr  5 10:41 entrydn.db2
-rw-------   1 root     other      540672 Apr  5 10:35 givenName.db2
-rw-------   1 root     other     6979584 Apr  5 10:41 id2entry.db2
-rw-------   1 root     other      974848 Apr  5 10:35 mail.db2
-rw-------   1 root     other       16384 Apr  5 10:41 numsubordinates.db2
-rw-------   1 root     other       81920 Apr  5 10:41 objectclass.db2
-rw-------   1 root     other       32768 Apr  5 10:41 parentid.db2
-rw-------   1 root     other      532480 Apr  5 10:35 sn.db2
-rw-------   1 root     other      540672 Apr  5 10:35 telephoneNumber.db2
-rw-------   1 root     other       16384 Apr  5 10:35 uid.db2
-rw-------   1 root     other       16384 Apr  5 10:35 uniquemember.db2
-rw-------   1 root     other      876544 Apr  5 10:35
vlv#snmccoupeopleoblueprintscom.db2
```

The file id2entry.db2 contains all the entries in the directory along with an ID number. The size of this file gives a good approximation of how large the directory database is. From the listing, you can see that the size of this file is approximately 7 Mbytes, which equates to about 700 bytes per entry.

Note – Since the size of the sample entry used in this example might be on the low side, you can use 1 Kbyte per entry to approximate the size of the database entries.

The other *.db2 files listed here represent the index files. If you add up the sizes of all index files, you come up with roughly 6 Mbytes. So the total database size would be 13 Mbytes.

Note – Index files can be smaller or larger than the example. For additional information on managing indexes, see "Performance Tuning" on page 179.

If you create a directory database with 100,000 entries using the same sample entry, the sizes look like this:

```
blueprints# cd install_dir/db
blueprints# ls -l
total 253668
-rw-------   1 root      other           18 Apr  5 11:18 DBVERSION
-rw-------   1 root      other        16384 Apr  5 11:15 aci.db2
-rw-------   1 root      other      7135232 Apr  5 11:18 cn.db2
-rw-------   1 root      other      7946240 Apr  5 11:18 dncomp.db2
-rw-------   1 root      other     13189120 Apr  5 11:18 entrydn.db2
-rw-------   1 root      other      5021696 Apr  5 11:18 givenName.db2
-rw-------   1 root      other           29 Apr  5 11:18 guardian
-rw-------   1 root      other     68558848 Apr  5 11:18 id2entry.db2
-rw-------   1 root      other      9666560 Apr  5 11:18 mail.db2
-rw-------   1 root      other        16384 Apr  5 11:18 numsubordinates.db2
-rw-------   1 root      other        81920 Apr  5 11:18 objectclass.db2
-rw-------   1 root      other        32768 Apr  5 11:18 parentid.db2
-rw-------   1 root      other      4775936 Apr  5 11:18 sn.db2
-rw-------   1 root      other      4923392 Apr  5 11:18 telephoneNumber.db2
-rw-------   1 root      other        16384 Apr  5 11:15 uid.db2
-rw-------   1 root      other        16384 Apr  5 11:15 uniquemember.db2
-rw-------   1 root      other      8364032 Apr  5 11:18
vlv#snmccoupeopleoblueprintscom.db2
```

As expected the id2entry.db2 file grew to almost 70 Mbytes and the total of the entries and indexes is about 130 Mbytes. This example gives you an idea of how much disk storage is required for the database. There are a number of other files which need to be taken into account. These files include database directory backups and log files.

Directory Backups

In addition to replication, it is wise to perform regular backups. Backups consist of a copy of all the files in the database directory. The backups are stored in separate directories, so several different snapshots can be stored.

Since backups require as much storage as the active directory database, you must allocate space for these. If multiple backups are stored, then the space requirement will grow proportionally with the number of backups.

Log Files

You need to allocate space for log files. These log files include:

- Transaction log
- Access log
- Error log
- Audit log
- Change log

Transaction logs are a way of maintaining database consistency even when the server crashes. Before each write operation is performed on the database, an entry is written to the transaction log. Since the write operation to the transaction log happens at about the same time as the write to the database, it is preferable to have the log on a separate disk volume for better performance.

The access log keeps track of who accesses the directory and what type of access is performed. The information contained in these logs is valuable when you determine what type of searches are performed the most so you know what indexes to optimize. A typical entry in this log is about 70 bytes. Therefore, a million searches would generate a 70-Mbyte file. Based on how active your directory is and how much data you want to collect, you can determine how much space to allocate for the access log. You can specify a size limit to prevent this file from growing too large. Writes to the access log are buffered, so disk write speed is not an important factor.

The error log records change in status activity as well as errors. The information stored here is useful for troubleshooting problems but usually doesn't need to be kept for a long period of time. Unless the directory server has a serious problem, this file will not grow very fast. Allocating 100 Mbytes is probably sufficient.

The audit log records certain events. The amount of data written to this log depends on what events you want to audit and how often those events occur.

The changelog on the Supplier tracks changes it needs to replicate on the Consumer. Unless a lot of update activity is going on, this log file will not grow very large.

Summary of Disk Storage Requirements

TABLE 7-1 summarizes the disk storage requirements.

TABLE 7-1   Disk Storage Requirements

Purpose	Size Estimate	Comment
Directory DB	1.5-2 Kbytes per entry	Separate volume
DB Backups	n * DB Size	n=number of backups
Transaction Log	8-20 Mbytes	Separate volume

TABLE 7-1   Disk Storage Requirements *(Continued)*

Purpose	Size Estimate	Comment
Access Log	100 Mbytes	Activity dependent
Error Log	10 Mbytes	Pruned often
Audit Log	0-10 Mbytes	Depends on usage
Changelog	1-10% of DB Size	Depends on # of updates

Be sure to consider storage needs for the directory database, the directory database backups, and the log files.

Directory Database

You should have enough RAM so the entire database, including indexes, can fit into memory. Ideally, everything should be cached so read speed is not important. In most environments, only a small percentage of activity will be writes, so the write speed is not that important.

Since the directory database must fit within a single file system, it should be large enough to accommodate future growth. Data availability is key here, so disk mirroring, or other RAID levels that provide redundancy, is recommended. Also, no other data should be kept on this volume.

Directory Database Backups

You perform database backups by copying the *.db2 files from the database directory to another directory. The backup storage device should be on a different volume than the active database and ideally on a different disk controller. Performance will be impacted somewhat if the two directories are on the same volume and controller, but the bigger concern is that if the active database volume becomes inoperative, then you do not want the backup volume to be inoperative also.

Log Files Storage

The transaction log is relatively small but is continually updated even for search operations. A storage device with a write cache is a benefit here for busy servers. The A1000, T3, etc. are good choices.

Writes to the access log are buffered, so there is little performance penalty with access logging turned on. The only consideration is the amount of space required, as long as it is not on the same volume as the directory database or transaction log.

Memory Sizing

The most important factor that determines directory performance is the availability of free memory. For peak performance, all directory data needs to be cached in memory. If data has to be retrieved from disk, performance will suffer dramatically.

Correctly sizing the directory server's memory requires some knowledge of which components of the directory use memory and how much each of these components uses. These components include:

- Server executables and database image backing files
- Database entry cache
- Database index cache
- Solaris file system cache

Server Executables

The directory server software includes four application executables:

1. `ns-slapd` — An instance of the directory server

2. `ns-admin` — The administration server

3. `jre` — Java runtime environment used by the Netscape Console

4. `dsypserv` — An NIS extension used for NIS interoperability

The `ns-slapd` process will use up most of the memory. Running with an empty directory database, the `ns-slapd` process only consumes 5-6 Mbytes, which includes all of the standard plug-ins. The NIS plug-in uses another 500 Kbytes. However, the database caches reside within this process space and will grow as they fill up. The database image backing files are also mapped into this space.

The `ns-admin` process uses up about 8 Mbytes of memory and does not grow in size. The Netscape Console is Java-based and so requires the Java runtime environment (`jre`). The size of this process is around 27 Mbytes. If the NIS extensions are used, the `dsypserv` process will be running and consuming about 2.5 Mbytes of memory.

Database Entry Cache

The database entry cache caches all the directory data. The total size of the database entries is close to the size of the `id2entry.db` file. The size will depend on the number of entries and the number of attributes each entry contains. For a relatively small entry, say, containing 15 attributes, plan on about 1 Kbyte per entry. Therefore, a 100,000-entry database would consume 100 Mbytes of space.

The size of the database entry cache can be configured but should be made large enough to fit all of the database entry data. The cache size will grow as entries are accessed until all entries are cached. This memory shows up as part of the `ns-slapd` process.

Database Index Cache

This cache is also referred to as the database cache, but the name is a little misleading. What is really contained in the cache are the database indexes. These indexes speed up search time by anticipating what type of searches will be most frequently done and caching the results. The number and size of indexes depend on how the directory data will be accessed. The size of the database indexes can approach the size of the database entries.

For peak performance, the database index cache should be large enough to contain all of the indexes. If configured correctly, this cache has a greater impact on performance than does the database entry cache.

Solaris File System Cache

Data that gets read from disk gets cached in the file system cache. Although directory data which doesn't fit into the database caches will still be cached in the file system cache, performance will not be as good as with the database cache. Therefore, it is better to make the database caches large and not rely on the file system cache. One exception to this advice is a directory database that is much larger than the system memory. In the case of a lot of paging activity, the file system cache will be more efficient handling the paging activity than will the database caches.

Summary of Memory Usage

TABLE 7-2 shows typical memory usage.

TABLE 7-2   Typical Memory Usage

Component	Estimated Size	Comment
ns-admin	8 Mbytes	Static size
jjre	25 Mbytes	Required for console
dsypserv	2.5 Mbytes	NIS extension

TABLE 7-2 Typical Memory Usage *(Continued)*

Component	Estimated Size	Comment
`ns-slapd`	6 Mbytes (no data)	Main directory process
DB Entry Cache	1 Kbyte x# of entries	Data dependent
DB Index Cache	Varies	Depends on complexity of searches; could reach DB Entry size

Estimating CPU Usage

Estimating how much CPU power will be needed is a difficult task. It is easy to see when a production system is overloaded, but predicting at what load level this overload occurs is tricky. If you already have a directory server running that you plan to upgrade, you can measure its CPU and use the measurement as a guide. However, if you do not have any historical data to go by, the best approach is to use benchmarks or testing results as a guide.

Industry-standard benchmarks are helpful when you are comparing two platforms but may not be representative of your environment. Homegrown or custom benchmarks are useful since you can design them to simulate your environment or what you think the environment might look like.

Unfortunately, there are not any widely accepted industry-standard LDAP benchmarks. The DirectoryMark benchmark from Mindcraft was developed to measure the effectiveness of an LDAP server in a messaging environment. However, it has not caught on as an industry standard benchmark as WebBench and SPECweb have for web servers. You can find more information on DirectoryMark on the Mindcraft Web site at:

```
http://www.mindcraft.com
```

To obtain sizing information for this book, we ran a series of custom benchmark programs. The following sections describe those benchmarks and provide the results.

LDAP Test Suite

The test suite runs with the standard LDAP schema that ships with the iPlanet Directory Server and client programs written with the iPlanet software development kit (SDK). The directory is populated with entries that have the following attributes:

cn:
givenName:
sn:

uid:
description:
telephoneNumber:
homePhone:
mobile:
pager:
userpassword:
ou:
mail:
departmentNumber:
facsimileTelephoneNumber:
initials:
title:

Random data is created for each entry by the creation of an LDIF file. The LDIF file is then imported into the directory database. Test runs included varying the number of entries, number of CPUs, type of connection, and type of encryption used during authentication.

TABLE 7-3 is a sample test matrix for these tests.

TABLE 7-3   Sample Test Matrix

Test/Profiles	Number of Entries	Number of CPUs	Cache Size
Linear CPU Scalability Simple read	100 Kbytes	1, 2, 4	200 Mbytes
# entries scalability Simple read Attribute update Entry add/delete Authenticate	10 Kbytes 50 Kbytes 100 Kbytes 200 Kbytes	1, 2, 4	200 Mbytes
Cache-size effect Simple read	100 Kbytes	2	200 Mbytes
Import performance Import			

The tests listed in TABLE 7-3 are:

Simple read: Client creates a persistent anonymous connection to the directory. Base-level searches select entries uniformly across the entire set of data in the directory. Search returns the user's email address based on the user ID. Measurement is queries/second.

Attribute update: Client creates a persistent authenticated connection to the directory. A single attribute is updated in entries selected uniformly across the entire set of data in the directory. That attribute is indexed with an equality index. Measurement is updates/second.

Entry add/delete: Client creates a persistent authenticated connection to the directory. Whole entries are added and deleted in a ratio of 75% adds, 25% deletes. Measurement is operations/second.

Authenticate: Client creates a persistent anonymous connection to the directory. User authentication is performed uniformly through the LDAP *authenticate* operation over that connection against the entire set of data in the directory. Measurement is authentications/second.

Results of Experimentation

The following tests were included in the experimentation:

- Configuration tests
- Simple read test with persistent connection
- Simple read test with nonpersistent connection
- Modify tests
- Authentication tests

Configuration

This server configuration (TABLE 7-4) represents what an organization's directory server might look like. The maximum memory configuration allowed tests to be run with increasingly larger directory sizes with sufficient available memory. The A1000 was chosen because of its write cache. This write cache helps speed up writes to the transaction log.

TABLE 7-4   Server Configuration

Server Type	Sun Enterprise 450 (E450)
CPU	4 x 400 Mhz
Memory	4 Gbytes
Disk Storage	A1000
Network	100BaseT

Tests were run with directory sizes of 10 Kbytes, 50 Kbytes, 100 Kbytes, and 200 Kbytes. These sizes were chosen to be representative of directory use within an organization. The iPlanet Directory Server is capable of scaling well past these sizes into millions of entries for E-Commerce applications.

Simple Read Test with Persistent Connection

This series of tests is aimed at measuring the directory search times as the directory grows in size and also measures the effect of adding additional CPUs (see FIGURE 7-1). The intent is to fit all the directory data in memory so that disk read speeds are not a factor.

In this series of tests, a persistent connection between the LDAP client and iPlanet Directory Server is established throughout the entire test run. The intent is to simulate an environment wherein an LDAP-enabled application is performing the directory searches.

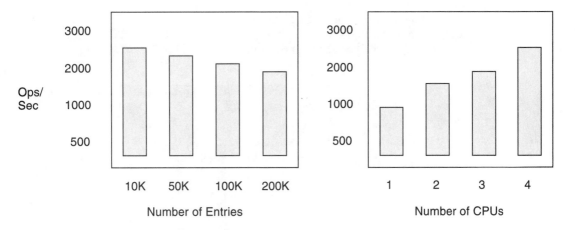

FIGURE 7-1 Simple Read Test with Persistent Connection

Read Test with Nonpersistent Connection

This series of tests shows the effect of using nonpersistent connections instead of persistent connections (see FIGURE 7-2). This setup simulates an environment in which an LDAP client is directly binding to the directory server, such as when a Netscape browser performs Address Book lookups.

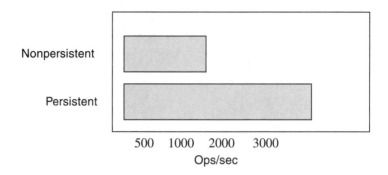

FIGURE 7-2 Nonpersistent Connections vs. Persistent Connections

Modify Tests

This series of tests demonstrates what directory update performance looks like. The tests simulate an environment wherein updates need to be performed on many entries, such as changing the telephone number prefix for a large group of employees. The effect of adding additional CPUs is shown.

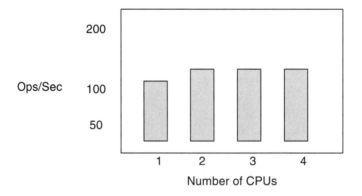

FIGURE 7-3 Effects of Additional CPUs

FIGURE 7-3 illustrates that write operations do not scale past two CPUs because they are limited by the speed of the disk.

Authentication Tests

This series of tests shows the authentication performance of the directory server with passwords stored in clear text, SHA encryption, and UNIX crypt encryption. It simulates an environment of a mail server having to authenticate a large number of email users in a short period of time.

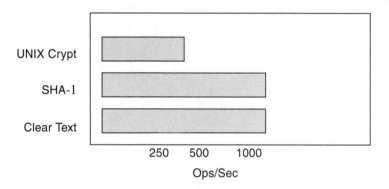

FIGURE 7-4 Authentication Performance of the Directory Server

As shown in FIGURE 7-4, the iPlanet Directory Server is optimized for storing passwords in SHA-1 format. UNIX crypt format is supported but runs only half as fast. The reason for this is that the crypt library is not multithread (MT) safe, so a mutex is required in a multithreaded environment.

Qualitative Observations Based on Test Results

Since the purpose of this experimentation is to provide guidelines on how to size your directory server, look at an interpretation of the results and evaluate its application to selection of the right server configuration.

- The iPlanet Directory Server is very fast at performing read or search operations. The peak was 2600 per second with 4 CPUs and a small, 10K entry, directory size.
- Read operations scale very well. Adding CPUs increased performance almost linearly.
- The search speed decreases as the directory gets larger. The greater the number of entries, the more time it takes to perform a search. However, this is not a linear degradation. Increasing the size by a factor of 10 decreased performance by only 40%.

- Write operations are slow compared to read operations. Increasing the number of CPUs does not increase performance.
- Authentication speeds vary somewhat, depending on how passwords are stored.
- Persistent connections require a lot less overhead than do nonpersistent connections.

Performance Tuning

Tuning the iPlanet Directory Server for better performance is much like tuning a database. Many of the concepts are similar, for example, using indexing for faster searches and database caching. Some simple things can be done, such as reducing the directory server code path by removing unneeded plug-ins.

This section looks at the role indexing plays in directory performance. If you are not well versed in database tuning concepts, then you can gain some background from the following overview of indexing.

Definition of Indexing

An index is a lookup table of entry ID numbers that correspond to certain search criteria. For example, if a search is made for a particular UID, then the UID index can be searched to find which entries have a matching UID.

Importance of Indexing

To understand the importance of indexing, it is helpful to understand the searching algorithm the directory server uses. When a search request is received, the directory server looks to see if any indexes match the search criteria. If, for example, an equality search for UID=jsmith is made and an equality index for the attribute UID exists, then the entry number can be retrieved directly from the index.

If an index does not exist for a particular search, then the directory server creates a candidate list that includes all the entries in the database. The directory searches the candidate list to see if there are any matches.

Index Types

TABLE 7-5 lists different types of indexes and the types of searches they are used with.

TABLE 7-5   Types of Indexes and Types of Searches

Index Type	Used When Search Contains	Example
Presence	Comparison against '*'	`(iscontractor=*)`
Equality	Comparison against some value	`(uid=jsmith)`
Approximate	Comparison uses the ~= operations for sound-alike searches	`(sn~=stevan)`
Substring	Comparison string contains the '*' as a wildcard	`(cn=*smith*)`
None available, always unindexed	Inequality comparisons	`(cn>smith)`

Different index types are used for different types of searches.

The Presence index is commonly used to determine if an ACI exists for a particular object. If an ACI exists, then access permissions need to be checked.

The Equality index is used in searches that require an exact match. A common example is a mail server, which bases the search for an entry on the UID of the person logging in. In this case, only an entry that matches exactly is of interest.

The Approximate index is used to retrieve entries that sound like the value being searched for. For example, a person's first name, may have multiple spellings, such as Stephen and Steven.

The Substring index is used to retrieve entries when only a portion of the total value is specified. An example of this is search for a name when only a sequence of characters in the name are known.

Viewing Indexes

The best way to view directory indexes is through the Directory Server Console. To summon the index screen, go to

Configuration —> Database —> Indexes

Two types of indexes are displayed: System and Additional.

System Indexes

FIGURE 7-5 shows the built-in system indexes.

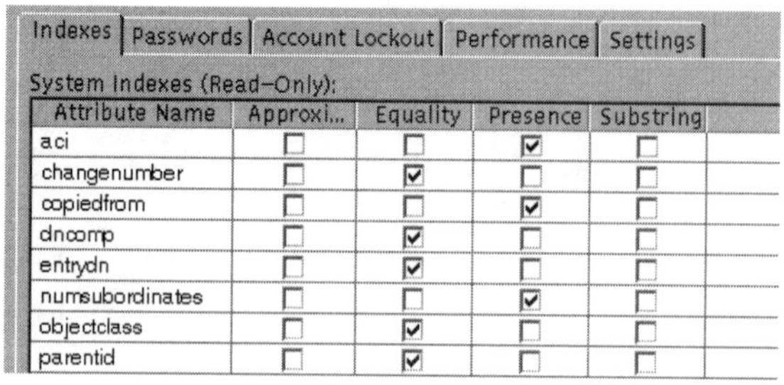

Attribute Name	Approxi...	Equality	Presence	Substring
aci	☐	☐	☑	☐
changenumber	☐	☑	☐	☐
copiedfrom	☐	☐	☑	☐
dncomp	☐	☑	☐	☐
entrydn	☐	☑	☐	☐
numsubordinates	☐	☐	☑	☐
objectclass	☐	☑	☐	☐
parentid	☐	☑	☐	☐

Tabs shown above table: Indexes | Passwords | Account Lockout | Performance | Settings. Section label: System Indexes (Read-Only):

FIGURE 7-5   Built-in System Indexes

These indexes are read-only and cannot be modified. TABLE 7-6 explains the use of these indexes.

TABLE 7-6   System Indexes

Attribute	Purpose
aci	Quickly obtains access control information
changeNumber	Tracks the replication
copiedfrom	Specifies source for replication
dncomp	Accelerates subtree searches
entrydn	Speeds up entry retrieval based on DN equality searches
numsubordinates	Specifies source for internal operations of the Directory Server Console.
objectclass	Accelerates subtree searches for internal administration purposes.
parentid	Speeds up one-level searches

Since these indexes cannot be modified, you do not need to know detailed information on how they work. The next category of indexes can be modified and are of more interest.

Additional Indexes

During the installation of the directory server, several indexes are created automatically; see FIGURE 7-6.

| Additional Indexes: | | | | |
Attribute Name	Approxi...	Equality	Presence	Substring
cn	☐	☑	☑	☑
givenName	☐	☑	☑	☑
mail	☐	☑	☑	☑
mailAlternateAddr...	☐	☑	☐	☐
mailHost	☐	☑	☐	☐
member	☐	☑	☐	☐
nsCalXItemId	☐	☑	☑	☑
nsLIProfileName	☐	☑	☐	☐
nswcalCALID	☐	☑	☑	☐
ntGroupDomainId	☐	☑	☑	☑
ntUserDomainId	☐	☑	☑	☑
owner	☐	☑	☐	☐
pipstatus	☐	☑	☐	☐
pipuid	☐	☑	☑	☑
seeAlso	☐	☑	☐	☐
sn	☐	☑	☑	☑
telephoneNumber	☐	☑	☑	☑
uid	☐	☑	☐	☐
uniquemember	☐	☑	☐	☐

FIGURE 7-6   Automatically Created Indexes

TABLE 7-7 shows the directory component or service that uses the index.

TABLE 7-7   Default Indexes

Attribute	Used By
cn	Common search parameter
givenName	User Account
mail	User Account
mailAlternative Address	NT Synchronization service
mailHost	Mail Server
member	Referential Integrity Plug-in
nsCalXItemId	iPlanet Calender Server
nsLIProfileName	Netscape Communicator roaming
ntGroupDomainId	NT Synchronization service
owner	Referential Integrity Plug-in
pipstatus	iPlanet Calendar Server
pipuid	Netscape Calendar Server
seeAlso	Referential Integrity Plug-in
sn	Common search parameter

TABLE 7-7 Default Indexes *(Continued)*

Attribute	Used By
telephoneNumber	Common search parameter
uid	Common search parameter
uniquemember	Referential Integrity Plug-in

The default indexes can be removed or modified. Removing indexes that are not used reduces the amount of memory required but does not significantly affect overall performance. Knowing which indexes are important and which are not is not always easy. The use of some indexes, such as those that support the NT Synchronization service, is obvious, and if you were not running the NT Synchronization service, you would remove those indexes.

If, however, a number of attributes are being used, but you do not know how often, you can monitor the usage of these attributes, as described in the next section.

Determining Which Indexes Are Important

You can determine the type of directory searches being performed by the directory server by looking in the access log for entries that contain the keyword SRCH. The following example shows what a typical SRCH record would look like.

```
blueprints# grep -i SRCH install_dir/slapd-instance/logs/access
05/Apr/2000:16:18:12 -0400] conn=18863 op=18885 SRCH
base="dc=blueprints, dc=com" scope=2 filter="(cn=John Smith)"
. . .
```

In this example, the search is being performed on the cn attribute. You can also see that it is an equality index. If this type of search appeared frequently in the access log, then an equality index on the cn attribute would help boost performance.

With the iPlanet Directory Server, you can be identify searches that reference unindexed attributes by examining the access log. Look for RESULT records that have a field that says notes=U. For example,

```
blueprints# grep -i "notes=U" install_dir/slapd-instance/logs/access
05/Apr/2000:16:18:12 -0400] conn=18863 op=18885 notes=U RESULT
err=0
```

By matching the connection (conn) and operation (op) fields with the corresponding SRCH record, you can determine which searches are being performed without indexes.

Cost of Indexing

Indexing can really help search performance, but at a cost. Indexes do consume memory, but the biggest cost in terms of resources is the increased write times. If an indexed attribute is added or modified, the associated index files also need to be updated.

In the case of a Substring index, a list of strings needs to be generated for each entry. Generation of the list can be very CPU intensive, especially for large string values. Also, if there are multiple index types, each type needs to be updated. For more information on tuning indexes for better write performance, see "Tuning Write Performance" on page 196.

Index Administration

Creating or modifying indexes is most easily performed through the Directory Server Console. If an attribute is already indexed, you can modify it by checking the appropriate boxes or you can remove it completely. To add an index, use the **Add Attribute** button under **Configuration** —> **Database** —> **Indexes**. All of the attributes defined in the directory should be listed in the **Select Attribute** window (see FIGURE 7-7).

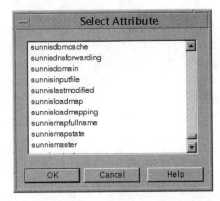

FIGURE 7-7 **Select Attribute** Window

Choose the attribute for which you want to create the index, then click the **OK** button. The attribute is then added to the **Index** screen where the type of indexing can be specified.

Indexing Summary

Indexing is a powerful tool for speeding up directory search times. However, too much indexing can have a negative effect on write performance. Before modifying or creating new indexes, you should examine the directory access log to determine what types of searches are more prevalent.

Since indexes pertain only to a particular instance of a directory server, a second server could be set up with replicated data but different indexes. The first server could be optimized for write access (minimum indexing), and the second server could be optimized for a wide variety of searches, although having lots of indexes does slow down directory replication.

Caching for Performance

To provide the quickest response to LDAP queries, the iPlanet Directory Server uses in-memory caches to cache database indexes and directory entries. The caches are managed to help ensure that the highest possible percentage of queries can be fulfilled from information stored in cache instead of from information retrieved from relatively slow disks.

Directory Caches

The iPlanet Directory Server uses two levels of cache to allow it to store information from the database in memory, and to circumvent the need to retrieve it from disk:

Database cache. The database cache caches pages from the database. It stores both database indexes and data. It is the lowest cache level. The size of the database cache is set by the administrator to a given amount of memory.

Entry cache. The entry cache caches the most recently accessed entries from the directory. It uses a least recently used algorithm to ensure that the most frequently accessed directory entries are always available in memory. Unlike the database cache size, the size of the entry cache is set by the administrator and is based on the maximum number of entries the cache should hold, not on the maximum amount of memory it should consume.

Evaluating Sizing Factors

To maximize directory read performance, you must cache as much directory data in memory as possible. By preventing the directory from having to read information from disk, you can eliminate the disk subsystem as a huge performance bottleneck.

There are three rules you must follow in maximizing read performance.

1. **Your database cache must always be large enough to hold the database's indexes.** As you will see, it should probably be set much larger than that, but you must always ensure that it is at least big enough to hold the directory indexes. If it is not, the directory will be forced to read indexes from disk for every search request. This behavior will quickly bring directory throughput to a virtual halt.

2. **Your database and entry caches must always fit into available physical memory.** If the sizes of the two caches combined is bigger than the amount of available physical memory on the machine, then the operating system will begin to swap the cache memory to disk. This can cause a significant amount of virtual memory *thrashing* that will quickly bring the directory and the entire system to a virtual halt.

3. **The database cache is more important than the entry cache.** When given a choice between allocating memory to the database cache or entry caches, you should generally prefer the database over the entry cache.

To maximize directory performance, you will want to allocate as much available memory to the directory caches as possible. You can achieve efficient operation by allocating memory between the caches in the ratio of 75% for the database cache, 25% for the entry cache. For example, if the system has 500 Mbytes of free memory during normal operation, allocate 375 Mbytes to the database cache, and 125 Mbytes to the entry cache.

Setting the Database Cache Size

You can set the size of the database cache through the Directory Server Console GUI or through a parameter in the `slapd.ldbm.conf` by editing the configuration file as shown below.

```
blueprints# cd install_dir/slapd-instance/config
blueprints# vi slpad.ldbm.conf
 . . .
suffix  "dc=blueprints,dc=com"
suffix  "o=NetscapeRoot"
directory       "/db_fs/db"
cachesize       100000
dbcachesize     100000000    <--- set size here in bytes
lookthroughlimit        5000
 . . .
blueprints# install-dir/slapd-instance/restart
```

Note – Be aware that the actual amount of memory used by the database cache can exceed the size you specify by up to 25% because of the additional memory required to manage the cache itself.

In any case, the database cache (with overhead) should not be set to consume over 2 Gbytes of memory, since it is not capable of using more memory than that.

Setting Entry Cache Size

Unlike the database cache, the entry cache size is set not by the amount of memory you would like it to consume but by the maximum number of entries you would like it to hold. The actual amount of memory it will consume is a function of the average entry size. For example, if your average entry size is 1 Kbyte, and you specify that the entry cache should hold a maximum of 10,000 entries, then the amount of memory the cache will consume will be (1 Kbyte/entry * 10,000 entries) 10 Mbytes + 25% for cache management overhead.

To determine the average entry size, you will need to use your best judgment of the data the directory will hold. You can determine the size of an entry by adding the sizes of all of its attributes. The sample entry below containing personal information for Cathy Miller is 387 bytes.

dn: uid=cmiller, ou=People, dc=blueprints, dc=com
cn: Cathy Miller
sn: Miller

givenname: Cathy
objectclass: top
objectclass: person
objectclass: organizationalPerson
objectclass: inetOrgPerson
ou: Tech Writing
ou: People
l: Chico
uid: cmiller
mail: cmiller@blueprints.com
telephonenumber: +1 408 555 4798
facsimiletelephonenumber: +1 408 555 9751
roomnumber: 4612
userpassword: BPs'r'Cool

To set the entry cache, edit the `slapd.ldbm.conf` file, as shown below.

```
blueprints# cd install_dir/slapd-instance/config
blueprints# vi slapd.ldbm.conf
. . .
suffix   "dc=blueprints,dc=com"
suffix   "o=NetscapeRoot"
directory        "/db_fs/db"
cachesize        100000        <--- set size here in # of entries
dbcachesize      100000000
lookthroughlimit         5000
. . .
blueprints#
```

Sizing the Database and Entry Caches

Although bigger caches are usually better, performance can degrade if `dbcachesize` is set too large. If you set the database cache too large and exceed the physical free memory available, the process will begin to page-out to disk. The result is severe performance degradation. You can detect this behavior by using `vmstat` and looking for excessive page-out activity.

Assuming the caches are not set too high to begin with, here is a technique you can use to fine-tune your database and entry cache sizes:

1. **Identify, using `vmstat`, the amount of free memory available when your system configuration is operating normally.**

2. **Use 75% of your free memory to allocate to your database cache.**

3. Divide that amount by 1.25 to account for the cache overhead, and use the result as the database cache size.

   a. If the result is larger than 1.6 Gbytes, reduce it to 1.6 Gbytes (the maximum dbcache size).

   b. If the result is smaller than the sizes of the database indexes (calculated by adding up the sizes of all *.db2 files in the directory database directory and subtracting the size of id2entry.db2), increase it to cover the sizes of the indexes. Do not exceed available memory, 1.6 Gbytes, or whichever is lower.

4. Use 25% of your free memory to allocate to the entry cache.

5. Divide that amount by 1.25 to account for cache overhead.

6. Divide the result by the average entry size, and use the result as the entry cache size (maximum number of cache entries).

7. Determine the size of an entry by adding up all of its attributes. Examine your data closely to determine average entry size.

Here is an example:

Assume the following system/directory parameters:

150 Mbytes available RAM (free memory)
Estimated 1 Kbyte entry size on average

Calculate DB cache size:

150 M * .75 = **112** Mbytes to allocate to db cache
112/1.25 = **90** Mbytes for db cache

Calculate entry cache size

150 - 112 = **38** Mbytes for entry cache
38/1.25 = **30** Mbytes avail for entries
30M/1 Kbytes = max **30,000** cache entries

Tuning Cache Sizes

Once you have set your initial cache sizes according to the aforementioned procedure, you should monitor your cache utilization from time to time to ensure efficient use. You can determine the effectiveness of your caches by examining the Database Performance Counters available through the Directory Server Console. To access this information, go to **Status —> Performance Counters**; under the **Database** tab the statistics shown in FIGURE 7-8 are displayed.

Summary Information	
Performance Metric	Current Total
Read–only status	0
Entry cache hits	985475
Entry cache tries	1114773
Entry cache hit ratio	88
Current number of entries in entry cache	50002
Maximum number of entries in entry cache	100000

Database Cache Information	
Performance Metric	Current Total
Hits	1465400933
Tries	1465424719
Hit Ratio	99
Pages read in	23766
Pages written out	269607
Read–only page evicts	0
Read–write page evicts	0

FIGURE 7-8 **Database** Tab Statistics

Note – The **Performance Counters** display data since the directory server was last started. To reset the counters, restart the directory server and delete the `*.share` backing files.

In FIGURE 7-8 you can see that the entry cache is set to 100,000 but it is only half full. Also, the database cache hit ratio is 99% which means that the indexes are essentially always cached. All the cache parameters are listed in TABLE 7-8.

TABLE 7-8 Cache Parameters

iPlanet Console Label	Monitor Entry Attribute	Meaning
Entry cache hits	`entrycachehits`	Number of requests filled from the entry cache
Entry cache tries	`entrycachetries`	Number of total requests to the entry cache.
Entry cache hit ratio	`entrycachehitratio`	Percentage of requests filled from the entry cache
Current number of entries in entry cache	`currententrycachesize`	Current number of entries in the entry cache
Hits (under database cache heading)	`dbcachehits`	Number of requests filled from the database cache.
Tries (under database cache heading)	`dbcachetries`	Number of total requests to the database cache.
Hit ratio (under database cache heading)	`dbcachehitratio`	Percentage of requests filled from the database cache.

These parameters can also be obtained from the command line, as shown below:

```
blueprints# ldapsearch -b "cn=monitor,cn=ldbm" -s base
"objectclass=*"
cn=monitor,cn=ldbm
objectclass=top
objectclass=extensibleObject
cn=monitor
database=ldbm
readonly=0
entrycachehits=985475
entrycachetries=1114773
entrycachehitratio=88
currententrycachesize=50002
maxentrycachesize=100000
dbchehits=1465400933
dbcachetries=1465424719
dbcachehitratio=99
dbcachepagein=23766
dbcachepageout=269607
. . .
```

Under optimal conditions, both the entry and database cache hit ratios will be above 95%. If either hit ratio is less than 95% and you have additional available physical memory, you should consider increasing your cache size to increase the hit ratio.

If you have been running your directory for several days and find that your entry cache is not filled to the maximum level, you might also consider lowering the size of your entry cache to just above the high watermark, and giving the freed memory to the database cache.

Setting the All IDs Threshold

Each index that the directory server uses comprises a table of index keys and matching entry ID lists. That is, for each index key there is a list of directory entry IDs that match the key. This entry ID list is used by the directory server to build a list of candidate entries that can match a specified search filter.

There is a size limit for each entry ID list. This size limit, called the All IDs threshold, is globally applied to every index key managed by the server. When the size of an individual ID list reaches this boundary, the server replaces that ID list with an All IDs token.

The All IDs token causes the server to assume that all directory entries match the index key. In effect, the All IDs token causes the server to behave as if no index is available for that particular search. The assumption is that some other aspect of the search filter will allow the server to narrow its candidate list before processing the list.

The default value for this parameter is 4,000. The All IDs mechanism is an important mechanism for improving search performance in those cases where the search results would yield most, if not all, directory entries. However, performance problems can occur if the All IDs threshold is set either too low or too high for your directory's size.

Tuning the All IDs Threshold Value

Stated again for emphasis: You should be very careful about changing the default All IDs threshold value for your server. With this in mind, here are some tips for tuning this parameter.

If your directory is reasonably stable in size, set the All IDs threshold to approximately 5% of the total number of entries stored in your directory. That is, if you have 1,000,000 entries in your directory, set the All IDs threshold to 50,000.

By default, the directory server is set to an All IDs threshold of 4,000. This value is ideal for a directory size of 80,000 entries. According to the advice given in the preceding section, this default value is acceptable for directories between 8,000 and 800,000 entries in size. If your anticipated directory size falls outside this range, change your All IDs threshold before populating your database. However, setting the All IDs too high can degrade search performance and increase memory footprint.

Setting Search Limit Parameters

Three search limit parameters let you manage the Directory Server performance by limiting the amount of resources the server allocates to client requests.

Size Limit (in entries) — Specifies the maximum number of entries the server will return to the client in response to a search operation. If this limit is reached, the server returns any entries it has located that match the search request, as well as an exceeded size limit error. The default value for this parameter is **2000**. Decreasing this value could reduce your average search time but will also limit the number of results returned on very large searches.

Time Limit (in seconds) — Specifies the maximum amount of real time the server spends performing a request. If this limit is reached during a search, the server returns any entries it has located that match the search request, as well as an exceeded time limit error. The default value for this parameter is **3600**. Decreasing this value produces results similar to those obtained by decreasing the **Size Limit** parameter.

Lookthrough Limit (in entries) — Specifies the maximum number of entries the server will check when seeking candidate entries in response to a search request. If this limit is reached, the server returns any entries it has located that match the search request, as well as an exceeded size limit error. The default value for this parameter is **5000**. Decreasing this value could reduce the average search time per request but will also produce more unmet requests. As a guideline, you should set this parameter at least 10% above your value for **Size Limit**.

Note – The values set on these parameters are hard limits on the resources that the server will apply to each request, but they are not enforced on the rootdn. In addition, an LDAP client can cause the server to actually use smaller values for **Size Limit** and **Time Limit**.

Changing Search Limit Parameters

You set the **Size Limit** and **Time Limit** parameters either by using the Directory Server Console or by editing the slapd.conf file.

From the Directory Server Console:

Go to the **Configuration** tab and highlight the top line in the left pane. On the right side of the screen, go to the **Performance** tab and observe the information there, shown in FIGURE 7-9.

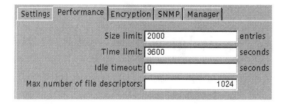

FIGURE 7-9   **Performance** Tab Information

Note – You should halt the Directory Server Console from the command line before you make the changes, then restart it.

To change these parameters from the command line:

```
blueprints# install_dir/slapd-instance/stop-slapd
blueprints# cd install_dir/slapd-instance/config
blueprints# vi slapd.conf
include "/opt/netscape/slapd-iplanet/config/slapd.at.conf"
include "/opt/netscape/slapd-iplanet/config/slapd.oc.conf"
include "/opt/netscape/slapd-iplanet/config/ns-schema.conf"
readonly        off
timelimit       3600          <----- change this line
sizelimit       2000          <----- change this line
lastmod on
idletimeout     0
. . .
blueprints# install_dir/slapd-instance/start-slapd
```

The **lookthroughlimit** can be changed either through the Directory Server Console or from the command line. However, using the Console will cause previously hand-edited data to be overwritten, so the command line method is recommended.

To change the **lookthroughlimit** parameter:

```
blueprints# install_dir/slapd-instance/stop-slapd
blueprints# cd install_dir/slapd-instance/config
blueprints# vi slapd.ldbm.conf
. . .
suffix   "dc=blueprints,dc=com"
suffix   "o=NetscapeRoot"
directory       "/db_fs/db"
cachesize       100000
dbcachesize     100000000
lookthroughlimit        5000        <---- change this line
. . .
blueprints# install_dir/slapd-instance/start-slapd
```

Considering Data Design Issues

You must look at three data design issues when deploying a directory:

- What are the number and types of attributes that will be stored as entries?
- How will the entries be organized into the directory hierarchy?
- What are the security rules that govern access to directory contents?

Design of the Entries

The number and type of attributes stored on entries can have a performance impact. When an entry is selected by a search, all of the entry's attributes are read into the entry cache even if only a few are requested by the client. This means that for a given amount of memory on a machine, you will be able to cache either a small number of large entries or a large number of small entries. Since the cache hit rate is increased as you cache greater numbers of entries, you will get better overall performance with smaller entries than with bigger ones.

The iPlanet Directory Server documentation recommends that you examine your schema for attributes that are redundant or unnecessary. Especially look for attributes that are excessively large. One small 20-character attribute will have negligible impact on entry size compared to the impact of a 50-Kbyte JPG photo.

You should take this suggestion in moderation, however. The directory is capable of managing entries with hundreds of attributes, with attribute values that are several megabytes in size. If your application requires that a lot of data be stored in the directory, you should not be discouraged from storing that amount of data. It is only important to understand the relationship between entry size and performance and to make sure that your machine has enough memory to provide a properly sized cache for your directory size.

Design of the Directory Hierarchy

The iPlanet Directory Server is designed so that the hierarchy structure will provide little or no impact on the performance of the directory. The directory can support branches that contain millions of entries all at the same level and as well as trees that are many levels deep, all without a significant impact on performance.

Design of the Security Rules

Using a large number of complicated Access Control Instructions (ACIs) can also impact performance. Although there is no hard limit on the number of ACIs you can use, strive for a simple ACI solution with as few ACIs as possible. As the number of ACI statements grows, the statements become difficult to manage and will also degrade performance. Most sites have 5-40 ACI statements in their directory and achieve acceptable performance.

Designing an LDAP Client

If you are building your own LDAP-enabled applications, remember that the design of your application can also affect search performance. Below is a list of tips to follow when you are designing your LDAP client:

- Avoid the use of `ldapdelete` followed by `ldapadd`. Use `ldapmodify` instead.
- Avoid configuring your client to always perform substring searches.
- Avoid retrieving attributes of an entry that your client does not need.
- Avoid multiple round trips to the directory when one trip will do. For example, in adjacent code, do not perform multiple searches for attributes in the same entry when the entries could be retrieved with a single search.
- Use a progressive, multilevel search that executes searches in order of complexity as described here:
  - Client searches for an exact match on an attribute and, if successful, returns the results and quits.
  - Client searches for a substring match and, if successful, returns the results and quits.
  - Client searches for a sounds-like match and returns the results and quits.

This type of phased approach to searching offers the best overall performance by minimizing the load on the iPlanet Directory Server.

Removing Unnecessary Plug-ins

The iPlanet Directory Server can be enhanced by the addition of features implemented as *plug-ins* which are contained in libraries loaded at runtime. If the features provided by the plug-ins are not used, there is only a small impact on performance. The memory footprint of the directory server will also be somewhat larger because of the inclusion of plug-ins.

It is wise to keep most of the default plug-ins, since removing them could have unwanted side effects. If, however, you are not using the Windows NT Synchronization service, it is safe to remove the two plug-ins associated with the service.

To remove plug-ins, from the Directory Server Console, go to the **Configuration** tab and expand the **Plugins** icon as shown in FIGURE 7-10.

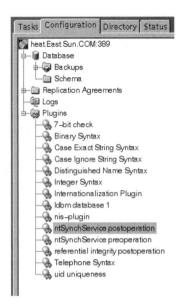

FIGURE 7-10 Expanded **Plugins** Icon

You can then click the plug-ins you want to delete, then uncheck the **Enable plugin** box. Since this operation modifies the `slapd.conf` file, you should halt the server, then restart after the change is made.

Tuning Write Performance

Compared with tuning the search performance of the directory, tuning the write performance is straightforward. The factor that most limits write performance is the amount of time it takes to update information in files on the physical disks of the machine where the directory is running. When a write operation of some type (add, update, or delete) is performed by the directory, the directory writes information to files in many different places:

- The appropriate indexes are updated.
- The update is noted in the transaction log.
- The access and audit logs are updated.
- The `changelog` is updated if replication is to be performed.

To guarantee the integrity of its data, the directory never considers a write operation complete until the Solaris operating system has confirmed that all of the appropriate files have been updated on physical media. Since disk access is thousands of times slower than memory access, write operations are often many times slower than reads, which are often completed out of the in-memory caches.

Considering this, center all write-tuning efforts around optimizing disk access. This optimization takes one of two forms:

1. It minimizes the amount of information that must be written to disk.

2. It increases the throughput of disk write operations by using faster disks, or spreading the load across spindles and controllers.

The following sections offer tips on tuning write performance.

Optimize Indexes

Although indexing makes searches much faster, the indexes must be updated by the directory for each write operation. This updating places a load on the server and increases the number of disk accesses that must be made for each directory update. When creating indexes, you must balance the needs of a fast search access to data against directory write performance.

The first optimization you can perform is to examine your indexes and remove any that are unneeded. If your applications never search on a particular attribute or do so infrequently, then putting an index on that attribute will only slow directory writes without providing any search performance gains. The directory, when first installed, is configured with a certain set of default indexes. You should always examine that list of indexes and remove any unnecessary ones.

It is important to consider the types of indexes the directory is maintaining. Each type of index, while useful for optimizing particular types of queries, is also associated with a particular cost whenever that index must be maintained. TABLE 7-9 illustrates the relative cost of maintaining certain types of indexes. The cost is expressed in terms of the number of logical database writes associated with maintaining the index for a given value.

TABLE 7-9   Relative Costs of Index Types

Type of Index	Relative Cost to Index a Value	Example Value: "first middle last"
Presence	1	1
Equality	1	1
Approximate	1 * number of words in value	3
Substring	1 * number of characters in value	17

You can see from TABLE 7-9, that substring indexes are potentially an order of magnitude (or more!) more expensive to maintain than equality or presence indexes. You should always be using the least expensive type of index that can accommodate the types of queries being made to an attribute. For example, if your applications will never be executing wildcard searches on a `uid` attribute, then you should not maintain a substring index for that attribute.

Increase Disk Throughput

An important part of write-performance tuning is finding ways to increase the throughput of the disks storing the directory data. This can be accomplished in two ways:

1. Increase the performance of individual disk subsystems.

2. Balance the write load across multiple disk subsystems.

The overall throughput of writing information to disk can be increased if the write load is spread across drives and controllers. The default installation of the directory places all directory data files under a single subdirectory. These files include the database and indexes, transaction logs, change database, and log files. This configuration usually results in all directory files being managed by a single disk volume.

In Chapter 4, "iPlanet Directory Server Installation and Configuration," procedures for relocating writable files are provided. Consult TABLE 7-10 to review the locations of the directives that control the location of each directory files that can be updated.

TABLE 7-10 Location of Files That Can Be Updated

File	Directive	Location
Database and indexes	directory	`slapd.ldbm.conf`
Transaction log	`db_logdirectory`	`slapd.conf`
Change log	`changelogdir` parameter or Netscape Console	`slapd.conf`
Log files	`accesslog, errorlog, auditfile` parameters, or Netscape Console	`slapd.conf`

Minimize Write Traffic

Since update performance is directly related to the amount of information that must be written to disk whenever an update occurs, anything that reduces or eliminates that disk traffic will speed updates. Here are some suggestions:

- Remove any unnecessary indexes, as discussed in "Optimize Indexes" on page 197.

- Minimize or eliminate logging. Turn off the access or audit logs if you don't use them regularly or don't require them for audit purposes.
- Eliminate the `changelog` db. If the directory is not a replication master, it doesn't need to maintain a change log. Turn it off through the Directory Server Console or through the `changelogdir` parameter in `slapd.conf`.

Checking the Schema

Schema checking is performed by iPlanet Directory Server to verify that all modifications conform to the current database schema. The database schema defines the type of information allowed in the database. Schema checking is an important feature that ensures you will be able to properly maintain the information after import. Schema checking works by default when database modifications are made by an LDAP client, such as `ldapmodify`, the directory server gateway, or when importing a database from an LDIF using the command line. The default value for this parameter is on.

Turning schema checking off can result in a slight increase in update performance. However, the amount of CPU time spent performing the schema check is a small fraction of the time spent waiting for disk writes to complete. For this reason, it's not recommended that the schema check be turned off during normal directory operation. However, turning it off can result in a large performance gain for imports. Also, on replica servers, you may want to turn schema checking off, since no application will directly modify the data on these servers.

If you do turn schema checking off, you will manually have to verify that your entries conform to the schema. Make sure that the attributes and object classes you create in your LDIF statements are both spelled correctly and identified in `slapd.conf`, `slapd.at.conf`, `slapd.oc.conf`, or a custom schema file that you are including in `slapd.conf`.

Tuning Import Performance

During a directory import with the `ldif2db` command, the directory performs a direct conversion of the entries in an LDIF file to a directory database and indexes. No LDAP operations are performed during this process, so the directory must be offline before an import can occur.

You can increase the performance of the import process by properly setting cache sizes and by turning off schema checking.

Setting Cache Sizes

During an import, the directory completely bypasses the LDAP processing logic and performs operations directly against the underlying database. The entry cache is completely unused during an import, and the database cache receives all of the activity.

You achieve maximum import performance by making the entry cache as small as possible (1,000 entries), and increasing the database to use as much available physical memory as possible.

Import Schema Checking

Turning off schema checking during an import may provide as much as a factor of two performance gain; however, you should never turn off schema check unless you are willing to sacrifice data integrity for speed. Leaving schema check off during import can result in an entry in the database that is impossible to modify once schema checking is turned back on. For this reason, you should not turn off schema checking unless you are certain that the entries in the LDIF file are valid for the directory's installed schema.

Troubleshooting Checklist

Here is a short checklist to help diagnose search performance problems:

1. Be certain that the directory is the problem.

If the machine running the directory is shared by other applications, the activities of those programs will naturally affect the performance of the directory. Before concentrating on tuning the directory, make sure that other programs are not the cause of your performance problem. For example, make certain that the "performance hiccup" that occurs at 9:00 every morning isn't caused by some other program's daily batch process.

2. Make sure that all searches are indexed.

Do you have RESULT records in the access log that have a notes=U field? If so, see "Optimize Indexes" on page 197.

3. Make sure that the machine isn't swapping.

Use `vmstat` to look at swap activity while the directory is running. If a significant amount of swapping is occurring, your cache sizes are probably set too large for the amount of available physical memory. See "Setting Cache Sizes" on page 200 for more information.

4. Make sure your caches are set large enough.

Optimal directory search performance is achieved by caching as much data in memory as possible. If your machine has unused physical memory, you can improve directory performance by increasing cache sizes. See "Setting Cache Sizes" on page 200, for more information.

5. Use server search parameters to keep runaway queries in check.

If the directory is receiving ad hoc queries from end-user applications, it is possible that the server can get bogged down executing thoughtless queries that return thousands of entries. You can limit the impact of these types of runaway queries by using the **Size Limit**, **Time Limit**, and **Lookthrough Limit** search parameters. See "Setting Search Limit Parameters" on page 191 for more information.

CHAPTER **8**

Deploying Highly Available LDAP Data Services

LDAP directory servers provide their own high availability features by performing directory data replication. With replication, the content of a directory tree, or sub-tree on one server, is duplicated on other servers. If one of the servers fails, the content is still available on the other servers. However, the current iPlanet Directory Server supports only a single-master replication model. This means that only one server at any one time is granted the access rights to update the content in the directory. If that server fails, updates cannot take place until the server is back online or a replica server is granted update permission. This chapter looks at a method for automatically switching over to a backup master directory server if the primary one fails. The software to do this is Sun Cluster 2.2 in conjunction with the Highly Available Data Services for the LDAP module.

Even with cluster deployments, LDAP replication plays an important role. Most companies are geographically dispersed with Wide Area Network (WAN) connections between sites. By positioning replicated LDAP directory servers at end points of WAN connections to service local users, you conserve precious bandwidth. The second part of this chapter presents LDAP replication architecture examples and deployment strategies for making LDAP data services available with the efficient use of network bandwidth.

iPlanet Directory Services 4.12 HA Architecture Models

This section provides working examples of the High Availability (HA) architecture that will enable you to understand what iPlanet Directory Server HA models are available and the concepts behind them. Since no single architecture fits every environment, we provide material about model availability to inform your decision about an architecture.

High Availability Strategy

When designing the architecture of a highly available directory strategy, you must be aware that availability comes at a price. It is generally thought that the more highly available a system is, the more its design and operations cost will be.

One of the major reasons for designing the architecture of highly available services is to prevent against the loss of business due to application service outages and downtime. In the case of directory services, unavailability of an application service can lead to loss of income, potential Internet subscribers, and even future revenues. The value of HA to directory services customers is directly related to the costs of downtime. This means that the higher the cost of downtime, the easier it will be to justify the additional expense of implementing HA. Take the case of Internet Service Providers (ISPs) who are core users of the directory services. They probably have service-level agreements with subscribers whereby they guarantee a certain level of availability. If ISPs do not meet this service-level agreement, they could incur financial penalties.

To provide HA solutions for your organization's directory services you must identify the goals of providing HA services. Possible goals might include performance, load balancing, and management. Once you understand your organization's goals, then you can look at some of the available options. Understanding the design goals will influence the way you design an architecture of an HA solution. Some of the more common approaches to designing high availability directory services include:

- Replication Models
- Referral Models
- Asymmetric HA (hot standby model)

Replication Models

Replication models support a single writable Supplier, and multiple read-only Consumer servers. The mechanism used is a simple replay-based replication scheme, in which a single-master server records the changes made to it and at some later time replays those changes to Consumer servers, which hold a read-only copy of the replicated subtree. Consumer servers may service `bind`, `unbind`, `search`, and `compare` operations on the replicated subtree, but they refer `add`, `delete`, `modify`, and `modifyRDN`/`modifyDN` operations to the master server, unless those operations come from the master server itself.

The Supplier server stores state information in a special attribute (the `copiedFrom` attribute) in the Consumer's copy of the entry at the top of the replicated subtree. Before commencing replay of changes, the Supplier retrieves the value of this attribute and sends only changes that have occurred since the last replication run.

Between these servers is a *Replication Agreement,* which must be configured before the servers can synchronize any data. Using the replication model enables us to avoid a situation whereby the loss of a single server causes the directory services to become unavailable. Once a server has been designated as the Supplier, all client updates are directed to that server. When a replica is initially created, it typically contains no directory data. To begin servicing client operations, initialize a replica. At a minimum, the replicated model should contain at least one backup server.

FIGURE 8-1 illustrates single-master directory replication architecture.

LDAP Client Sends Directory Updates

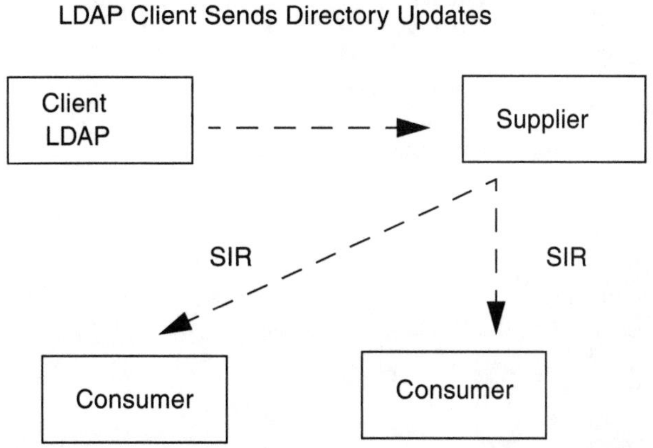

FIGURE 8-1   Single-Master, Directory-Replication Architecture

A higher-performance replication architecture is based on the same principle as FIGURE 8-1. To deploy that architecture, you would deploy directory services and the appropriate directory clients in the form of a workgroup. The idea behind workgroup architecture is that a Supplier server replicates its directory tree out to the multiple Consumers that are located in the workgroup in multiple LANs. The benefit of such an architecture is that it allows clients of the directory service to be much closer to the directory server that services their needs.

FIGURE 8-2 shows high-performance, single-master, directory-replication architecture.

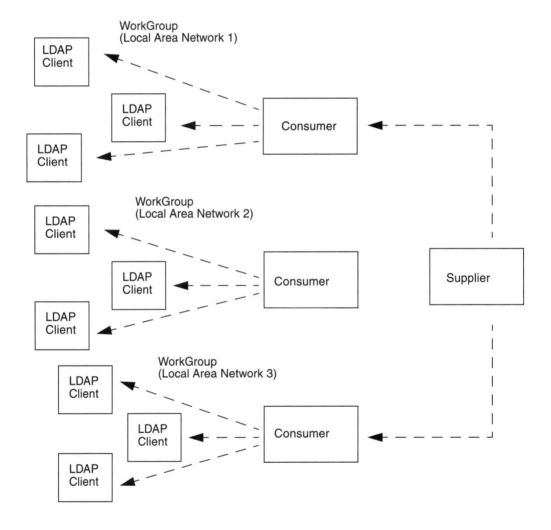

FIGURE 8-2 High-Performance, Single-Master, Directory-Replication Architecture

The replication hub directory architecture (FIGURE 8-3) builds upon the two previous architectures: a single-master directory, serves as a dedicated Supplier server to maintain all of the directory data. Any update requests that come from clients are handled by the Supplier server. The one major difference in the replication hub directory architecture is how the Supplier server replicates its content out to a replication master server. This replication hub server is a Consumer server of the Supplier server, and its function is to replicate changes that are made and send these changes out to the other Consumer servers. In turn, these directory Consumer servers will serve requests to clients.

One of the big advantages of the replication hub directory architecture is that the Supplier server can be taken offline for tasks such as routine maintenance.

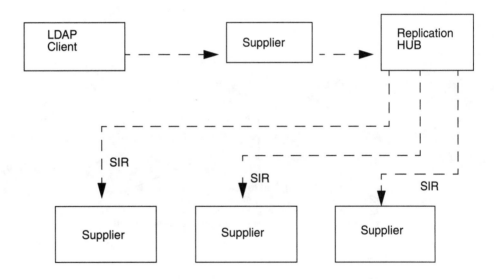

FIGURE 8-3   Master and Replication Directory Hub Architecture

Referral Models

Referral models are helpful because they enable HA architecture to scale to millions of users. For example, consider the not-unusual case of a company that has thousands of divisions located around the world. One major issue that this type of organization faces is the undesirability and impracticality (from management's viewpoint) of putting all the organization's entries into one directory server.

FIGURE 8-4 illustrates the basic referrals mechanism and how it works.

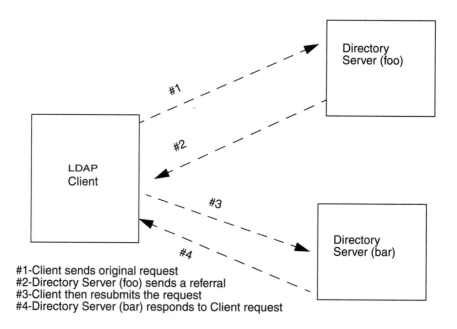

#1-Client sends original request
#2-Directory Server (foo) sends a referral
#3-Client then resubmits the request
#4-Directory Server (bar) responds to Client request

FIGURE 8-4   Basic Referrals Mechanism

A better approach to solving such management issues is to enable all divisions within your organization to manage their own directory server for its local user entries. The reason this architecture works so well is that users at the local division are only concerned with local entries. If the local division users want to find information pertaining to a user located outside the local division, they will then be referred automatically to a directory of directory servers. This server uses its directory tree to determine where to refer client requests.

FIGURE 8-5 illustrates a replication referrals mechanism.

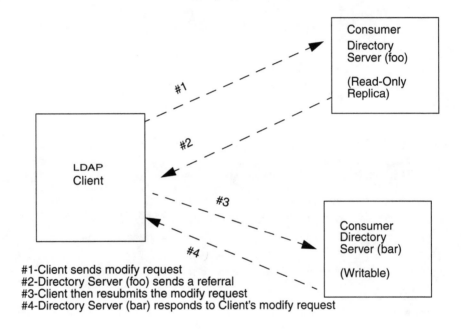

#1-Client sends modify request
#2-Directory Server (foo) sends a referral
#3-Client then resubmits the modify request
#4-Directory Server (bar) responds to Client's modify request

FIGURE 8-5 Replication Referrals Mechanism

FIGURE 8-6 shows a referral mechanism beyond the local division server.

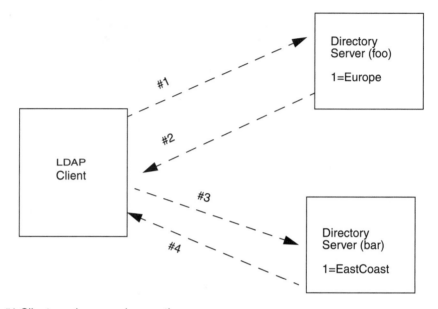

#1-Client sends a search operation
#2-Directory Server (foo) references and searches for entry
#3-Client then resubmits the search operation
#4-Directory Server (bar) responds to Client search operation with additional entries

FIGURE 8-6   Referral Search beyond the Local Division

Overview of Sun Cluster 2.2 Software

In general, clusters perform two mutually exclusive roles: clustering for high availability, and clustering for performance. Although Sun Cluster software can increase performance of some applications such as database servers, its primary benefit to an LDAP directory service is increased availability. In this role, Sun Cluster software is configured in a *shared nothing* architecture. What this means is that at any time a *resource* is owned by only one of the cluster nodes. If that node fails, then the ownership of its resources is transferred to a working node.

Sophisticated clustering software such as Sun Cluster needs to perform many housekeeping functions such as cluster creation and membership monitoring. While these are important functions, they are not discussed here. Instead the focus is on how the failover of the LDAP data service works.

Logical IP Addresses

The basic concept behind clustering for HA is the notion of a floating Internet Protocol (IP) address that is temporarily assigned to a server providing a service such as an LDAP directory server. Clients of this service use the logical IP address, rather than the server's actual IP address, to access the server. In the event of a cluster node failure, the logical IP address associated with the LDAP data service is transferred to a working node.

The convenience of referencing services by their logical IP address rather than the actual one is that the client need not know what physical server is actually providing the service. For example, an LDAP client such as a messaging application would always reference the LDAP server by its logical IP address and would be unaware if this IP address was transferred to another cluster node.

FIGURE 8-7 shows what a typical Sun Cluster HA configuration might look like. Two public networks are used for redundancy, and logical addresses are used by clients accessing services on the servers. The physical hosts are called phys-hahost1 and phys-hahost2; however LDAP clients only address these servers by their logical IP addresses.

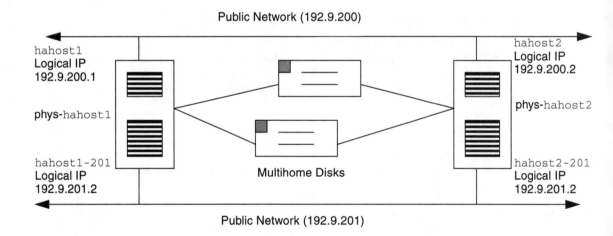

FIGURE 8-7   Typical Sun Cluster HA Configuration

In the FIGURE 8-7 configuration, both phys-hahost1 and phys-hahost2 are capable of running instances of the iPlanet Directory Server. The directory database files reside on the multihomed disks which are mirrored. At any time, the disks are owned by only one of the hosts. In the event of a failure, the ownership of the disks (and database) is transferred to the working node. The logical IP address associated with the directory service is also transferred.

Data Services for Sun Cluster

To run a particular application, such as the iPlanet Directory Server, in a Sun Cluster environment, the following software is required:

- Sun Cluster core components
- HA Data Services (for that application)

The Sun Cluster core components provide the necessary framework for running the application-specific software, or *data services*. The core components are responsible for maintaining a cluster configuration database and other services such as a heartbeat signal between cluster nodes. These core components must be configured before the data services can be installed and configured.

The data services provide functions specific to a particular service or application. For example, the Sun Cluster HA for Netscape LDAP data service manages the failover of the iPlanet Directory Server. This service is added as a Solaris package after the core Sun Cluster components are installed.

The HA Data Service for LDAP performs the following functions:

- Monitors the health of the directory service
- Controls the stopping and starting of the directory service
- Attempts to restart a failed directory server on the same node
- Stops the directory server on one cluster node, restarts it on another

---

Caution – Once the HA Netscape LDAP data service is configured with the Sun Cluster software, the directory server is no longer started or stopped manually, because the data service provides those functions.

Building a Sun Cluster with HA LDAP Data Services

While it is possible to build and configure a Sun Cluster without professional assistance, we strongly recommend that you seek the services of a consultant with Sun Cluster experience. Since you are deploying a Sun Cluster to increase service availability, it is well worth the investment to have an expert perform the initial set-up. To give you an idea of what is involved in setting up a Sun Cluster, we outline below some of the basic steps.

Building a Sun Cluster starts with identifying a Sun-supported hardware configuration. This configuration usually consists of two (or more) similar servers both of which are physically connected to one or more *multihomed* disk storage devices. The storage devices contain information such as the directory database and log files. Since the log files are usually kept on a different disk drive than the directory tree, several physical disk drives are typically deployed.

The multihomed storage devices are physically accessible by all the cluster nodes, but only one cluster node has control over it at any time. If the LDAP directory service fails, the control of the multihomed storage devices is transferred to another cluster node.

Another important consideration is the communication channels between the nodes. Separate channels are used for cluster communication, the *heartbeat* signal, and client access to the directory service itself. If the heartbeat or communication channels fail, then the cluster will not function properly. Each node would think that the other node has failed. Therefore, using redundant network interface controller (NIC) cards is critical.

LDAP Fault Monitor

The HA LDAP data service contains a fault probe that periodically checks to see if the directory service is functioning properly. The fault probe is run on both the active node and the standby node. On the active node, an `ldapsearch` command is executed on the node running the LDAP service; then the probe waits for the successful completion. On the standby node, the probe attempts to *telnet* into the port (default is 389) on the node that the LDAP server is running on. If the attempted telnet session times out, then the standby node is assumed to have failed.

The following is a section of the shell script used as the fault probe in HA LDAP Data Services.

```
INST_MON=$INST_MON_DIR/ldapsearch
PROBE_INTERVAL='get_config_param $INST_NAME PROBE_1_INTERVAL'
PROBE_TIMEOUT='get_config_param $INST_NAME PROBE_1_TIMEOUT'
while : ; do
#
# Take a nap here
# In the first iteration, this has the advantage of allowing time
# for slapd to start.
#
sleep $PROBE_INTERVAL

#
#  Remote probe, just try to connect to slapd
#  Local probe, connect to slapd with "cn=monitor" if [ "$LOCAL"
= "yes" ]; then hatimerun -t $PROBE_TIMEOUT $INST_MON -h $LHOST
-p $LPORT -b "cn =monitor" -s base "objectClass=*" > /dev/null
2>&1 else hatimerun -t $PROBE_TIMEOUT telnet -e'e' $LHOST $LPORT
<< TELEND > /dev/null 2>&1 equit TELEND fi
```

iPlanet Directory Server 4.12 Installation

No changes are required to the iPlanet Directory Server software to run in the Sun Cluster environment; however, there are compatibility issues, so it is recommended that you consult the Sun Cluster documentation. You must enter specific configuration parameters and install components in the proper order. The following steps summarize the process.

1. Load the core Sun Cluster components.

2. Install the HA Data Services for LDAP package SUNWscns1.

3. Install the HA Data Services Update, Patch-ID# 108109-xxx.

4. Install the iPlanet Directory Server 4.12 software on each cluster node.

5. Run the Sun Cluster configuration command: hadsconfig(1M).

When installing the iPlanet directory Server 4.12 software as noted in Step 4, you must change the following default parameters:

- Specify the *logical* host name instead of the *physical* host name of the server on which the software is being installed.
- Change the default server root directory, /usr/netscape/server4, to a directory that resides on the multihomed disk.

- Change the base install directory: The pathname should be the location, at which the start and stop scripts, `start-slapd` and `stop-slapd`, reside.

These parameters are also used for input to the `hadsconfig` command.

In addition to changing the default parameters, you set the following parameters to the preferred operation of the HA LDAP Data Service.

- **Name of the instance** — Multiple instances of the iPlanet Directory Server can be run simultaneously in the Sun Cluster environment. For administrative purposes, assign each instance a unique name tag.
- **Takeover flag** — This parameter specifies whether you want to failover this instance of the directory service to another cluster node. In most cases, you want this parameter set to y for yes.
- **Probe interval** — This is the time between fault probes. Since the fault probe executes an `ldapsearch` command, an additional load is placed on the directory server and network. The trade-off is between adding the additional load versus the time it takes for the Sun Cluster software to recognize there is a problem. The default is 60 seconds.
- **Probe time-out** — This is the time after which the fault probe will time out. Setting this value too low may cause a false failover trigger, so you must take care to set this value correctly. The default is 30 seconds.

Configuring the Sun Cluster HA for iPlanet Data Services

After you have installed the Sun Cluster HA for Netscape packages and the Netscape Directory Server, you are ready to configure the LDAP data service package. Sun Cluster HA for Netscape allows configurable instances that are independent of each other. Sun Cluster data services are configured with the `hadsconfig`(1M) command.

To configure HA data services for LDAP:

1. **Run the `hadsconfig`(1M) command to configure the service.**

```
phys-hahost# hadsconfig
```

2. **Register the Sun Cluster HA for LDAP data service by running the `hareg`(1M) command.**

If you installed the data service packages on all potential masters of a logical host but not on all hosts in the cluster, use the -h option and specify the logical host name.

```
phys-hahost# hareg -s -r nsldap -h logicalhost
```

3. **Run the hareg -Y command to enable all services and perform a cluster reconfiguration.**

```
phys-hahost1# hareg -Y
```

LDAP Cluster Deployment Options

Once you have decided to deploy your LDAP directory server in a Sun Cluster environment, you will need to decide what deployment model is right for you. You can either use the hot standby model or run services on all cluster nodes with the active server model.

Asymmetric (Hot Standby Model) HA

The basic asymmetric architecture consists of two clustered host machines, commonly referred to as *nodes*. These two nodes are represented by one logical IP address and an associated host name. The basic idea behind one logical IP address and host name is that the cluster services can then be referred to singularly. In this type of configuration, only one node in the cluster is ever active at any given time, which means that the hot standby node stays potentially idle most of the time. The obvious disadvantage to this type of architecture is the cost involved in having a server idle most of the time. Both cluster nodes share a logical disk array that is configured and designated to this shared volume. In this architecture, only one instance of the directory server will run on the active node.

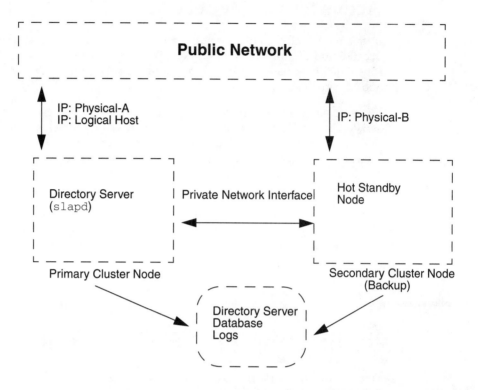

FIGURE 8-8   A Directory Server Asymmetric High Availability Model

In the architecture of FIGURE 8-8 the active node is Physical-A. If a failover occurs, the active node then becomes Physical-B. At the same time, the shared volume is switched to the secondary node in the cluster (backup node). In turn, the directory services that were running on the primary node will be stopped and will be started on the secondary node. The advantage of this architecture is that it dedicates a resource exclusively to the primary node with no resource contention. The disadvantage of the asymmetric HA model architecture is that the secondary node is idle most of the time.

In this model, two identical servers are configured and sized with enough capacity to handle the load effectively. One server in the cluster is active all the time, and the other server is idle. If the primary server fails, then the secondary server takes over.

The advantage of this model is that server performance does not degrade in the event of a failure. The disadvantage, of course, is that the resources on the standby server are not doing productive work. However, a manual switchover can be initiated so that periodical maintenance can be performed on a server without affecting service.

Active Server Model

In this model, all the cluster nodes have active services running on them. However, because you cannot have two master LDAP directory servers active at the same time, you either have to run two different instances of the LDAP server or run another type of service.

For example, you could have two separate directory trees, each with its own master server. One of the master servers could be active on each cluster node. In the event of a cluster node failure, the LDAP server on that node would failover to the healthy node. Similarly, you could have an LDAP server active on one node and a web server active on another node. If either service failed, then the LDAP server would failover to the other node.

The problem with this model is that running the additional service or services on the second node requires additional system resources. If sufficient resources are not available on the node to which the services failover, then the performance of all services will be degraded.

Redirecting LDAP Client Requests

How LDAP clients locate servers is application dependent. Web browsers with built-in LDAP capability generally only allow you to specify a single server for a particular Address Book. If that server is not operational, the client will not automatically try another server. Other clients, like the Solaris 8 LDAP client, allow you to specify a list of potential servers and a time out period during which to try another one if the first one does not respond.

A simple technique for client failover is DNS round robin, which rotates through a list of IP addresses, returning a different one for different lookup requests. The theory is that if a client attempts to contact a server and is unsuccessful, it will try again by performing a new DNS lookup. This time, the client receives an address of a different server, with luck, one that is operational. The problem is that clients often cache IP addresses so they will not have to do subsequent DNS lookups, which defeats the purpose of a DNS round robin.

An alternative method is to deploy some kind of LDAP redirector, which routes a received client request, to an appropriate LDAP server. The iPlanet Directory Access Router (iDAR) is an example of a redirector. The iDAR also acts as a load balancer, by sending requests to the least busy server. If a server is not responding, then no further requests are forwarded to it until it is operational again. More discussion on iDAR can be found in Chapter 11, "Directory Services Consolidation."

## CHAPTER 9

Preventive Maintenance

Proper maintenance procedures are a critical element in keeping the directory server running trouble free. Log file examination and pruning, scheduled backups, directory schema updates, and proper access control are all important maintenance functions. If you know the proper procedures to perform, these functions can save time and prevent unnecessary downtime.

This chapter discusses both routine and less frequently performed procedures such as relocating the directory to larger disk partitions. Sample scripts are also provided to perform bulk modifications on the directory database.

Directory Log Files

Log files play an important role in determining the health of your directory server. However, they do tend to grow in size and will need occasional pruning. There is sometimes a trade-off between the amount of data that is logged and the effect of that logging has on overall directory performance.

The iPlanet Directory Server provides three types of logs to help you manage your server and tune performance better. These logs include:

- Access Log
- Error Log
- Audit Log

The following sections discuss the format of the data maintained in these logs, the method for viewing the contents, and the settings for pruning parameters.

Access Log

If access logging is turned on, every time a client performs a directory operation, that event is written to the access log. For each client access two types of records are recorded:

- Operation requested
- Result of the operation

The operation requested can be a `search`, `add`, `delete`, or `modify` function. For a search operation, which is the most common, the following data is recorded in the operation record.

Date/Time — When the operation was performed.

Connection number — What connection the operation was performed on. If the clients are using persistent connections, there will be many entries with the same connection number.

Operation number — A sequence number identifying the operation that took place on the connection.

Search base — Where in the DIT the search began.

Scope — How many levels of the DIT were searched.

Filter — Search criteria specified.

Following the operation record in the access log is the result of that operation. For a search operation, the following data is written to the access log:

Date/Time — This should correspond to the operation record timestamp.

Connection number — The same connection as the operation record.

Operation number — The same number as operation record.

Error code and tag number — 0 for no error; see Appendix D, "Error Codes" for nonzero return codes.

Number of entries returned — If the search was successful, the number of entries that matched the search criteria.

Search time — The time in seconds it took to perform the search.

A typical pair of access records looks like this:

```
[05/Apr/2000:16:18:12 -0400] conn=18868 op=19154 SRCH
base="dc=blueprints,dc=com" scope=2 filter="(uid=cmiller)"

[05/Apr/2000:16:18:12 -0400] conn=18868 op=19154 RESULT err=0
tag=101 nentries=1 etime=0
```

In the example, you can see that the `conn=` and `op=` fields match, so you know the result matches the operation performed. The result was successful, with one matching entry returned.

Viewing the Access Log

View the access log from either the command line or the Directory Server Console. The same information is displayed regardless of which method you use.

To View the Access Log from the Command Line

```
blueprints# cd install_dir/slapd-instance/logs
blueprints# more access
[05/Apr/2000:16:18:12 -0400] conn=18872 op=19387 SRCH
base="dc=blueprints,dc=com" scope=2 filter="(uid=tbialaski)"
[05/Apr/2000:16:18:12 -0400] conn=18873 op=19438 RESULT err=0
tag=101 nentries=1 etime=0
[05/Apr/2000:16:18:12 -0400] conn=18868 op=19154 SRCH
base="dc=blueprints,dc=com" scope=2 filter="(uid=bsmith)"
[05/Apr/2000:16:18:12 -0400] conn=18870 op=19358 SRCH
base="dc=blueprints,dc=com" scope=2 filter="(uid=mmoore)"
[05/Apr/2000:16:18:12 -0400] conn=18868 op=19154 RESULT err=0
tag=101 nentries=1 etime=0
[05/Apr/2000:16:18:12 -0400] conn=18870 op=19358 RESULT err=0
tag=101 nentries=1 etime=0
[05/Apr/2000:16:18:12 -0400] conn=18867 op=19095 SRCH
base="dc=blueprints,dc=com" scope=2 filter="(uid=mhaines)"
[05/Apr/2000:16:18:12 -0400] conn=18872 op=19387 RESULT err=0
tag=101 nentries=1 etime=0
[05/Apr/2000:16:18:12 -0400] conn=18874 op=19446 SRCH
base="dc=blueprints,dc=com" scope=2 filter="(uid=cmiller)"
...
blueprints#
```

You can view the archive access logs by specifying the archive name, which has an extension of YearMonthDayTime. For example,

```
access.20000405-153437
```

To View the Access Log from the Directory Server Console

1. **On the Directory Server Console, choose the Status tab, then click the Logs icon in the navigation tree in the left pane.**

2. **Choose the Access Log tab in the right pane.**

   This tab displays the last 25 entries in the access log by default.

3. To refresh the current display, click Refresh. Click the Continuous check box if you want the display to refresh automatically every 10 seconds.

4. To view an archived access log, choose it in the Select Log pull-down menu.

5. To display a different number of messages, enter the number you want to view in the Lines to show text box and then click Refresh.

6. You can tell the server to display only messages containing a specific string. To do this, enter the string in the Show only lines containing text box and then click Refresh.

FIGURE 9-1 shows the access log being displayed.

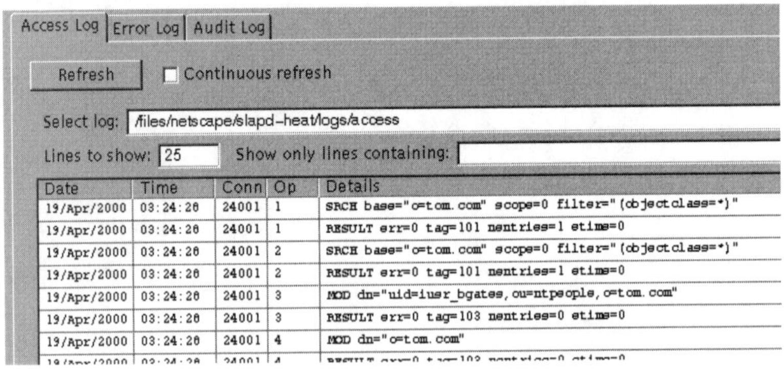

FIGURE 9-1   **Access Log** Tab and the Resulting Details

Access Log Configuration Options

Access logs can provide helpful troubleshooting information, but they also take up disk space and consume system resources. The actual load that access logging places on the system is minimal, so turning off access logging does not improve system performance. However, the size of the access log can grow very quickly on a busy server. Every 2,000 accesses adds an additional 1 Mbyte to the log, so it is not wise to let the log keep growing.

There are a number of configurable parameters you can use to limit the amount of space the access log will consume. You can specify a size limit, after which the access log is written to an archive file. An archive file can also be created after a specified period of time, perhaps daily or weekly. The next section explains how to configure the various options.

Enabling Access Logging and Specifying Log Location

1. **On the Directory Server Console, choose the Configuration tab and then click the Logs icon in the navigation tree.**

2. **Choose the Access Log tab in the right pane.**

3. **To enable access logging, click the Enable Logging check box.**

   Clear this check box if you do not want the server to maintain an access log.

   You can also disable access logging manually by changing the **accesslog-logging-enabled** parameter in the `slapd.conf` file as follows:

   accesslog-logging-enabled *off*

4. **Enter the full path and file name you want the server to use for the access log in the text box provided. The default is:**

   install_dir/`slapd-`*instance*/`logs/access`

Note – Access logging is enabled/disabled immediately through the Directory Server Console. If manually edited in the `slpad.conf` file, the change does not take effect until the directory server is restarted.

Setting Log Creation Policies

Log file creation policies are established through the same screen as the one that enables access logging. FIGURE 9-2 shows where the parameters are set.

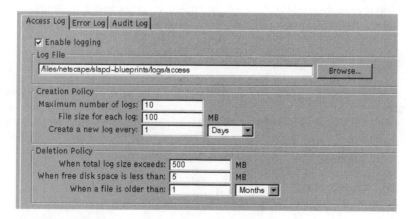

FIGURE 9-2   **Access Log** Tab and Parameter Settings

You can establish creation and deletion policies by changing the values in the following fields.

Creation Policy

Maximum number of logs: Total of access logs + number of archive logs. This number should be set to greater than 1 or else the access log will grow indefinitely. Once the maximum number is reached, the oldest log file is deleted.

File size for each log: A new log file is created when this limit is reached. Enter -1 for no limit to be set.

Create a new log every: The default—every day—is handy if you want to see what the activity was on a particular day.

Deletion Policy

When total log size exceeds: When the sum of all the log files reaches this size, the oldest log file is deleted.

When free disk space is less than: Deletes the oldest log file if the free space on the disk partition the logs are stored on falls below the specified threshold.

When a file is older than: Deletes log files when they reach a specified age.

Error Log

The error log contains detailed messages of errors and events the server experiences during normal operations such as start up and shut down. The error log record is in the format of:

```
date time details
```

The error log is enabled by default and can be disabled, but disabling is not recommended. Unless there is a serious problem, the error log does not grow substantially and uses few system resources. Similar parameters for controlling the size of the access log can be set for the error log.

Viewing the Error Log

View the error log from either the Directory Server Console or the command line. From the Directory Server Console follow these steps:

1. On the Directory Server Console, choose the Status tab and then click the Logs icon in the navigation tree.

2. Choose the Error Log tab in the right pane.

   This tab displays the last 25 entries in the error log by default.

3. To refresh the current display, click Refresh. Click the Continuous check box if you want the display to refresh automatically every 10 seconds.

4. To view an archived error log, choose it in the Select Log pull-down menu.

5. To specify a different number of messages, enter the number you want to view in the Lines to show text box and click Refresh.

6. You can tell the server to display only messages containing a specific string. To do this, enter the string in the Show only lines containing text box and click Refresh.

From the command line:

```
blueprints# cd install_dir/slapd-instance/logs
blueprints# tail -f errors
[06/Apr/2000:08:22:53 -0400] - slapd got shutdown signal
[06/Apr/2000:08:22:54 -0400] - slapd shutting down - signaling
operation threads
[06/Apr/2000:08:22:54 -0400] - slapd shutting down - waiting for
20 threads to terminate
[06/Apr/2000:08:22:54 -0400] - slapd shutting down - waiting for
housekeeping to close down
[06/Apr/2000:08:22:54 -0400] - Waiting for 4 database threads to
stop
[06/Apr/2000:08:22:55 -0400] - All database threads now stopped
[06/Apr/2000:08:22:55 -0400] - slapd stopped.
...
blueprints#
```

Audit Log

The audit log is useful for tracking changes to the directory database and the directory server configuration. If a problem arises with the directory at a particular time, checking the audit log is a good place to start to see if the problem coincided with the directory malfunction.

The following is an example of an entry made in the audit log.

```
blueprints# cd install_dir/slapd-instance/logs
blueprints# tail -f audit
time: 20000420100730
dn: ou=Managers,dc=blueprints,dc=com
changetype: add
ou: Managers
objectclass: top
objectclass: organizationalunit
creatorsname: cn=Directory Manager
modifiersname: cn=Directory Manager
createtimestamp: 20000420140730Z
modifytimestamp: 20000420140730Z
...
blueprints#
```

From the log, you can see that a change was made to the directory tree at 10:07 on April 20. At this time, a new ou called Managers was added by the Directory Manager.

Audit Log Configuration

The procedure for enabling the audit log and managing the creation of archive log files is similar to the procedures for the access and error logs. You set the parameters through the Directory Server Console by going to the Configuration—>Logs—>Audit Log tab.

Managing Database Transaction Logging

Whenever a directory database operation such as a write is performed, the server logs the operation by default to the transaction log. For best performance, the operation itself might not be performed immediately. Instead, it is stored in a temporary memory cache on the directory server until the operation is completed. If the server experiences a failure, such as a power outage, and shuts down abnormally, the information about recent directory changes that were stored in the cache are lost. However, when the directory server restarts, it automatically detects the error condition and uses the database transaction log file to recover the database.

Although database transaction logging and database recovery are automatic processes that require no intervention, you may want to tune some of the database transaction logging parameters for best performance. These parameters include:

- Location of the database transaction log
- Database checkpoint interval
- Durable transactions

The following sections show how to modify these parameters.

Changing the Location of the Database Transaction Log

In Chapter 4, "iPlanet Directory Server Installation and Configuration," the postinstallation section explains how to move the transaction log. Moving the transaction log file, which is stored in the *install_dir*/slapd-*instance*/db directory, to another disk drive is recommended for two reasons:

1. The purpose of the transaction log is to aid in the recovery of a directory database that was shut down abnormally, possibly as a result of a system failure. If the problem was caused by a disk failure on the disk volume where the directory database resides, you would also lose the transaction log.

2. Storing the database transaction log on a separate physical disk will improve directory server performance.

You specify the location of the database transaction log file by adding the db_logdirectory parameter to the end of the slapd.ldbm.conf file as shown here.

```
blueprints# cd install_dir/slapd-instance/config
blueprints# vi slapd.ldbm.conf
...
directory        "/db_fs/db"
cachesize        100000
dbcachesize      100000000
lookthroughlimit       5000
readonly         off
mode     0600
db_logdirectory /log_fs/log <- change this line
...
blueprints#
```

After you complete the change, restart the directory server to cause the changes to take effect.

Changing the Database Checkpoint Interval

Whenever a directory database operation such as a write or modify is performed, the operation is logged to the directory server database transaction log. For best performance, the results of the operation itself may not be written to disk immediately. Instead, they are stored in a temporary memory cache on the directory server. At specific intervals, the directory server writes the previously cached data out to the disk and logs a checkpoint entry in the database transaction log. By indicating which changes have already been written to the directory, checkpoint entries tell the directory server where in the database transaction log to begin recovery, thus speeding up the recovery process.

By default, the directory server is set up to send a checkpoint entry to the database transaction log every 60 seconds. Increasing the checkpoint interval can increase the performance of directory server write operations. Increasing the checkpoint interval can also significantly increase the amount of time required to recover the directory database after a disorderly shutdown and can waste disk space due to overly large database transaction log files. Therefore, you should only modify this parameter if you are familiar with database optimization and can fully assess the impact of the change.

To modify the checkpoint interval, you add the `db_checkpoint_interval` parameter using a range from 10 to 300 to the end of the `slapd.conf` file. The parameter is specified in seconds.

```
blueprints# cd install_dir/slapd-instance/config
blueprints# vi slapd.conf
. . .
db_checkpoint_interval 120 <- Add this line
. . .
blueprints#
```

Enabling Durable Transactions

By default, durable database transaction logging is enabled. This means that every time a write is performed on the directory, a corresponding entry is physically written to the database transaction log disk. To improve performance, you can disable durable transaction logging. When you do so, every directory database operation is logically written to the database transaction log file, but it may not be physically written to disk immediately. That means that if a directory change was written to the logical database transaction log file but not physically written to disk at the time of a system crash, you cannot recover the change. When durable transactions are disabled, the recovered database is consistent but does not reflect the results of any LDAP write operations that completed just before the system crash.

You can disable durable transactions by adding the db_durable_transactions parameter to the end of the slapd.conf file and set its value to off.

```
blueprints# cd install_dir/slapd-instance/config
blueprints# vi slapd.conf
...
db_durable_transactions off <- Add this line
...
blueprints#
```

Backing Up and Restoring the Directory Database

Backing up the directory database is essential even though your directory server is protected with redundant hardware such as RAID. If the directory data becomes corrupted for some reason and is not detected right away, the corruption will be copied to the mirrored disk. In cases like this, you need to restore the directory database to a known good state.

The fastest way to back up the directory database is to copy the database and associated index files to another disk volume. For archive purposes, the backed-up files can then be backed up to tape. It is also wise to maintain more than one backup copy rather than deleting the old one when a fresh backup is performed. This practice is easy to follow since a new directory is created by default each time a new backup is performed.

You can perform backups while the directory server is running; however, the server must be offline while you perform a restore. You can initiate a backup from the Directory Server Console or from the command line. In most cases, the command line is preferable since it can be run from an automated script. If, however, you want to back up the database before performing some risky directory operation such as updating the schema, using the Directory Server Console is quick and convenient.

The following sections discuss how to back up and restore both from the Directory Server Console and from the command line.

Backing Up the Database from the Directory Server Console

When you back up your database from the Directory Server Console, the server copies the entire database and associated index files to a backup location. To perform an online backup of your database from the Directory Server Console,

1. **On the Directory Server Console, choose the Tasks tab.**

2. **Click Back Up the Directory Server. The Backup directory dialog box is displayed.**

3. **Choose a directory name where you want the backup stored in one of two ways: In the Directory text box, type the name of the directory in which you want the backup placed; or, click Use default and let the server provide a name for the backup directory. If you choose to use the default, the backup files will be placed in the following location:**

   install_dir/slapd-*instance*/bak/*backup_directory*

   where *backup_directory* is a directory given the name of the backup. By default, the backup directory name identifies the time and date when the backup was created in the format YYYY_MM_DD_HHMMSS.

4. **Click OK.**

Backing Up the Database from the Command Line

You can back up your database from the command line by using the db2bak command line script. This script assumes you are using the slapd.conf file located in *install_dir*/slapd-*instance*/config.

To perform an online backup of your directory from the command line:

```
blueprints# cd install_dir/slapd-instance
blueprints# ./db2bak backup_dir
```

Note – If a directory is not specified on the command line, the default *install_dir*/slapd-*instance*/backup_dir is used where backup_dir is in the YYY_MM_DD_HHMMSS format.

Restoring the Database from the Directory Server Console

If your database becomes corrupted, you can restore it from a previously generated backup by using the Directory Server Console. This process consists of copying the database and associated index files from the backup location to the database directory.

Caution – Restoring your database overwrites your existing database files.

To restore your database from a previously created backup:

1. **On the Directory Server Console, choose the Tasks tab.**

2. **Click Restore Directory Server. The Restore Directory dialog box is displayed.**

3. **The Directory Server Console lists all backups in the default directory (*install_dir*/ slapd-*instance*/bak/*backup_name*) in the Available Backups list box. You can either select the backup from this list or, from the Directory text box, enter the full pathname to a location containing a valid backup.**

4. **Click OK.**

Note – If the server is running, you are prompted to shut it down. The restore cannot continue while the server is running.

Restoring Your Database from the Command Line

You can restore your database from the command line by using the bak2db command line script. This script assumes you are using the slapd.conf file located in *install_dir*/slapd-*instance*/config, where *install_dir* is the directory where you installed the directory server and *instance* is the name of your directory server.

To restore your directory from the command line:

```
blueprints# cd install_dir/slapd-instance
blueprints# ./stop-slapd
blueprints# bak2db backup_dir
blueprints# ./start-slapd
```

Deleting Database Backups

By default, the Directory Server Console places the backup files that it creates in a directory under *install_dir*/`slapd-`*instance*/`bak`. If you want to remove old backups, you can manually delete the files from this directory by using a Solaris utility like the `rm -r` command or you can create a *cron* script that deletes the directory and its contents.

Restoring Databases That Include Replicated Entries

If you are restoring a database that is supplying entries to other servers, then you must reinitialize all of your Consumer servers. A message will be logged to the Consumer servers' log files stating that reinitialization is required. If you want re-initialization to occur automatically, you can modify the `ORCauto` parameter.

If you are restoring a database containing data received from a Supplier server, then one of two situations can occur:

1. **Change log entries have not yet expired on the supplier server**. If change log entries have not expired on the Supplier server since the local database backup was made, then you can simply restore the local Consumer server and continue with normal operations. This situation is likely to occur only if the backup was done within a period of time that is shorter than the value you have set for the `Max Changelog Age` parameter in `slapd.conf`.

2. **Change log entries have expired on the Supplier server since the time of the local backup**. In this case, the Consumer server will automatically be re-initialized.

If the Consumer server needs to be initialized, then the database needs to be placed in read-only mode, as described in the next section.

Placing a Database in Read-Only Mode

You must put a database in read-only mode if you are manually initializing a Consumer server. When a database is in read-only mode, you cannot create, modify, or delete any entries. If your directory server manages multiple databases, you can place all of them into read-only mode at the same time by placing your entire server in read-only mode.

If you want to place a database into read-only mode from the command line, set the `slapd.conf` read-only parameter to on. You must shut the server down before you edit the configuration files.

To place a database into read-only mode from the Directory Server Console:

1. **On the Directory Server Console, choose the Configuration tab.**

2. **Click the Database icon in the navigation tree in the left pane.**

3. **Choose the Settings tab in the right pane.**

4. **Click the Make Database Read-Only check box.**

5. **Click Save.**

Exporting and Importing the Database with LDIF

An alternative to the backup and restore procedures described in the previous section is to export and import directory data in LDAP Data Interchange Format (LDIF). This method is useful if you want to copy part of the directory tree to another server.

Chapter 4, "iPlanet Directory Server Installation and Configuration" describes the procedures for initializing the directory by importing data in LDIF format. This is a common method for importing data from legacy data sources such as NIS maps. In this scenario, the maps are converted to LDIF format; then the LDIF file is imported into the directory.

Note – The process of converting data to LDIF requires that some kind of filtering program be written. The procedure for writing such a filter is beyond the scope of this book. Tips to get started can be found on the `iplanet.com` Web site.

You can perform the export and import of LDIF either through the Directory Server Console or through the command line. Since the procedure for using the Directory Server Console is discussed in Chapter 7, "Capacity Planning and Performance Tuning," the focus here is on using the command line tools.

Exporting Databases to LDIF from the Command Line

The directory database is exported to LDIF with the `ns-slapd` command executed from the `db2ldif` keyword. Below is the full syntax for running this command.

`ns-slapd db2ldif -f` *slapd.conf* `-a` *output_file* `[-d` *debug_level* `-n -r -s` *include_suffix* `-x` *exclude_suffix*`]`

where:

slapd.conf — Is the location of the directory server configuration file. The default location of the `slapd.conf` file is *install_dir*/`slapd-`*instance*/`config`.

-a — Is the location of the output file in which the server saves the exported LDIF. If a path is not specified, the file is created in the current directory.

-d — Optional debug level

-f — Is the `slapd.conf` configuration file to use for the conversion process. The default location of the `slapd.conf` file is *install_dir*/`slapd-`*instance*/`config`.

-n — Optionally specifies that entry IDs are not to be included in the LDIF output. The entry IDs are necessary only if the `db2ldif` output is to be used as input to the `db2index` command.

-r — Optionally used to import the LDIF file into a Consumer server. The **-r** flag causes the server to include the `copiedFrom` attribute and its contents in the LDIF output. The replication process requires this information. If the **-r** option is used, you also need to use the **-s** option to specify the suffix you want exported. You must shut down the server before using this option to export.

-s — Optionally specifies the suffix or suffixes to include in the export. Multiple **-s** arguments can be specified. If an **-s** or **-x** argument is not specified, then the server exports all suffixes within the database. If you use both **-x** and **-s** arguments with the same suffix, the **-x** operation takes precedence. If you intend to import the LDIF file into your configuration directory, make sure that you also use **-s** to include `o=NetscapeRoot`.

-x — Optionally specifies a suffix or suffixes to exclude in the export. You can specify multiple **-x** arguments.

Here is an example of the command:

```
blueprints# ns-slapd db2ldif -f /files/netscape/slapd-
blueprints/config/slapd.conf -a output.ldif -s dc=blueprints,
dc=com -s "o=NetscapeRoot"
```

The db2ldif Script

If you want to export the entire directory to LDIF, you can use a script called db2ldif. The script is located in *install_dir*/slapd-*instance* directory. If the script is run with a file name as an argument, then the LDIF output is sent that file. Otherwise, a default file of the form: YYYY_MM_DD_HHMMSS.ldif is created.

For example:

```
blueprints# cd install_dir/slapd-instance
blueprints# ./db2ldif
blueprint# ls ./ldif
2000_04_17_224244.ldif
blueprints#
```

Importing Databases from LDIF

You can import an LDIF file either by running the ns-slapd command with the ldif2db keyword or by running the ldapmodify command. To import an entire database run the ldif2db script, which executes the ns-slapd command with the ldif2db argument. For example:

```
blueprints# cd install_dir/slapd-instance
blueprints# ./stop-slapd
blueprints# ./ldif2db -i ./ldif/2000_04_17_224244.ldif
blueprints# ./start-slapd
```

Import a directory subtree from an LDIF file by using the ldif2db command. However, for importing small numbers of entries (less than 10,000) run the ldapmodify command.

For example:

```
blueprints# ldapmodify -D "cn=Directory Manager" -w mypassword -
c -a -f somefile.ldif
```

Note – You cannot import an LDIF file that contains a root entry unless you bind to the directory as the rootDN (Directory Manager). The reason is that access to the root entry is the top of the tree and by definition does not contain any ACIs.

## CHAPTER 10

Managing Directory Services

The contents of a directory are not static. Directory entries are constantly being added, deleted, and modified. After the directory service is installed and running, new uses for it will be discovered, requiring changes to the directory database structure. Setting proper access control on new directory data objects is also an ongoing process as the nature and sensitivity of directory data changes. As more applications and clients begin to rely on the availability of the directory service, monitoring its health and taking corrective action is critical to a successful implementation.

This chapter looks at the tools and techniques for managing your constantly changing directory server. The specific areas covered are:

- Establishing access control policies
- Managing the directory schema
- Monitoring directory resource consumption
- Managing with SNMP
- Managing the LDAP directory server with BMC PATROL

Establishing Access Control Policies

Before populating the directory database, it is wise to map out an access control policy. In the Solaris UFS file system, permissions are set on directories and files to establish what access rights are permissible. User and group ownership is assigned to determine who has access to directories and files. Finer grained access control can be obtained by the use of the Solaris access control list (ACL).

The same access rights can also be applied to the directory, but the tools for applying them are much different from the Solaris tools you may be used to. This mechanism is far more flexible but can also be far more complex to administer. To help you to better understand how to administer directory access control, we first review the security access model and define some of the common terminology you will encounter.

LDAP Security Model Review

At the top of the directory information tree (DIT) is the *root*. Under the root are containers in the form of suffixes or organization units (ou). Data entries, which have attributes associated with them, appear under an ou. Access permissions can be set at any level of the DIT: root DN, ou, entry, or attribute. These permissions are set by the creation of access control instructions (ACIs), which are associated with any one of the directory entities.

A directory client establishes its identity when a connection is first made to the directory server. This operation is called *binding* and requires some form of authentication, which users do by one of the following methods:

- Simple bind by supplying a DN and password
- SSL using client certificates
- Anonymous binding
- Directory server defined with SASL

The simple bind is the most common method. Once a user is authenticated, an attribute, such as the uid and group membership, can be used to grant or restrict access.

An ACI can be set at any level in the DIT, including the attribute level. Once an ACI is created for a directory entity, all the children of that entity inherit it. An ACI different from the parent can be assigned to a child entry, but the precedence rule applies. This rule states that a **deny access** always takes precedence over the **allow access** directive. For example, you can permit read access to everyone for the whole directory, but limit access in a subtree by creating an ACI with **deny access** set. Likewise, a single attribute, such as an employee's salary, can be protected with an ACI.

Access Control Instructions

An access control instruction is an attribute that can be assigned to any entry in the directory. By default, no ACI attributes are assigned. With no ACI attributes assigned, the default is to deny access rights to all users. An ACI can be assigned in these ways:

- From the Directory Server Console
- By creation of an LDIF file
- Through an LDAP URL from Netscape Communicator

Using the Directory Server Console is the simplest method, but for large bulk imports, LDIF statements may be more convenient. For remote online updates, you can use a web browser to create or modify ACIs.

> **Note –** During the iPlanet Directory Server installation, a special account called `Directory Manager` is created. This user has complete directory access rights and is not affected by ACIs.

ACI Format

The ACI is composed of three parts:

- **Targets** — The object, object attribute, or group of objects to which access is being controlled.
- **Permissions** — The rights that are allowed or denied
- **Bind Rules** — The persons who can access the directory, time (hours or days) when they can access the directory, and the location from which the directory can be accessed.

The target can be expressed as an entry such as `ou=Sales` or as a wildcard targeting all matching entries. Permissions and Bind Rules are set as a pair and collectively referred to as an Access Control Rule (ACR).

Access Rights

Unlike the Solaris file system, which permits read, write, and execute permissions, ACIs provide a number of access rights that can be assigned to directory data.

- **Read** — Read data.
- **Write** — Add, delete, modify attributes.
- **Add** — Create new entries.
- **Delete** — Delete entries.
- **Search** — Search for data. The user must have both search and read permission.
- **Compare** — Comparison operations. User cannot see the value.
- **Selfwrite** — Add or delete self. Use for group management.
- **Proxy** — Access target with rights from another entry.
- **All** — Do everything. Specified entry has all rights.

Bind Rules

Bind rules define the following:

1. The users and groups that can access the directory

2. Location from which an entity must bind

3. Time or day access is allowed

4. Access based on authentication method

Use rule 1 to specify a particular user, all authenticated users, nonauthenticated (anonymous) users, or users belonging to a particular group. Define access for special cases such as parent access and self-access in this rule.

Specify an IP address or fully qualified DNS name in rule 2. You can use wildcards to limit the location to specific subnets. A particular time of day like 8:00 a.m. to 5:00 p.m., or a day of the week like Monday through Friday, can be specified in rule 3 to limit user access to those hours.

If SSL or SASL authentication is available, specify either of these types as a requirement in rule 4. In this situation, the default is *not* to require any particular type of authentication.

Access is defined by specifying a bind rule of `userdn = "ldap:///anyone`. You can see that there is no restriction on when a client can access the resource. The ACI format is as follows:

```
aci: (<target>) (version 3.0;acl"<name>";<permission><bind rule>;)
```

- `<target>` — Defines the object, attribute, or filter you are using to define what resource to control access to.
- `version 3.0` — Required string that identifies the ACL version.
- `acl "<name>"`— Name for the ACI. This `<name>` can be any string that identifies the ACI. This ACI name is mandatory.
- `<permission>` — Defines that actual access rights and whether they are allowed or denied.
- `<bind rule>` — Identifies the circumstances under which the directory login must occur, and in what order for the ACI to take affect.

Example Anonymous Access ACI statement:

```
aci: (target ="ldap:///dc=blueprints,dc=com")(targetattr
!="userPassword")(version 3.0;acl"Anonymous read-search
access";allow(read,search,compare)(userdn ="ldap:///anyone");)
```

Creating Access Control Instructions

The easiest way to create a new ACI and modify existing ones is through the Directory Server Console. Use the following procedure to create a new ACI.

▼ Adding a New ACI through the Directory Server Console

1. **Log in as Directory Manager (or user with equivalent authority).**

2. **From the Directory Tab, right-click the entry in the navigation tree for which you want to create an ACI.**

   The **Properties** menu is displayed.

3. **Choose the Set Access Permissions Menu Item.**

   The **ACI** selector box is displayed. Existing ACIs can be edited or deleted from this box.

4. **Click New.**

   The **Set Access Permissions** window is displayed. At this point you can modify or add rules. FIGURE 10-1 shows the **Rights** pop-up menu used for adding access rights.

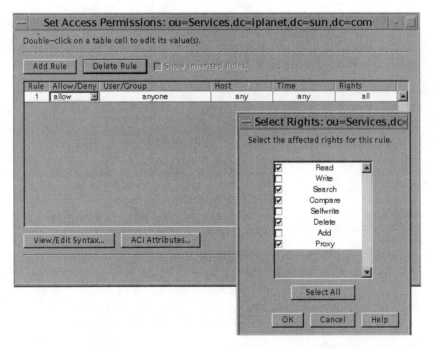

FIGURE 10-1 **Rights** Pop-up Menu in the **Set Access Permissions** Window

5. **Modify the rule to create the desired permissions.**

   The following options are available:

   - **Allow/Deny** — Pull-down menu, pick one.

- **User/Group** — Double-click to choose users and groups to either include or exclude from access. Also use to add users and groups to the list.
- **Host** — Double-click to enter a DNS host name or IP address to include or exclude from access. You can enter a wildcard as part of the IP address to limit or deny access to a particular range of IP addresses or subnet.
- **Time** — Double-click to choose a range of hours to allow or deny access and a day of the week. Add new rule or ACI to specify a range of days.
- **Rights** — Check the boxes shown.
- **View/Edit Syntax** — Use this form to change the name of the ACI from the default **Unknown** and to edit previously defined ACIs.
- **ACI Attributes** — Use this option to assign access rights to a particular attribute or a range of attributes.

ACI Best Practices

ACI is flexible and can be a useful tool. However, if misused, ACIs can create problems. Here are some tips to avoid potential problems.

1. Limit the number. Processing ACIs creates additional overhead, so for better performance, keep the number of ACIs to a minimum.

2. Keep them simple. Complicated rules are often hard to decipher and can lead to unintended results.

3. Limit one rule per ACI. If a simple ACI won't do, then it is better to create multiple ACIs with a single rule each. This practice makes it easier for someone else to understand what access rights were intended.

Managing the Directory Schema

Before an LDAP client can interact with an LDAP directory server, it must be aware of how the directory data is stored. Data can be stored as strings, numbers, and in some cases, multiple values. Rules for matching values during searches are also established, for example, whether a compare operation is case sensitive. The format of directory data and the rules for how that data is used are defined in the directory schema.

The schema is a set of files that are read by the directory server when it starts. Every object class and attribute that the directory can store is defined in the schema files. To ensure that any LDAP client can interoperate with any LDAP server, a set of standard schema definitions has been defined. The definitions include the mandatory object classes and attributes that all compliant LDAP servers must support.

However, although fairly comprehensive, the standard schema may have to be extended to accommodate data particular to a company. This section looks at where schema files reside and describes how to add new object classes and attributes that LDAP-enabled applications require.

The Schema Files

On the iPlanet Directory Server all schema files reside in the *install_dir*/slapd-*instance*/config directory. The schema definition is divided into two files:

- slapd.oc.conf — Contains object class definitions
- slapd.at.conf — Contains attribute definitions

All the standard object class definitions that all LDAP directory servers are expected to have are contained in the slapd.oc.conf file. The standard attributes, in addition to those defined by Netscape, are contained in the slapd.at.conf file. However, the Netscape-defined object classes that use the attributes contained in the slapd.at.conf file are not in the slapd.oc.conf file. These object classes are defined in separate files which have the schema.conf extension. For example:

```
blueprints# cd install_dir/slapd-instance/config
blueprints# ls *schema*
java-object-schema.conf
ns-admin-schema.conf
ns-calendar-schema.conf
ns-certificate-schema.conf
ns-common-schema.conf
ns-compass-schema.conf
ns-delegated-admin-schema.conf
ns-directory-schema.conf
ns-legacy-schema.conf
ns-mail-schema.conf
ns-mcd-browser-schema.conf
ns-mcd-config-schema.conf
ns-mcd-li-schema.conf
ns-mcd-mail-schema.conf
ns-media-schema.conf
ns-mlm-schema.conf
ns-msg-schema.conf
ns-netshare-schema.conf
ns-news-schema.conf
ns-proxy-schema.conf
ns-schema.conf
ns-value-schema.conf
ns-wcal-schema.conf
ns-web-schema.conf
blueprints#
```

These schema files are placed here as a convenience for use with Netscape (iPlanet) applications such as messaging and calendaring servers. They are not required for normal directory operation.

The files `slap.oc.conf` and `slapd.at.conf` should never be modified. Instead, you can make necessary modification in two files included for that purpose.

- `slapd.user_at.conf` — User-defined attributes
- `slapd.user_oc.conf` — User-defined object classes

These files are created during the iPlanet Directory Server installation but do not contain data unless additional object classes and attributes are added. If, for example, the NIS extensions are installed, the new object class and attribute definitions appear in `slapd.user.at.conf` and `slapd.user.oc.conf`.

How Schema Files Are Read

When the iPlanet Directory Server starts, it reads the `slapd.conf` file. Contained in this file is the location of the schema files. The pertinent lines are shown below.

```
blueprints# cd install_dir/slapd-instance/config
blueprints# more slapd.conf
. . .
include "/usr/netscape/blueprints/slapd-blueprints/config/
slapd.at.conf"
include "/usr/netscape/blueprints/slapd-blueprints/config/
slapd.oc.conf"
include "/usr/netscape/blueprints/slapd-blueprints/config/ns-
schema.conf"
. . .
userat  "/usr/netscape/blueprints/slapd-blueprints/
slapd.user_at.conf"
useroc  "/usr/netscape/blueprints/slapd-blueprints/config/
slapd.user_oc.conf"
. . .
blueprints#
```

If you make changes to any of the files shown, you need to restart the server for the changes to take effect.

Modifying the Schema

When new LDAP-enabled applications are deployed, there is a good chance that the directory schema needs to be modified. Since you should not modify the core set of schema definitions for risk of losing compatibility with other LDAP implementations, you should always create a new object class when you want to add attributes.

In most cases, if you are extending the schema to support a new application, the application developer or vendor will supply either a sample schema file or a schema installation script that modifies the existing schema files. Besides modifying the schema files directly, use the Directory Server Console to create new object classes and attributes.

Note – The schema is accessible via LDAP in Planet Directory Server 4.12 in read-only mode. Future versions of the iPlanet Directory server may support write mode as well.

Obtaining an Object Identifier

If you do decide to extend the schema by defining a new schema element, you should register your schema and get the appropriate OIDs to uniquely identify it.

In a test environment you do not need OIDs. You can use an OID that you fabricate, just as long as you do not publicly publish your schema.

If you have a schema that you think is valuable to the world, you may want to standardize it by submitting it to the IETF. Sun does have an official owner of the Sun LDAP OID tree.

▼ Creating Attributes from the Directory Server Console

To create attributes from the Directory Server Console, follow these steps:

1. **Under the Configuration tab, select the Database icon.**

2. **Under the Schema tab, choose Attributes.**

3. **Click the Create button.**

   A form like that shown in FIGURE 10-2 is displayed.

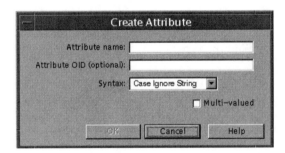

FIGURE 10-2 **Create Attribute** Window

4. **Fill in the form with the following values:**

   Attribute name: Unique name

   Attribute OID: Object Identifier

   Syntax: One of the following types:
   - Case Ignore String
   - Binary
   - Telephone Number

- Case Exact String
- Distinguished Name

▼ Creating Object Classes from the Directory Server Console

To create object classes from the Directory Server Console, follow these steps:

1. **Under the Configuration tab select the Database icon.**

2. **Under the Object Classes tab select the Schema folder.**

3. **Click the Create button.**

   A form like that shown in FIGURE 10-3 is displayed.

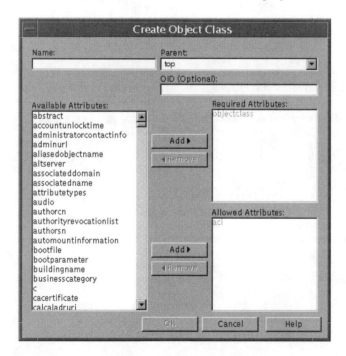

FIGURE 10-3 Create Object Class Window

4. **Fill in the top part of the form and choose the attributes you want to include in the new object class.**

   Name — Choose a unique name for this object class. It cannot be the same as an existing object class.

Parent — The parent object class from which this new object class will inherit its attributes. If this object class is not related to any previously defined object class, then the parent is top.

OID — Object Identifier. OIDs are registered dotted decimal numbers much like Internet addresses. In most cases, this part is left blank.

Required Attributes — These attributes must be defined in any entry of this object class.

Allowed Attributes — An entry may or may not have these attributes defined.

Note – New attributes must be created before they can be added to an object class.

Monitoring the Directory Server

Careful monitoring of your directory server is important to prevent unnecessary outages due to overload conditions. Solaris utilities such as `vmstat` and `iostat` provide an overall assessment of the health of the system. To get a better understanding of what is going on with the directory itself, the iPlanet Directory Server includes some performance monitoring tools. These tools are explained here.

Monitoring Resources

The following tables show available performance monitoring parameters of three categories: overall server performance (TABLE 10-1), current resources being consumed (TABLE 10-2), and the status of current connections (TABLE 10-3).

TABLE 10-1 Server Performance Monitoring

Resource	Usage Since Startup	Average/Minute
Connections	Total number of connections to this server since server startup.	Average number of connections per minute since server startup.
Operations initiated	Total number of operations initiated since server startup. Operations include any client requests for server action, such as searches, adds, and modifies in the directory tree. It is likely that multiple operations will be initiated for each connection.	Average number of operations per minute since server startup.
Operations completed	Total number of operations completed by the server since server startup	Average number of operations per minute since server startup.
Entries sent to clients	Total number of entries sent to clients since server startup. Entries are sent to clients as the result of search requests.	Average number of entries sent to clients per minute since server startup.
Bytes sent to clients	Total number of bytes sent to clients since server startup.	Average number of bytes sent to clients per minute since server startup.

TABLE 10-2 Current Resource Usage Table

Resource	Current Total
Active threads	Current number of active threads used for handling requests. Additional threads can also be created by internal server tasks, such as replication.
Open connections	Total number of open connections. Each connection can account for multiple operations and, therefore, multiple threads.
Remaining available connections	Total number of remaining connections that the server can concurrently open. This number is based on the number of currently open connections and the total number of concurrent connections that the server is allowed to open.

TABLE 10-2 Current Resource Usage Table *(Continued)*

Resource	Current Total
Threads waiting to write to client	Total number of threads waiting to write to the client. This happens anytime the server must pause while sending data to a client. Reasons for this pause can include a slow network or client, or an extremely large amount of information being sent to the client.
Threads waiting to read from client	Total number of threads waiting to read from the client. Threads wait if the server starts to receive a request from the client and the transmission of that request is halted for some reason. Generally, threads waiting to read are an indication of a slow network or client
Thread Concurrency	Number of threads running concurrently.
Databases in use	Total number of databases being serviced by the server. Currently, this value is always 1.

TABLE 10-3 Connection Status Table

Table Header	Description
Time opened	The time on the server when the connection was initially opened.
Started	The number of operations initiated by this connection.
Completed	The number of operations completed by the server for this connection.
Bound as	The distinguished name used by the client to connect to the server. If the client has not authenticated to the server, the server displays the error code "not bound in this field."
Read/Write	The state of the server currently blocked (or not) for read or write access to the client. Possible values include: **Not blocked** – The server is idle, actively sending data to the client or actively reading data from the client. **Blocked** – The server is trying to send data to the client or read data from the client but cannot. The probable cause is a slow network or client.

▼ Monitoring Server Performance from the Directory Server Console

The easiest way to view the monitoring parameters is from the Directory Server Console. To view these parameters:

1. **Click Performance Counters under the Status tab.**

2. **Click the Server tab.**

3. **To continually refresh the screen with new data, check the Continuous refresh check box.**

   FIGURE 10-4 shows the performance counters.

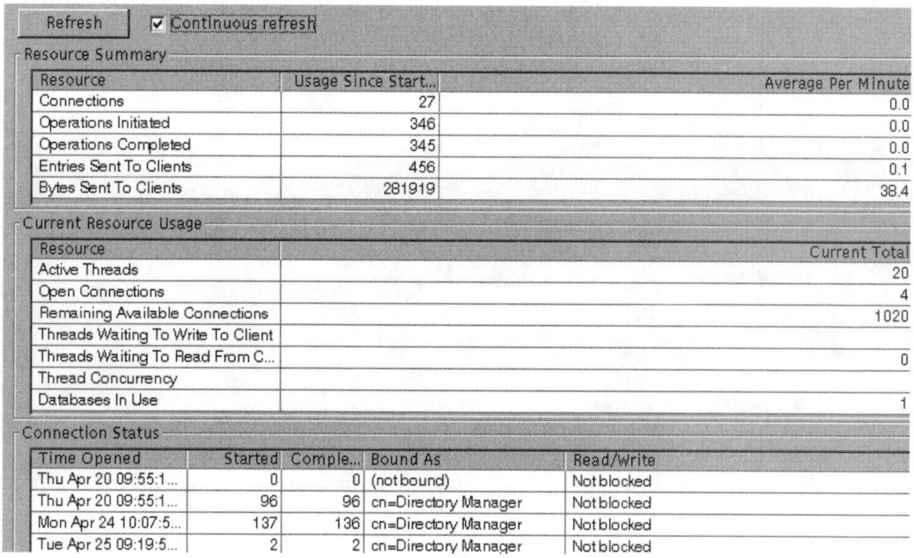

Refresh	☑ Continuous refresh		

Resource Summary

Resource	Usage Since Start...		Average Per Minute
Connections	27		0.0
Operations Initiated	346		0.0
Operations Completed	345		0.0
Entries Sent To Clients	456		0.1
Bytes Sent To Clients	281919		38.4

Current Resource Usage

Resource		Current Total
Active Threads		20
Open Connections		4
Remaining Available Connections		1020
Threads Waiting To Write To Client		
Threads Waiting To Read From C...		0
Thread Concurrency		
Databases In Use		1

Connection Status

Time Opened	Started	Comple...	Bound As	Read/Write
Thu Apr 20 09:55:1...	0	0	(not bound)	Not blocked
Thu Apr 20 09:55:1...	96	96	cn=Directory Manager	Not blocked
Mon Apr 24 10:07:5...	137	136	cn=Directory Manager	Not blocked
Tue Apr 25 09:19:5...	2	2	cn=Directory Manager	Not blocked

FIGURE 10-4 Performance Counters

Monitoring the Server from the Command Line

You can monitor service activity from any LDAP client by performing a search and specifying the following parameters:

```
objectClass=*
```

and a search base of

```
cn=monitor
```

and a scope of

```
base
```

For example:

```
blueprints# ldapsearch -h blueprints.com -s base -b"cn=monitor"
"(objectclass=*)"
cn=monitor
objectclass=top
objectclass=extensibleObject
cn=monitor
version=Netscape-Directory/4.12 B00.193.0352
threads=20
currentconnections=5
totalconnections=28
dtablesize=1024
readwaiters=0
opsinitiated=1992
opscompleted=1991
entriessent=2102
bytessent=1887388
currenttime=20000425182927Z
starttime=20000420135517Z
nbackends=1
dataversion=blueprints.com:389 020000316143827 42241
ldapserverconfigdn=cn=ldap://:389,dc=blueprints,dc=com
backendmonitordn=cn=monitor,cn=ldbm
blueprints#
```

When you monitor your server's activities in this way, you see the following information:

version — The directory server's current version number.

threads — Current number of active threads used for handling requests. Additional threads can also be created by internal server tasks, such as replicating or writing to logs.

currentconnections — Number of open connections to the server.

totalconnections — Number of connections handled by the directory server since it started.

dtablesize — Number of file descriptors available to the directory server. Each connection requires one file descriptor: one for every open index, one for log file management, and one for ns-slapd itself. Essentially, this value lets you know how many more concurrent connections can be serviced by the directory server.

writewaiters — Number of threads waiting to write data to a client.

readwaiters — Number of threads waiting to read data from a client.

opsinitiated — Number of operations the server has initiated since it started.

opscompleted — Number of operations the server has completed since it started.

entriessent — Number of entries sent to clients since the server started.

bytessent — Number of bytes sent to clients since the server started.

currenttime — Time when this snapshot of the server was taken. The time is displayed in Greenwich Mean Time (GMT) in UTC format.

starttime — Time when the server started. The time is displayed in GMT in UTC format.

nbackends — Number of back ends (databases) the server services. Currently this value is always 1.

Monitoring Database Activity

A number of database metrics can be extracted from the directory. Many of these were discussed in Chapter 7, "Capacity Planning and Performance Tuning," but to review, we summarize these metrics in TABLE 10-4, TABLE 10-5, and TABLE 10-6.

TABLE 10-4 Database Performance Metrics

Performance Metric	Current Total
Read-only status	The state of the database—whether currently in read-only mode. Your database is in read-only mode when your read-only `slapd.conf` parameter is set to on.
Entry cache hits	The total number of successful entry cache lookups. That is, the total number of times the server could process a search request by obtaining data from the cache rather than by going to disk.
Entry cache tries	The total number of entry cache lookups since the directory server was last started. That is, the total number of search operations performed against your server since server startup.

TABLE 10-4 Database Performance Metrics *(Continued)*

Performance Metric	Current Total
Entry cache hit ratio	Ratio of the number of entry cache tries to successful entry cache lookups. This number is based on the total lookups and hits since the server was last started. The closer this value is to 100% the better. Whenever a search operation attempts to find an entry that is not resident in the entry cache, the directory server has to perform a disk access to obtain the entry. Thus, as this ratio drops towards zero, the number of disk accesses increases and directory server search performance drops. Refer to Chapter 7, "Capacity Planning and Performance Tuning," for tuning information.
Current number of entries in entry cache	The total number of directory entries currently resident in the entry cache.
Maximum number of entries in entry cache	The maximum number of directory entries that are allowed to be maintained in the entry cache. This value is managed by the Maximum Entries in the Cache parameter in `slapd.ldbm.conf`.

TABLE 10-5 Database Cache Information

Performance Metric	Current Total
Hits	The number of times the database cache successfully supplied a requested page.
Tries	The number of times the database cache was asked for a page.
Hit ratio	The ratio of database cache hits to database cache tries. The closer this value is to 100%, the better. Whenever a directory operation attempts to find a portion of the database that is not resident in the database cache, the directory server has to perform a disk access to obtain the appropriate database page. Thus, as this ratio drops towards zero, the number of disk accesses increases and directory server performance drops. Refer to Chapter 7, "Capacity Planning and Performance Tuning," for tuning information.
Pages read in	The number of pages read from disk into the database cache.

TABLE 10-5 Database Cache Information *(Continued)*

Performance Metric	Current Total
Pages written out	The number of pages written from the cache back to disk. A database page is written out to disk whenever a read-write page has been modified and then subsequently evicted from the cache. Pages are evicted from the database cache when the cache is full and a directory operation requires a database page that is not currently stored in cache.
Read-only page evicts	The number of read-only pages discarded from the cache to make room for new pages.
Read-write page evicts	The number of read-write pages discarded from the cache to make room for new pages. This value differs from Pages Written Out in that these are discarded read-write pages that have not been modified.

TABLE 10-6 File-Specific Table

Performance Metric	Current Total
Cache hits	Number of times that a search result resulted in a cache hit on this specific file. That is, a search that required data from this file was performed and the required data was successfully obtained from the cache.
Cache misses	Number of times that a search result failed to result in a cache hit on this specific file. That is, a search that required data from this file was performed and the required data could not be found in the cache.
Pages read in	Number of pages brought to the cache from this file.
Pages written out	Number of pages for this file written from cache to disk.

Monitoring the Database from the Directory Server Console

To view the database activity from the Directory Server Console, follow this procedure:

1. **Click Performance Counters under the Status tab.**

2. **Click the Database tab.**

3. **To continually refresh the screen with new data, Check the Continuous refresh box.**

FIGURE 10-5 is an example of the output.

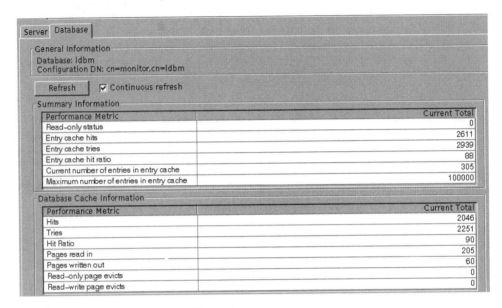

FIGURE 10-5 Database Output Example

Monitoring the Database from the Command Line

You can monitor your directory server's database activities from any LDAP client by specifying the following parameters:

```
objectClass=*
```

and a search base of

```
cn=monitor,cn=ldbm
```

and a scope of

```
base
```

For example:

```
blueprints# ldapsearch -h blueprints.com -s base -b
"cn=monitor,cn=ldbm" "(objectclass=*)"
cn=monitor,cn=ldbm
objectclass=top
objectclass=extensibleObject
cn=monitor
database=ldbm
readonly=0
entrycachehits=2611
entrycachetries=2939
entrycachehitratio=88
currententrycachesize=305
maxentrycachesize=100000
dbchehits=2046
dbcachetries=2251
dbcachehitratio=90
dbcachepagein=205
dbcachepageout=60
dbcacheroevict=0
dbcacherwevict=0
dbfilename-0=uid.db2
dbfilecachehit-0=46
dbfilecachemiss-0=3
dbfilepagein-0=3
dbfilepageout-0=6
...
blueprints#
```

When you monitor your server's activities in this way, you see the following information:

database — The type of database you are currently monitoring.

read-only — State of the database, that is, whether in read-only mode. A value of 0 means the server is not in read-only mode; 1 means it is in read-only mode.

The other parameters displayed are listed in TABLE 10-7 along with a cross-reference to the performance metric it represents.

TABLE 10-7 Displayed Parameters

Parameter	Performance Metric
entrycachehits	Entry cache hits
entrycachetries	Entry cache tries
entrycachehitratio	Entry cache hit ratio
currententrycachesize	Current number of entries
maxentrycachesize	Maximum number of entries
dbchehits	Hits
dbcachetries	Tries
dbcachehitratio	Hit ratio
dbcachepagein	Pages read in
dbcachepageout	Pages written out
dbcacheroevict	Read-only page evicts
dbcacherwevict	Read-write page evicts
dbfilecachehit	Cache hits
dbfilecachemiss	Cache misses
dbfilepagein	Pages read in
dbfilepageout	Pages written out

Managing with SNMP

The Simple Network Management Protocol (SNMP) has been around for a number of years and is widely deployed. Originally designed to manage network devices, SNMP can also manage other items such as applications and services.

Using the directory server MIB and network management software, such as Sun MC, you can monitor your directory server like all other managed devices on your network.

The SNMP protocol runs in the application layer of the Open Systems Interconnection (OSI) stack, which allows network devices to read, write, and act on management data. The management information resides in a special object data store and includes everything from the make and architecture of a machine to the average number of data bytes transmitted. You will find that companies such as Sun will add new object definitions as the need arises. A data structure named Management Information Base (MIB) defines SNMP objects.

Network devices, can generally be grouped into either managed devices or Network Management Servers (NMSs). It is also likely that the managed server will also function as a managed device. Each managed device contains a local object data store and runs an SNMP application known as an agent. On a Solaris host, the agent is a daemon. Your installed version of Solaris will determine whether you have the SNMP agent or not. The agent updates the local object data store as events transpire and also responds to commands from their network management servers.

FIGURE 10-6 depicts specific elements of a SNMP network, with the Local Area Network (intranet), and Wide Area Network (Internet) all supporting the Internet protocol (IP).

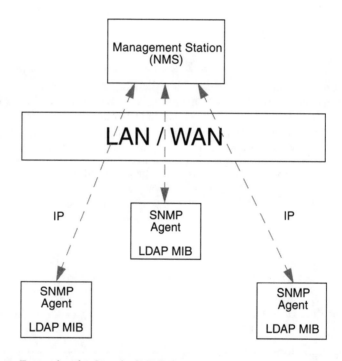

FIGURE 10-6 Example of a Simple SNMP Environment

Three devices illustrate a simplistic view of the type of protocols that the device would use, all over IP. The other device located at the top of FIGURE 10-6 is the server that will act as the management host. The purpose of this host is to query and if necessary update the agents running on the other three networked devices. You will notice that the application running on the management station talks to the SNMP protocol layer, which in turn uses IP port 161 to send and receive information from managed devices.

The three devices located in FIGURE 10-6 all have an SNMP agent installed and running, enabling them to be managed devices that can perform actions based on commands from the management station. What happens here is the management station receives commands that arrive as IP packets on the default port of 161. The SNMP protocol interprets these packets and directs the agent to read and write objects in an MIB data store.

SNMP describes this functionality using one or more MIBs. The Abstract Syntax Notation One (ASN.1) describes objects within an MIB. SNMP v2, which is the current version of SNMP, and uses MIB-II specification (RFC1213 contains a complete definition).

Using LDAP MIB

The iPlanet Directory Server has its own management information base. The directory server's MIB is a file called `netscape-ldap.mib`. This MIB contains definitions for variables pertaining to network management for the directory server. These variables are known as managed objects. Using the directory server MIB and network management software, such as Sun MC, you can monitor your directory server like all other managed devices on your network.

The directory server MIB has an object identifier of `iso.org.dod.internet.private.enterprises.netscape.nsldap` that is, `nsldap OBJECT IDENTIFIER ::= { 1.3.6.1.4.1.1450.7 }` which is located in the *install_dir*/`plugins`/`snmp` directory.

You can see administrative information about your directory server and monitor the server in real time by using the directory server MIB. The directory server MIB is divided into three distinct tables of managed objects:

- Operations Table
- Entries Table
- Interaction Table

Note – Before you can use the directory server's MIB, you must compile it along with the MIBs that you will find in *install_dir*/`plugins`/`snmp`/`mibs`.

Operations Table

The Operations Table provides statistical information about directory server access, operations, and errors. TABLE 10-8 describes the managed objects stored in the Operations Table of the `netscape-ldap.mib` file.

TABLE 10-8 Operations Table

Managed Object	Description
dsAnonymousBinds	The number of anonymous binds to the directory since server startup.
dsUnauthBinds	The number of unauthenticated binds to the directory since server startup.
dsSimpleAuthBinds	The number of binds to the directory server that were established by a simple authentication method such as password protection since server startup.
dsStrongAuthBinds	The number of binds to the directory server that were established by a strong authentication method such as SSL or an SASL mechanism such as Kerberos since server startup.
dsBindSecurityErrors	The number of bind requests that have been rejected by the directory server because of authentication failures or invalid credentials since server startup.
dsInOps	The number of operations forwarded to this directory server from another directory server since server startup.
dsReadOps	The number of read operations serviced by this directory server since application start. The value of this object is always 0 because LDAP implements read operations indirectly through the search operation.
dsCompareOps	The number of compare operations serviced by this directory server since server startup.
dsAddEntryOps	The number of add operations serviced by this directory server since server startup.
dsRemoveEntryOps	The number of delete operations serviced by this directory server since server startup.
dsModifyEntryOps	The number of modify operations serviced by this directory server since server startup.
dsModifyRDNOps	The number of modify RDN operations serviced by this directory server since server startup.

TABLE 10-8   Operations Table *(Continued)*

Managed Object	Description
dsListOps	The number of list operations serviced by this directory server since server startup. The value of this object will always be 0 because LDAP implements list operations indirectly through the search operation.
dsSearchOps	The total number of search operations serviced by this directory server since server startup.
dsOneLevelSearchOps	The number of one-level search operations serviced by this directory server since server startup.
dsWholeSubtreeSearchOps	The number of whole subtree search operations serviced by this directory server since server startup.
dsReferrals	The number of referrals returned by this directory server in response to client requests since server startup.
dsChainings	The number of operations forwarded by this directory server to other directory servers since server startup. The value of this object is always 0.
dsSecurityErrors	The number of operations forwarded to this directory server that did not meet security requirements.
dsErrors	The number of requests that could not be serviced because of errors (other than security or referral errors). Errors include name errors, update errors, attribute errors, and service errors. Partially serviced requests are not counted as errors.

Entry Table

The Entry Table (TABLE 10-9) provides statistical information about directory entries and the entry cache.

TABLE 10-9 Entry Table

Managed Object	Description
dsMasterEntries	The number of directory entries for which this directory server contains the master entry. The value of this object is always 0.
dsCopyEntries	The number of directory entries for which this directory server contains a slave copy. The value of this object is always 0.
dsCacheEntries	The number of entries cached in the directory server.
dsCacheHits	The number of operations serviced from the locally held cache since application startup.
dsSlaveHits	The number of operations that were serviced from locally held replications (shadow entries). The value of this object is always 0.

Interaction Table

The Interaction Table (TABLE 10-10) provides statistical information about communications with peer servers.

TABLE 10-10 Interaction Table

Managed Object	Description
dsIntIndex	Statistical data is kept for the last 5 peer directory servers with which this directory server has attempted to communicate. This object provides a unique identifier used to delimit the information about the interaction with a specific peer directory server.
dsName	The distinguished name of the peer directory server identified by the corresponding dsIntIndex object.
dsTimeOfCreation	The amount of time since this directory server first attempted to contact the peer directory server identified by the corresponding dsIntIndex object. If this attempt was made before the NMS was initialized, the object will contain a value of 0.

TABLE 10-10 Interaction Table *(Continued)*

Managed Object	Description
dsTimeOfLastAttempt	The amount of time since this directory server last attempted to contact the peer directory server identified by the corresponding dsIntIndex object. If this attempt was made before the NMS was initialized, the object will contain a value of 0.
dsTimeOfLastSuccess	The number of times this directory server has failed to contact the peer directory server identified in the corresponding dsIntIndex object since the last successful contact.
dsFailuresSinceLastSucces	The number of times this directory server has failed to contact the peer directory server identified in the corresponding dsIntIndex object since the last successful contact.
dsFailures	The total number of times this directory server has failed to contact the peer directory server identified by the corresponding dsIntIndex object.
dsSuccesses	The total number of times this directory server has successfully contacted the peer directory server identified by the corresponding dsIntIndex object.
dsUR	The URL of the peer directory server identified in the corresponding dsIntIndex object.

Managing the LDAP Directory Server with BMC PATROL

Third-party products, such as BMC PATROL from BMC, can be used to monitor the directory service. This section describes the Knowledge Module (KM) developed to monitor the iPlanet Directory Server.

iPlanet Directory Server KM Overview

The iPlanet Directory Server (part of the iPlanet Messaging KM) Knowledge Module allows the administrator to continually monitor and automatically react to critical data centers, thus decreasing the likelihood of a failure as administrators are made aware of potential application problems before they become critical.

The iPlanet Directory Knowledge Module conforms to standard PATROL
Knowledge Module design and operation, ensuring that the PATROL architectural
integrity is maintained. The Knowledge Module is designed to run on servers that
conform to the iPlanet E-Commerce Solutions environment, such as the iPlanet
Directory and Messaging servers.

Introduction to BMC PATROL

PATROL monitors and manages distributed systems with the ultimate goal of
increasing the availability of servers and applications that run on them. As with any
other technology, you need to understand from an architectural point of view how
components work and fit together. This understanding will enable you to address
the management of LDAP directory services. It is important to understand each
component of PATROL, as well as its own objectives and key terms.

First, look at the behind-the-scenes functioning of PATROL, including how the
Agent works, how the Agent communicates with the Console, and how knowledge
is distributed in the PATROL environment.

Basic PATROL Architecture

When you understand the functions of the main components, you understand how
PATROL can do all the things it does. The PATROL product comprises four main
components:

1. PATROL Agent

2. PATROL Event Manager

3. PATROL Knowledge Modules

4. PATROL Console

Here are some key terms that are used in the PATROL components.

Agent — A process that resides on the server—basically, the monitoring engine. The
Agent carries out most of PATROL's duties.

Console — Software that runs on your workstation to provide your view into the
PATROL Agents.

Discovery — The process of finding, recognizing, and then establishing monitoring
relationships with target objects (databases, applications, etc.). It is what makes
PATROL self-configuring.

Knowledge — The collection of all monitoring definitions and rules, for example,
which Module guides the Agent in performing its duties.

Event — A situation that requires manual intervention; a communication that takes place between an Agent and a Console; a change in the state of a PATROL object.

Event Management — The process of assigning responsibility for the investigation of a system-related problem and then tracking activities associated with this event through to closure.

Commit — The process of globalizing changes made to the PATROL environment from a Developer Console and then piping the change to the Agent(s).

FIGURE 10-7 illustrates PATROL architecture.

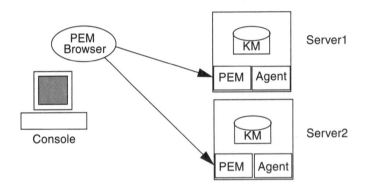

FIGURE 10-7 Basic PATROL Architecture

Basic PATROL Agent

The Agent is the workhorse of PATROL. At Agent startup, the Agent reads a discovery script from its local file system. Once discovery has taken place, the appropriate KMs are loaded. Everything the Agent monitors and executes automatically is based on the rules within the KM.

It is important to note that Agents live within the boundaries of resources that you allocate to them. This allocation is done at installation. The more resources you allocate to the Agent, the faster it becomes. The PATROL Smart Agent technology was developed to consume as few resources as possible (on your server, as well as your network). The fewer the applications or features of those applications you monitor with PATROL, the fewer the resources the Agent needs to accomplish its tasks.

The Agent process is made up of several logical modules. It is this modular approach that facilitates addition of new functionality over time.

Basic PATROL Event Manager (PEM)

The PATROL Event Manager (PEM) enables you to view and manage events that occur on monitored system resources and that are sent by PATROL Agents. PEM is a PATROL tool that helps automate this process. The Agent communicates events to all interested consoles via the event broadcast mechanism.

Basic PATROL Knowledge Modules

The knowledge module has three distinct characteristics. At Agent startup, a Knowledge Module is loaded from a file on the Agent's local file system. Similarly, at Console startup, a Knowledge Module is also loaded. The only time a KM is moved around over your underlying network is when a Developer Console updates knowledge stored at each Agent.

A Knowledge Module comprises two major components: discovery rules and scripts. The discovery rules implement the scope defined by the KM developer. The discovery rules define to the PATROL environment how to determine whether the *objects* that you want to manage exist and are currently active in the target environment. Once the objects have been discovered, the scripts provide PATROL the intelligence required to implement the purpose of the KM.

Parameters are the monitoring component of PATROL. A parameter monitors the individual units of performance of the targeted application (e.g., CPU utilization, file system capacity). Associated with parameters are alert ranges, and associated with alert ranges are recovery action scripts.

Basic PATROL Console

The PATROL Console is where the PATROL user initiates ad hoc commands that are executed on the Agents. Ad hoc commands are sourced (the actual command scripts are stored at the Console), and when triggered by the PATROL user, the command scripts are sent to an Agent (or multiple Agents simultaneously) for execution. This approach allows a PATROL Console user to not only view alerts from the agent but also to take troubleshooting, administrative, or corrective actions from the same platform. These stored commands make up the administrator's toolkit, the chief benefit of running a PATROL console.

The PATROL Console running in developer mode is the tool used to manage, update, and modify the PATROL environment's monitoring knowledge. The other option for the PATROL Console is the Operator Console. This is the type of console that you encounter in production environments. It has all the capabilities to monitor and take action, but none of the authority necessary to access the Agent's knowledge and change the way PATROL is configured.

Basic iPlanet Directory PATROL Architecture

FIGURE 10-8 illustrates the iPlanet Directory PATROL architecture.

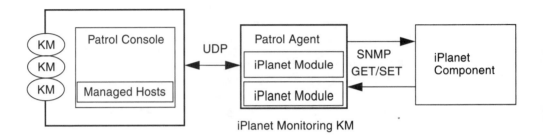

FIGURE 10-8 Basic iPlanet Directory PATROL Architecture

iPlanet Directory PATROL Components

The iPlanet Directory Services Knowledge Module, which is a component of the iPlanet Messaging Server 4.15, is made up of a set of modules which are accessed in an hierarchical manner. The entry-level module is the access point to the other directory modules.

IMS4_DIRECTORY

FIGURE 10-9 IMS4 Directory Services Knowledge Module Icon

This module (FIGURE 10-9) houses several properties of its own including the ability to automatically discover an LDAP service running on the default port of 389, as well as the configuration of other LDAP instances that are not running on this well-known LDAP port. It is also possible to stop, start, and restart the LDAP service from a menu option. Double-clicking this module will present you with the view in FIGURE 10-10.

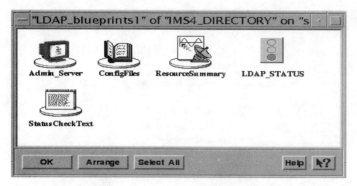

FIGURE 10-10 Directory Knowledge Modules

FIGURE 10-10 presents the remaining directory knowledge modules, which include the Configuration files, Connectivity, Connection Status, Admin Server Status, and Resource Summary. In addition to these modules, the SNMP modules monitor the process status of the master agent and subagent.

It is easy to make mistakes when modifying the configuration files. If a modification error has occurred, the Knowledge Module will alert you of the condition that one of the configuration files has changed. The following configuration files are currently monitored:

- `slapd.conf`— Main LDAP configuration file
- `slapd.at.conf`—Where the standard LDAP attribute types are defined
- `slapd.oc.conf`—Where the standard LDAP Object Classes are defined
- `slapd.user_at.conf`—Where the LDAP user-defined attributes are defined
- `slapd.user_oc.conf`—Where the user-defined Object Classes are defined

The Resource Summary module enables system administrators to take a quick glance at what the LDAP server has been doing. The resources that are currently monitored are LDAP connections, which are the total number of connections made to a particular LDAP server, the total number of all LDAP operations to an LDAP server, how many LDAP operations were completed by the LDAP server, the total number of entries based on the search requests that were sent to the clients, and the total amount of bytes also sent to the clients.

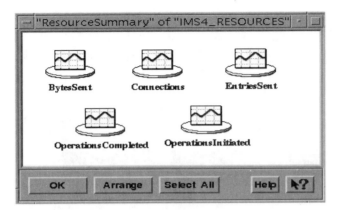

FIGURE 10-11 Resource Summary Modules

In addition to the modules in FIGURE 10-11, the Knowledge Modules support the current resource usage of an LDAP server, including the current number of active threads of an LDAP server, the number of open connections, and how many connections the LDAP server can open. The Knowledge Module also provides some general server information, such as the version of the LDAP server software you are running.

Checking Memory Usage with pmap

The Solaris 8 operating environment includes a utility called pmap which is handy for determining which processes are using up memory. Since the database and entry cache sizes are dynamic, the amount of memory consumed by the directory server will change over time.

To run pmap on the directory server process, specify the PID of the ns-slapd process. For example:

```
blueprints# ps -e | grep ns-slapd
 24626 ?        1:05 ns-slapd
blueprints# pmap 24626
...
0012E000   6408K read/write/exec     [ heap ]
...
 total     33136K
...
blueprints#
```

The output from pmap is quite voluminous, so only a couple of lines are shown. You will notice that as the directory caches grow in size, the size of the heap grows. Eventually, this value will reach the maximum value specified in the configuration files. This is a good check to see if the actual cache size matches what you think it was set at. For additional information on pmap see the man page, pmap(1M).

## CHAPTER 11

Directory Services Consolidation

Most corporate information technology (IT) infrastructures are composed of heterogeneous hardware and software platforms. Some systems may have been chosen because they provided the best solution at the time, whereas others may have been inherited through a merger or acquisition. Whatever the reasons for the system composition, corporate IT managers have to cope with maintaining a multitude of applications requiring several different data stores.

Examples of disparate applications and data stores are:

- LDAP-enabled applications, such as messaging and web servers
- Relational Database — Oracle, Sybase, etc.
- Microsoft Exchange
- e-Directory from Novell
- Windows NT Directory Services (NTDS)
- Lotus Notes
- NIS and NIS+ from Sun

Consolidation of all these data stores into a single repository is a daunting task. This activity must be well planned to prevent critical data from becoming inaccessible. Another aspect of consolidation is the simplification of the security access methods deployed by different applications. This chapter examines tools, technology, and the methodology available to make data consolidation a reality.

Benefits of Consolidation

The obvious benefit to consolidation is the ability to present a consistent view of data, such as employee information, across a wide range of applications. The data about an employee may be maintained in a Human Resources (HR) database, messaging system database, operating system naming service, and a company-wide address book. In many cases, the same data fields are maintained in all these places. If the employee transfers to another department, updates need to occur in all these data stores. This creates extra work and may lead to conflicting data being stored.

Another benefit to directory consolidation is providing a single interface that new applications can be written to. With a single view of the data, the application developer does not have to worry about how the data is formatted and what access protocol to use.

LDAP as a Consolidation Choice

Having made the decision to consolidate, you must next figure out how. There are numerous approaches, but consolidation built around LDAP technology makes the most sense. LDAP has a wide industry adoption and is gaining popularity, particularly in the E-Commerce market. Unlike relational databases, LDAP technology makes it easy to distribute data around your company. It is also easily extended to include new data objects.

Once you decide to build your consolidation strategy around LDAP, you must next decide how to deploy this technology. A number of alternatives are explained in the following section.

Consolidation Approaches

There are essentially three approaches. In most cases, it makes sense to deploy a combination of these.

1. Convert all your data to LDAP directory data.

2. Deploy gateway services that act as a front end to the LDAP directory.

3. Deploy a synchronization service.

Converting all your data is not practical in some cases, but when you have multiple LDAP-enabled applications each with its own directory, you can consolidate this data, as described later. Gateway services are difficult to implement and not widely available. Synchronization services have several advantages which we discuss later. We also later discuss the iPlanet Meta-Directory Server product, which combines synchronization and the ability to join disparate data sources to create a single LDAP view.

Consolidation of LDAP-Enabled Applications

Even when different applications are using LDAP as their primary data store, there are some caveats you must be aware of when merging the data into a single LDAP directory.

- Incorporating the application-specific schema
- Creating a common Directory Information Tree (DIT)
- Resolving ACI conflicts

Most applications will extend the standard LDAP schema to include additional object classes and attributes. If the applications are all written by a single vendor, for example iPlanet, chances are the schema extensions are compatible. In fact, the iPlanet Directory Server ships with schema files that are used to support the iPlanet suite of products. However, if you plan to have your directory support other applications that require schema extensions, you must watch out for conflicts.

Many applications are hard-coded to look for particular distinguished names (DNs) in the DIT. For example, the application might expect user profiles to reside in a particular organizational unit within a particular branch of the tree. Another application might expect user profiles to reside somewhere else. Unless these conflicts are resolved, a separate subtree must be created for each application.

Different organizations may have different security requirements and therefore may set different access control levels on the directory contents. In some cases, this can present a conflict. For example, if an application needs write permission to a directory subtree which has access control instructions that prohibit writing, the application will fail.

Mapping Attributes

Applications that need to use an existing schema but refer to attributes by a different name can include a mapping file. A mapping file equates its attributes to the attributes it uses internally. The file can also contain a naming context mapping so the application data can be placed anywhere in the DIT. An example of an application that provides attribute mapping is the NIS extensions for Solaris. In this application, you define the place where the NIS map data is stored by modifying a mapping entry.

Another method for mapping attributes is to deploy an LDAP directory router, which has that capability, as a front end to your directory servers. The iPlanet Directory Access Router provides attribute mapping and is discussed in "iPlanet Directory Access Router" on page 284.

LDAP Gateways

LDAP gateways provide front ends to an existing directory service that uses LDAP directories as their data store. With gateways, clients use the same protocol they normally would, only instead of communicating with a *real* server, they communicate with the gateway server. Unlike synchronization services, discussed below, the only data store for gateways is the LDAP directory.

A good example of an LDAP gateway is `ypldapd` from PADL Software. The `ypldapd` software acts as a gateway between NIS and an LDAP directory by emulating the Solaris `ypserv` process. NIS clients bind to the server running `ypladpd` just as they would to a server running `ypserv`. However, instead of retrieving information from NIS maps, they retrieve it from an LDAP directory server.

Another example of a gateway is the dynamic DNS implementation in Windows 2000. DNS records can be optionally maintained in Active Directory instead of DNS `db` zone files. DNS requests are serviced in a manner transparent to the client.

LDAP gateways are attractive because all the directory data resides in one place. There is no danger of getting data out of sync. However, since you are not maintaining the original data store, you cannot use management tools that work against that data. Instead, you must be use LDAP-based tools.

Also, it is difficult to provide all the functionality of the directory server you are replacing. For example, directory replication may not be available between a gateway and the native service such as NIS, since NIS data is propagated from masters to slaves as `dbm` files.

LDAP Synchronization

An alternative to an LDAP gateway is a synchronization service. Instead of using an LDAP directory as its sole data store, the synchronization service also maintains data in the data store of the original directory server. Updates are performed on one data store, then the changes are propagated to the other one. In some synchronization services, all data is mastered on only one of the directory servers. This process is referred to as one-way synchronization. Other synchronization services allow updates to be performed on either server and are referred to as two-way synchronization services.

Password Synchronization

As discussed in Chapter 3, "Security Models," there are many different authentication schemes. For protection, these schemes store passwords in an encrypted format by employing a particular hashing algorithm. Since it is likely that the two directory servers being synchronized use different hashing algorithms, the passwords must be decrypted, then encrypted with a new algorithm.

Some encryption algorithms, such as *crypt*, use a one-way hash, which means they cannot be decrypted on the server. The only way to get around this restriction is to intercept the password before it is encrypted on one server, then send the unencrypted password to the server being synchronized. An example of this technique is the NT Synchronization Service, which installs a special DLL on a Windows NT Domain Controller. All password changes are trapped by the DLL, which sends the unencrypted password to the iPlanet Directory Server.

Two problems can arise when password synchronization is deployed. The first problem is that in some cases passwords are sent over the network in clear text. However, you can solve this problem by setting up a secure SSL connection between the two synchronizing directory services. The second problem is that one-way hashed passwords can only be reset when users change their passwords. While this is not an insurmountable problem, it can inconvenience the users.

NIS Extensions for Solaris

The iPlanet Directory Server NIS extensions are an LDAP synchronization service between NIS and LDAP.

NT Synchronization Service

The NT Synchronization Service, which is available for the iPlanet Directory Server, synchronizes user account data maintained in the Windows NT SAM database with data maintained in the directory. For additional details see Chapter 12, "Microsoft Windows Interoperability."

iPlanet Meta-Directory Server

The iPlanet Meta-Directory Server is really a combination of a gateway and a synchronization service. Data from various sources can be synchronized with an LDAP directory, and incoming LDAP requests can be redirected, or linked, to an external data source. How different data sources are handled is determined by the type of Meta-Directory connector written for the data source.

Originally developed for Windows NT, the Meta-Directory Server now runs in the Solaris operating environment. The Meta-Directory Server is not a replacement for a directory server; instead, it works in conjunction with one. The iPlanet Directory Server bundled with the Solaris operating environment is fully compatible with the Meta-Directory Server, which must be purchased separately.

Since the Meta-Directory is a complex product with many features, it is not practical to present here a detailed explanation of how it works. Instead, we present an overview and some possible deployment scenarios.

How Meta-Directory Works

Conceptually, the Meta-Directory software creates a unified view of an LDAP directory that is composed of data from different data sources. This view is referred to as the MetaView and is what applications accessing the Meta-Directory see. The concept is simple, but the underlying technology required to create the unified view is quite complex.

A component called the `JoinEngine` collects data from `ConnectorViews` and then merges that data to create the unified view. A `ConnectorView` is created from special software, called *connectors*, which is written specifically to interface with a particular directory service. For example, an SQL connector would interface directly to a relational database.

Data can also be collected outside the context of the `JoinEngine` by indirect connectors. Indirect connectors use a synchronized copy of the directory to provide the `JoinEngine` with access to data in an external directory. Both direct and indirect connectors are available with the Meta-Directory software.

The Meta-Directory uses a trigger mechanism, which is written as part of a connector, to detect changes on the data source. The changes are recorded in a `changelog`, which is consulted to construct the `MetaView` of the data.

Meta-Directory Connectors

Connectors come in two types: direct and indirect. Direct connectors can access the data source directly through either LDAP or SQL, which are the two protocols that Meta-Directory Server supports. If the data source does not support either of these protocols, then an indirect connector is used. The indirect connector synchronizes a data source with data in an LDAP directory. The LDAP directory is then used to create the `MetaView`.

Connectors are available with the Meta-Directory Server product and from third parties. A description of some of the more popular connectors are provided in this section.

LDAP Connector

The LDAP connector is a direct connector to the location of the data in an LDAP directory. An LDAP connector is effectively built into the iPlanet Directory Server when the Meta-Directory schema is added to the directory schema. The Meta-Directory server may or may not reside on the same system to which the LDAP connector points.

Database Connector

The database connector is a direct connector to data residing in an SQL-accessible database. Supported databases are Oracle, Sybase, and the Microsoft SQL Server. A trigger mechanism detects changes in specified tables and columns in the connected database. Each insert, update, and deletion of rows in the selected tables results in a series of changes in the `changelog`.

A setup of customized scripts is created for the database server during the Meta-Directory Server configuration. The scripts are run against the target database to create a second database, which is populated with changes made to tables in that database.

Database connectors can be either one-way or two-way. LDAP search queries directed to the Meta-Directory Server can be forwarded to the connected database for data retrieval, and, if desired, database tables can be updated through LDAP. Whether a two-way flow of data is permitted depends on the particular database connector being deployed.

Directory Connector for Lotus Notes

The Directory Connector for Lotus Notes is an indirect connector that allows a two-way flow. It propagates any entry changes made in Lotus Notes to those same entries stored in the LDAP directory. If you make a change in the MetaView to an entry linked with a Lotus Notes entry, the change will (if the configuration allows it) be reflected in the Lotus Notes ConnectorView and propagated to Lotus Notes through the Directory Connector for Lotus Notes.

Directory Connector for Microsoft Exchange

The Directory Connector for Microsoft Exchange allows a two-way flow of data between Microsoft Exchange and its corresponding Indirect ConnectorView. It propagates any entry changes made in Microsoft Exchange to those same entries stored in the Indirect ConnectorView, so that they can be relayed to any corresponding entries in the MetaView. If you make a change in the MetaView to an entry linked with a Microsoft Exchange entry, the change will (if the configuration allows it) be reflected in the Microsoft Exchange ConnectorView and propagated to Microsoft Exchange through the Directory Connector for Microsoft Exchange.

Universal Connector

The Universal Connector allows a two-way flow of data between a variety of external directories and their corresponding Indirect ConnectorViews. It provides a Perl programming interface, which you can configure to connect to applications not previously supported by the Meta-Directory. It enables you to create, modify, or delete records in the external data repository.

The Universal Connector is interesting because you can use it to access data contained in flat files. Solaris system data that resides in /etc files can become a data source with some Perl programming.

Deploying iPlanet Meta-Directory

The iPlanet Meta-Directory Server can be deployed alongside other directory consolidation tools. Although it is possible to write a connector for almost any data source, if an alternative exists, you should use it. For example, a Universal Connector for NIS data could be written, but available iPlanet NIS extensions provide that function. Likewise, the iPlanet NT Synchronization Service provides synchronization between LDAP and Windows NT user account data.

Unified Login and Single Sign-on

Directory consolidation by itself may provide a unified `login`, but it does not provide single sign-on (SSO) capability. A unified `login` is achieved since the same name and password are used for all directory-enabled application logins. However, this does not mean that each application will not prompt the user for a name and password.

Single sign-on is achieved by only requiring the user to log in once. When the user attempts to access an application after already being authenticated, a special identifier is passed to the new application, verifying that the user has already been authenticated. Since there is no single standard way of performing SSO, all participating applications must be written with the same method. In this section, we examine two methods:

- Kerberos
- Netegrity SiteMinder

Kerberos and LDAP

Chapter 3, "Security Models," presented an overview of Kerberos. Although Kerberos technology is orthogonal to directory services, Kerberos can be used to create an SSO environment with or without the presence of a directory service. However, for web-based applications, the use of Kerberos is somewhat limited. If, for example, you want to provide access to partners outside your company, they would not be able to contact the Key Distribution Center (KDC) as required by Kerberos.

The directory service can use Kerberos as an authentication service, provided it is equipped to do so. However, at the time this book was written, the necessary Kerberos module for the iPlanet Directory Server was not available.

SiteMinder

The SiteMinder product was developed by Netegrity to address the problem of managing logins to heterogeneous web-based services. For example, users that access a web service hosted on a Microsoft IIS Web server are authenticated by a Windows NT domain controller, which maintains user account information. If the same users want to access web services on an iPlanet Web server running on a Sun server, they have to be authenticated by another mechanism, usually through LDAP. Since there is no way to pass authentication verification between these two systems, users must log in twice.

SiteMinder solves this multiple login problem by providing a central point for all authentication. Instead of being authenticated by each web service, users are authenticated by SiteMinder instead. After the user is authenticated, a special encrypted *cookie* is created and used for subsequent logins to different web-based services and applications. Even though users are automatically authenticated, you can curtail their access rights to specific resources by establishing access control policies through SiteMinder's security policy management features.

How SiteMinder Works

The SiteMinder product provides more than single sign-on capability. A full description of all these features can be found at the Netegrity Web site: `http://www.netegrity.com`. Included here is a brief description of how SiteMinder works, to give you an idea of how it would be deployed in a corporate environment.

The SiteMinder software consists of two main components:

- SiteMinder Policy Server
- SiteMinder Web Agent

The Policy Server provides authentication, among other services, to web-based applications. The Web Agent is integrated with a standard web server and is the component that allows the web server to be managed by SiteMinder. It intercepts all requests for resources (URLs), then decides whether the specified resource is under SiteMinder's control. If it is, the Policy Server is contacted.

The Policy Server acts as a front end to whatever authentication method is being deployed within your organization. These include:

- Basic authentication (user-name/password)
- Basic authentication over SSL
- Authentication schemes

  - ACE/Server (Security Dynamics)
  - CryptoCard
  - RADIUS Proxy
- Forms-based authentication
- X.509 certificates
- Custom or third-party schemes

Use some of these schemes in combination to provide stronger authentication. You can establish priority levels for finer control over resources. For example, if users are authenticated by a method that has a lower priority than the resource they are accessing, then an attempt to authenticate them at a higher level is made. Conversely, if users are already authenticated at a high-priority level, then no further authentication is required.

FIGURE 11-1 illustrates how single sign-on is achieved with SiteMinder.

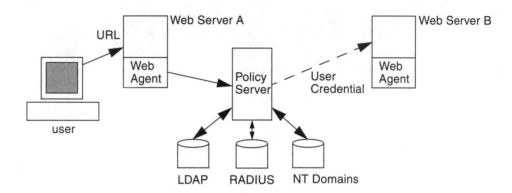

FIGURE 11-1 SiteMinder Single Sign-on

In FIGURE 11-1, the user accesses an URL that is located on Web server A, which has the SiteMinder Web Agent running on it. The agent checks to see if the requested URL is under SiteMinder control, and if it is, the agent contacts the Policy Server, which authenticates the user according to established policy rules. Once the user is authenticated, an encrypted cookie or user credential is created and passed to the other web servers under SiteMinder control.

When the same user tries to access a URL on Web server B, the Web Agent can then grant access according to the user credential it was passed, eliminating the need for a second user login.

Limitation of SiteMinder

SiteMinder was designed to work in a web server environment, where authentication is triggered upon a URL request. When a user logs into a computer, authentication is handled by the underlying operating system, instead of being initiated by a web server. Since there is no way to pass the authentication information to SiteMinder from the operating system, the user would have to log in again to gain access to web service applications.

Even though SiteMinder is a valuable tool for creating an SSO environment between disparate web applications, the user is still required to log into the platform from which the web applications will be launched. SiteMinder also requires that an agent be installed on each web server that will participate in the SSO environment. The agents are written with web server extension APIs such as ISAPI for Microsoft IIS and NSAPI for iPlanet Web server, and so must be provided by Netegrity.

iPlanet Directory Access Router

Although the iPlanet Directory Access Router (iDAR) does not provide directory consolidation by itself, it can be used to address some consolidation issues. For example, if two LDAP-enabled applications are expecting different directory schemas, use the iDAR to map the schema of one directory server to another. Response filtering provides an approach to consolidating internal and external directories. Instead of maintaining separate directories with protected data on one, deploy the iDAR to block external access to sensitive data.

Additional information about particular features can be obtained from the iPlanet Web site at: http://www.iplanet.com.

iDAR Overview

Functionally, iDAR is an LDAP access router located between LDAP clients and LDAP directory servers. Requests from LDAP clients can be filtered and routed to LDAP directory servers, based on rules defined in the iDAR configuration. Results from the directory server can be filtered and passed back to clients, again based on rules defined in the iDAR configuration. This process is totally transparent to the LDAP clients, which connect to the iDAR just as they would to any other LDAP directory server.

The iDAR provides enhanced high availability, security, and client compatibility features for both extranet and intranet directory infrastructures, including:

- Automatic load balancing
- Transparent server failover and failback
- Automatic referral following
- Extranet/intranet access control groups
- Secure client and server authentication
- Dynamic query and response filtering
- Dynamic schema mapping
- Directory-based or file-based configuration
- Configurable logging

The iDAR coexists with and complements new and existing LDAP directory infrastructures and integrates seamlessly with directory-enabled applications already deployed in both company extranets and intranets. It can be deployed to leverage the existing investment in a corporate directory infrastructure. The iDAR will interoperate with any LDAP-compliant directory server. The iDAR will work with the iPlanet Directory Server, and it is compatible with any LDAP-enabled and conformant directory, whether it's a native LDAP directory, an LDAP-enabled X.500 directory, or an LDAP-enabled relational database.

The iDAR implements the LDAP v3 Internet specification and also supports the older and less functional LDAP v2 specification for compatibility with already deployed directory-enabled client applications that use LDAP v2. In the Solaris operating environment, the iDAR server runs as a separate system server process. The server is multithreaded and can handle thousands of LDAP client requests while applying access control rules and protocol filtering rules to each request. The iDAR provides protection to private directory information from unauthorized access, while making it safe for organizations to publish their public information. Fine-grained, access control policy on LDAP directories can be established, such as control over who can perform different types of operations on different parts of the Directory Information Tree (DIT). The iDAR can also be configured to disallow certain kinds of operations typically performed by web trawlers and robots to collect information.

Unlike a web proxy server, the iDAR does not operate in a reverse proxy mode. It does not forward connections to arbitrary servers on the Internet from clients inside the firewall. Neither does it cache search results. The predominant reason for this is the problem of applying access controls to the data. These controls are currently only applied in the LDAP directory server where the access controls are maintained. The Directory Access Router has no knowledge of the directory server access controls.

iPlanet Directory Access Router Feature Set

The iDAR feature set provides three distinct functions:

- High availability
- Firewall-like security
- Client-server compatibility

High Availability

The iDAR supports high availability directory deployments by providing both automatic load balancing and automatic failover and failback among a set of replicated LDAP directory servers. For extranet and intranet environments, it is often necessary to ensure that mission-critical directory-enabled clients and applications have 24x7 access to directory data. The iDAR maintains connection state information for all directory servers that it knows about and dynamically performs proportional load balancing of LDAP operations across a set of configured directory servers. Should one or more directory servers become unavailable, the load is proportionally redistributed among the remaining servers. When a directory server comes back online, the load is proportionally reallocated dynamically.

For example, suppose directory server A is configured to receive 40% of the LDAP client load; server B, 20%; server C, 20%; and server D, 20%. If directory server B fails, iDAR will recognize that server A is configured to carry twice the load of servers C and D and will redistribute the 20% load from server B such that server A now receives 50%, server C, 25%, and server D, 25%. When directory server B is recovered, iDAR automatically detects this and reverts to the original load percentages configured across all four servers.

Network layer IP load balancing devices don't have access to the LDAP protocol layer. However, the iDAR integrates load balancing with access control, query filtering, and query routing and can make more intelligent decisions about application-layer access control and LDAP routing.

Firewall-like Security

The iDAR provides flexible, external, directory access control facilities that enhance the basic access control provided by a directory server. The access control mechanisms allow different users and communities of users to be associated with specific access groups to which administrator-defined security restrictions and query filters will be applied. The administrator can control access to entries based on LDAP authentication information, IP address, domain name, and other criteria. The server also supports secure authentication, using Internet standard security mechanisms including both challenge-response, protected-password authentication, and digital certificate-based strong authentication and data encryption. For protected passwords, the CRAM-MD5 and DIGEST-MD5 SASL mechanisms are supported. For strong authentication and data confidentiality, support is available for both the Netscape alternate port 636 Secure Sockets Layer (SSL) mechanism and the Internet standard Transport Layer Security (TLS) mechanism. RSA, Digital Signature Standard, Triple-DES, and Diffie Hellman cryptographic algorithms are supported.

One of the significant security features the iDAR provides is the protection of the number of connections established between LDAP clients and the LDAP directory server. You can protect your LDAP directory server from connection attacks by configuring the iDAR to monitor a number of specific metrics: the number of simultaneous client operations, the number of operations a client can request per connection, and the number of connections for a particular client group. The iDAR can also time out inactive clients.

The systems administrator can configure the iDAR with specific threshold limits not to be exceeded for the given metrics. The iDAR monitors these metrics and helps ensure that the thresholds are not exceeded.

These features can help prevent denial-of-service attacks and flood attacks that are so commonplace in the industry today. If the iDAR detects that a threshold has been reached, it starts refusing connections to the directory server and prevents the directory server from being attacked and overwhelmed.

Client-Server Compatibility

The iDAR provides intelligent query routing by making query routing decisions that are based on LDAP DNs and group access rights, including identification of mobile users by their authentication credentials. In addition, the iDAR can automatically follow LDAP referrals that may be returned by a directory server in support of highly distributed and scalable directory services. Automatic referral following is a significant advantage for large-scale directory deployments, where it is necessary to physically distribute directory information among a set of directory servers, but to have the distributed directory appear to users as one logical directory. The iDAR supports this type of deployment scenario by enabling the directory architect to logically unify otherwise distributed directory data in support of scalable distributed directory services.

The iDAR supports any compliant LDAP v2 or LDAP v3 client application. Support is provided for schema rewriting to accommodate client applications with fixed schemas that do not always match the directory server's schema. For example, the Microsoft Outlook email client has a fixed schema that expects the directory server to implement Microsoft-defined attributes, which may not match a company's more general schema requirements. The schema rewriting capability allows the directory system administrator to implement a general-purpose company schema and then dynamically map specific elements of that schema into the set of attribute types that are required by the less functional client application. The iDAR is otherwise schema agnostic and accepts any attribute types and object classes defined by a large set of standard and ad hoc industry schema definitions, including RFC1274, X.520, X.521, LIPS, PKIX, `inetOrgPerson`, and DEN.

CHAPTER **12**

Microsoft Windows Interoperability

One of the advantages of standard technology like LDAP is the opportunity it creates for dissimilar operating environments to interoperate. The business computing landscape is composed of heterogeneous systems, since no single computing architecture addresses all computing needs. These systems include UNIX-based servers and workstations and Microsoft Windows clients and servers. Each of these systems maintains its own data store, which is sometimes duplicated to enable users to access resources on either system.

This chapter focuses on how Solaris-based systems can share information with Windows-based systems by deploying LDAP technology. The first part of this chapter looks at how the user account data can be synchronized between a Windows NT server and a Solaris server running the iPlanet Directory Server. The second part of the chapter examines the directory services in Microsoft's newest operating system, Windows 2000, and how they can interact with Solaris directory services.

Windows NT Interoperability

One of the most important roles a directory plays is being the keeper of user account information, including the user's identity. When a user logs into a computer or application, the directory is consulted to provide user information that is used for controlling access and locating personal resources such as mail boxes and home directories. The ability to share this user account data between different operating environments is highly desirable.

This section focuses on how user account information is managed in a Windows NT environment and how that information can be made available to the Solaris operating environment. The key technology that allows this flexibility is a feature of the iPlanet Directory Server called the NT Synchronization Service.

Windows NT Security Model

In the Windows NT environment, user account information is kept in the Security Account Manager (SAM) database. This database is maintained on special Windows NT servers called Domain Controllers, of which there are two varieties: primary (PDC) and backup (BDC). The difference between the two is that the BDC maintains only a read-only copy of the SAM database, whereas the PDC has write privileges.

When a user logs into a computer running Windows NT, the login ID along with the user's password is passed to either a BDC or a PDC for authentication. If the user is successfully authenticated, then a token called a security ID (SID) is passed back along with information about the user. Based on the SID, Windows NT servers can determine what access rights a user has to its resources.

Besides the login process, other applications can use the SAM database for authorization and retrieval of user profile information. For example, a Microsoft Exchange server would contact a BDC or PDC to verify the identity of an email user, then retrieve information about the user.

How the NT User Account Information Is Made Available to Solaris Server

Several approaches can be implemented to allow information to be accessed from both the Windows NT and Solaris operating environments. One approach is to port the PDC and BDC code from Windows NT to the Solaris operating system, which is how the Solaris PC NetLink product was architected. Another approach is to provide a synchronization service between the SAM database and a different type of directory store, like an LDAP directory.

The approach used in the iPlanet Directory Server is the latter one. That is, provide a two-way synchronization service that updates the LDAP directory whenever changes are made on the Windows NT side, and vice versa. Since the SAM database is not based on LDAP, the structure of the data stored in it is different from the structure of the same data stored in the iPlanet Directory Server. To make the synchronization service work, the data from the Windows NT environment needs to be mapped to an LDAP structure.

Mapping NT User Account Information to LDAP

The schema for two object classes—`ntUser` and `ntGroup`—that support Windows NT user accounts ships with the iPlanet Directory Server. Some of the LDAP attributes contained in these object classes correspond directly to Windows NT user account fields. These are shown in TABLE 12-1.

TABLE 12-1 Windows NT to LDAP Mapping

Directory Server Attribute	NT User Account Field
`cn` or `commonName`	`full_name`
`description`	`comment`
`uid`	`name`
`userPassword`	`password`

For each Windows NT user account as well as for Windows NT groups, an equivalent LDAP entry is created with these mapped fields. Also, if an `ntUser` LDAP entry is created, an equivalent Windows NT user account is created.

How the Synchronization Service Works

The NT synchronization service consists of a process, `ns-dssynch.exe`, running on a Windows NT domain controller and the iPlanet Directory Server, with the NT synchronization plug-in enabled, running on a Sun server. The `ns-dssynch.exe` process captures changes to the SAM database, then sends them to the iPlanet Directory Server over a predefined port number. A special DLL running on the Windows NT server traps password changes before they are encrypted and sends them in clear text to the directory server.

Note – Since passwords are sent to the directory server in clear text, it is recommended that the synchronous service be set up on a secure port that uses SSL.

At scheduled times, changes made to user accounts on the NT side are propagated to the directory server. The equivalent LDAP entries are then updated.

NT Synchronization Service Installation

Two components are required to run the NT synchronization service. One component runs on the Sun server and is installed by default. The other component, which runs on the Windows NT server, is not contained on the Solaris companion CD and must be downloaded from the iPlanet Web site:

www.iplanet.com

The iPlanet Directory Server for NT software, which you download, is contained in a ZIP file that you should install on the NT Server. Once you unZIP the file, run setup.exe on the Windows NT domain controller and follow these steps:

1. **Choose the Custom installation option.**

2. **Check these components for installation:**
   - Netscape Server Family Core Components
   - Netscape Directory Server 4.0 Synch Service

3. **When the configuration screen appears, fill in the appropriate information:**
   - **Host** — Name of the Sun server.
   - **LDAP Port** — Either the secure or insecure port on the Sun server.
   - **Administrator DN** — The account as which the Synchronization server will log into the directory server. There must be write permission in the subtree where the entries are kept.
   - **Administrator password** — Password for login DN.
   - **Directory base for NT Users** — The container on the directory server where account information is stored. This container must be created manually on the server.
   - **Directory base for NT Groups** — The container on the directory server where group information is stored. This must be created manually.
   - **Enforce UID uniqueness in subtree** — A specified subtree prevents the creation of entries with the same UID.
   - **Synchronization plug-in port** — The port number configured on the directory server for synchronization. Port 5009 is the default.

FIGURE 12-1 shows the **Directory Server Settings** tab of the **Configuration** tool. You can run this tool after the installation to change parameters.

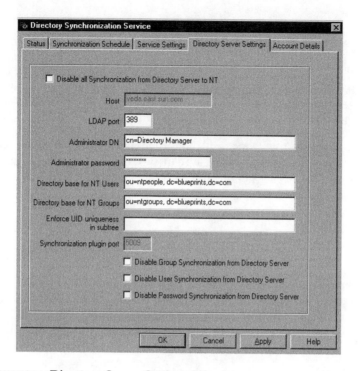

FIGURE 12-1 **Directory Server Settings** Tab

After the installation on the NT server completes, modify the **Netscape Directory Synchronization** service on the NT server so you can log in as an NT administrator.

On the directory server:

1. **In the Directory Server Console, highlight the** `rootDN` **and go to Configuration—>Settings.**

2. **Under settings:**

   a. **Check Enable NT Synchronization Service.**

   b. **Enter number in Synchronization port: field.**

3. **Create the containers (ou=) for the NT users and groups.**

Windows 2000 Interoperability

With the release of Windows 2000, Microsoft placed the directory service at the core of its operating environment. The directory service, called Active Directory, is used by the core operating system to store user account and system resource data and by the BackOffice suite of products as their data store.

The goal of Active Directory is to provide a scalable, easily accessible, central repository for both operating system and application data. To achieve this goal, Active Directory brings together several standards-based technologies:

- DHCP
- DNS
- LDAP
- Kerberos
- Public Key Infrastructure

Although similar technologies exist in the Solaris environment, implementation differences do not allow the technologies to be freely mixed and matched. This section focuses on how Active Directory services are structured, how the technology components interact, and how Solaris-based services can interoperate.

Active Directory Services Architecture

Before discussing how Active Directory services interoperate with Solaris directory services, it is useful to take a look at their architecture. FIGURE 12-2 depicts the major components of Active Directory services.

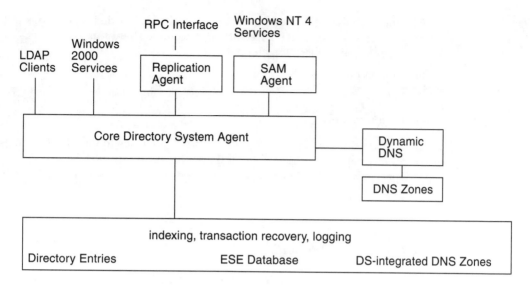

FIGURE 12-2 Active Directory Services Major Components

The core of the directory server is referred to as the Directory System Agent (DSA). Each controller in an Active Directory environment is a DSA that runs on its own computer. The DSA is the control center of Active Directory and is the integration point for other services and agents. All updates to the database and searches are performed by the DSA. The DSA also communicates with other DSAs in the network, which together form an Active Directory services domain.

The database that Active Directory uses is based on the Extensible Storage Engine (ESE) database. This is an Indexed Sequential Access Method (ISAM) database similar to the one in which Microsoft Exchange stores data. The ESE database has built-in indexing features, along with other database features such as transaction logging and recovery. All directory data resides in this database. It includes user accounts, Kerberos credentials, public keys, digital certificates, etc. If the Windows 2000 DNS server is deployed, the DNS zone data is also maintained in the directory.

The DSA interfaces with other services. LDAP-enabled applications can interface directly with the DSA, although this is not the recommended interface for applications. Windows 2000 clients and services access the DSA through a set of APIs called the Active Directory Service Interface (ADSI). This is Microsoft's preferred interface and is discussed in "How Applications Access Active Directory Services" on page 302.

A replication agent performs multimaster replication between multiple DSAs. A SAM agent provides backward compatibility to Windows clients, using NT Lan Manager (NTLM) authentication.

To examine how Active Directory services work in greater detail, let's look at the different aspects of the Active Directory architecture. These functional areas can be expressed in terms of these four models:

- Information model
- Security model
- Access model
- Replication model

As these models are described, you will notice similarities to the LDAP models discussed in Chapter 2, "Solaris Naming Services Architecture." This is not a coincidence; X.500 and LDAP concepts are used throughout the Active Directory implementation.

Information Model

The directory information model defines how data is stored and how objects are named. Basically, two types of naming constructs are used in Active Directory:

- LDAP, or X.500
- DNS

LDAP or X.500 Integration

The LDAP, or X.500, information model names and stores directory entries. The Active Directory structure looks very much like the LDAP Directory Information Tree (DIT). It is an inverted tree with a root entry, or suffix, at the top. Below the root entry are containers, such as organization units (ou) which contain directory entries. The entries are defined as objects that have attributes associated with them. Associated with the attributes are values that can be single or multivalue. As is the case with LDAP directory servers, the Active Directory schema defines the objects and rules that determine the attribute values that can be used.

DNS Integration

DNS plays an important role in Active Directory services. Clients locate Active Directory controllers by examining service resource (SRV RR) records. Clients of Active Directory services search these records to locate the nearest controller. The directory *naming context*, or Active Directory *partition*, as Microsoft calls it, maps to the DNS domain name of a company and its subdomains. To do this, the domain component (dc) naming convention identifies the root object. This naming is not mandatory, but it does eliminate confusion between Active Directory domains and DNS domains if you make the names the same.

Although not directly related to the naming model, the Windows 2000 version of DNS supports dynamic updates of zone records. What this means is that when a DHCP server assigns an IP address to a client, that IP address is automatically updated in the DNS database. Likewise, when a DHCP address lease expires, the entry is removed from the DNS database. Using dynamic DNS eliminates the need for WINS servers and databases.

Active Directory Naming

The Active Directory namespace is similar to that found in the iPlanet Directory Server. At the top of the tree is a root identifier specified by dc=, under which is an organization specified by o=, as depicted in FIGURE 12-3.

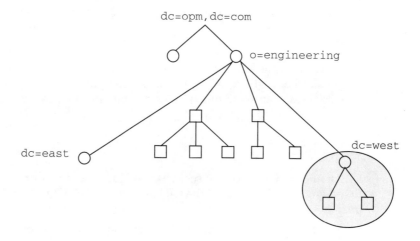

FIGURE 12-3 Active Directory Namespace

In FIGURE 12-3, the Active Directory domain is mapped to the company's DNS domain name which is opm.com. This technique is convenient since nearly all companies have a registered DNS domain name. Under the top-level domain are the subdomains called east.opm.com and west.opm.com. Deployments of Solaris directory services follow a similar pattern.

The east and west portions of the tree actually reside in a different Active Directory domain. In the next section, we see how these different Active Directory domains are tied together.

Domains, Trees, and Forests

In Windows NT Server 4.0, directory data, such as user account information, is maintained by a domain controller, as discussed in "Windows NT Security Model" on page 290. These controllers are responsible for maintaining their own namespace. Since it is not always practical to keep all of your company data in a single domain, you will generally deploy multiple NT domains. To share data between these domains, you set up a trust relationship between two cooperating domains. You must do this manually, and the trust relationships soon become an administrative nightmare to maintain.

With Windows 2000, domain controllers still maintain their own namespace, but the trust relationships between domain controllers have been improved. You can now establish automatic trust relationships by deploying domain *trees* and domain *forests*.

A domain tree is a set of domains that form a contiguous namespace through a set of hierarchal relationships. In FIGURE 12-3, opm.com is the parent domain of east.opm.com and west.opm.com. Together they form a domain tree.

A domain forest is a set of domains or domain trees that do not form a contiguous namespace but do have an implicit trust relationship between them. Domains in a domain forest share a common schema, configuration, and the Global Catalog.

Global Catalog

By default, Active Directory services configures the first domain controller in the first domain in the forest as the Global Catalog. The Global Catalog has several purposes:

- It enables users to browse for the names and addresses of all other users in the domain forest.
- It enables users and applications to use resources and objects in remote domains.
- It enables public key authentication and encryption functions.

Significantly, the Global Catalog provides a way to centrally maintain information about users and universal groups for access control purposes.

Security Model

The initial authentication of a user at login time takes place through the client's LDAP connection to the Active Directory server. Either Kerberos, or public key-based Transport Layer Security (TLS) protocols running alongside the LDAP *bind* operation provide authentication of all users. Once users are authenticated, their identities are mapped to a Windows 2000 account. Optionally, Kerberos or TLS can encrypt all LDAP traffic between the user and Active Directory services.

After a user is authenticated, every directory activity is subject to access controls. Access controls are stored as a binary value called a security descriptor, with the object they protect. This security descriptor contains a security identifier (SID) that identifies the principal to whom the access control entry (ACE) applies, and also contains information on the type of access the ACE grants or denies.

Note – The generation of an SID is specific to Microsoft's Active Directory implementation and not a standard LDAP concept. Therefore, a Solaris directory server cannot generate an SID, preventing it from authenticating a user for operating system use. However, LDAP-enabled applications running on Windows clients can be authenticated by a Solaris server.

Access Model

The access model describes how authorization to access particular objects takes place. FIGURE 12-4 shows the access control process in Windows 2000.

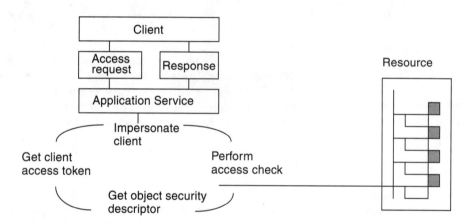

FIGURE 12-4 Access Control Process in Windows 2000

In the Windows 2000 security model, clients access objects through services. They never directly access to the objects. Controllers authenticate the user's identity at login time by using Kerberos or another method negotiated under LDAP's Simple Authentication and Security Layer (SASL). The client is granted a Kerberos Ticket-Granting Ticket (TGT) and service tickets for application servers. For access control, application servers use the client security context information to impersonate the client and look up its user or group SIDs in local permissions tables such as the file system. If the access check succeeds, the client can use the requested objects.

Replication Model

Active Directory services use a multimaster replication model that is far more difficult to set up and manage than is the single-master model on which the iPlanet Directory Server 4.12 is based. In the single-master model, all changes for a particular naming context are made on one server. The changes are then propagated to replication partners. In the multimaster model, changes can be made on any server in the domain.

Another factor that increases the complexity is that domains can be arranged in trees and forests. The replication service must therefore be aware of the topology and determine what data needs to be replicated.

In the simple case where multiple controllers at a single site are serving the same domain, replication is set up automatically. An Active Directory process called the Knowledge Consistency Checker (KCC) is responsible for mapping out the Active Directory domain controller topology and determining how replication should be performed. The main heuristics used in this case are the network mask of the controller to determine what subnet the controller is on and the routing information to determine how many hops there are between controllers.

For example, if there are three Active Directory domain controllers called A, B, and C, A might replicate to B, B to C, and C to A. The KCC would automatically set up this replication scheme. However, the scheme could later be manually modified. What gets updated and when are determined by an update sequence number (USN) which is stored with every entry. There is also a pause interval between controllers, so updates can be batched together and make more efficient use of network bandwidth. If changes are marked *urgent*, they can be sent out immediately instead of pausing. An example of an urgent change would be the revocation of a user's account.

Another issue with the multimaster model is maintaining consistency. For example, if a user account is created at the same time on two different controllers with the same login name, a conflict will exist during replication, since each user must have a unique login name. In this case, the Active Directory service will automatically change the login to a unique name for one of the entries. In the event a container was removed on one controller while an entry was created in it on another controller, that entry will be placed in a lost and found area.

If replication is performed between sites in different geographical regions, the network bandwidth of the link between them must be factored in. Active Directory services will try to do the right thing, but manual inspection is recommended. In this case, the replication partner pulls the updates. Also, there is no controller-to-controller notification going on as is the case within a site.

Active Directory domains can be grouped together in trees and forests as discussed earlier. The relationships among domains in a domain tree are established by a common schema and configuration. The schema defines the rules for allowable data types and values, and the configuration lets each controller know how the other ones are configured. Both the schema and configuration containers need to be replicated to maintain the tree relationship.

Forests are similar to trees but do not have an explicit hierarchal relationship. An identical schema can be used but is not required. However, to create a trust relationship that can be automatically maintained, you must replicate a subset of the tree. User accounts are an example of what would be replicated.

Note – The main advantage of multimaster replication is that if one server goes down, a replication partner can assume all its duties including the task of performing updates. Clustering the iPlanet Directory Server master replication server creates the same environment.

How Active Directory Clients Interact with Servers

Active Directory services servers support both NTLM and Windows 2000 style login and authentication. The login process for a Windows client is as follows:

1. The Client obtains an IP address and an address of a DNS server from DHCP.

2. The DNS server is searched for a Service Resource Record (SVR RR) which contains the IP address of an Active Directory domain controller.

3. The Client initiates the domain controller logon process.

4. Credentials are obtained from a Kerberos key server.

5. An LDAP bind operation that involves a Kerberos exchange, whereby the client presents credentials, takes place.

In the Active Directory services environment, DHCP plays the same role it did in previous releases. However, DHCP is integrated with Dynamic DNS, so DNS is updated whenever DHCP assigns an IP address or a DHCP lease expires. Essentially, this mechanism replaces WINS.

Windows clients locate a domain controller by consulting a DNS server and looking for particular service records. Every controller within a domain is listed. The client picks the one on the same subnet it resides on.

Legacy clients can use the same protocol for logging on as before. This protocol sends a password to the controller along with a login name. If the client supports Active Directory services, then the handshake is different. The client first needs to obtain security credentials from a Kerberos server. Then, the client attempts to bind to the domain controller by using Kerberos authentication or some other SASL-defined security method. Part of the Kerberos ticket is the client's SID.

Once the client is logged in, an object that impersonates the user is used for access control. The client never has direct access to any resources.

How Applications Access Active Directory Services

The Microsoft preferred interface is the Active Directory Service Interface (ADSI). The following operations are supported in ADSI:

- Binding to the domain controller
- Access to directory data
- Complex searches

Additionally, ADSI provides interfaces to other directories including LDAP and NetWare.

Alternatively, applications can use LDAP to access Active Directory Services but need a supported security method like Kerberos. ADSI also provides a number of enhancements that LDAP does not. These include automatic locating of the directory server entry (DSE) of a domain server.

Solaris Directory Services and Active Directory Services Interactions

At the time this Sun BluePrint was written, Windows 2000 had recently been released, so there has been little interoperability certification between Solaris directory services and Active Directory services. However, since there is common technology between the two environments, there is an opportunity for some degree of interoperability.

This section looks at the level of interoperability that is desirable and at potential issues.

Signing On Only Once

We would like a user to be authenticated once upon login and then automatically be authenticated for all applications the user accesses. However, this aim is difficult to achieve because two processes actually take place: authentication and authorization.

Authentication is the process of verifying whether users are who they say they are. The authentication scheme Windows 2000 uses is Kerberos, which is also available in the Solaris operating environment. So, in theory, a Windows 2000 client could authenticate through a Solaris Kerberos server, but that approach would not necessarily give the user access to Windows 2000 resources.

Authorization is required for user access to system resources. Windows NT authorizes users by checking the client's SID against an access control list (ACL). The client receives the SID as part of a Kerberos ticket. Since the way the SID is generated is proprietary, the Solaris Kerberos server cannot attach an SID to the ticket.

Note – The SID that Active Directory Services uses is not the same as the one stored in a PDC's SAM database. Therefore, even though the Solaris PC NetLink software can function as a PDC, it cannot generate Windows 2000-style SIDs.

You can achieve single sign-on for Kerberos-enabled applications. Use the same Kerberos ticket with applications running on either Solaris or Windows 2000 servers. However, the user typically needs to log in to a system before running applications, so a true single sign-on environment would not be achieved.

Joining a Windows 2000 Tree or Forest

We might also want to create a contiguous namespace consisting of an Active Directory tree of which both Windows 2000 and Solaris servers are a part or share data by joining an Active Directory forest. However, both of these capabilities require security mechanisms that have recently been published by Microsoft but have not yet been implemented in the Solaris operating environment. Another way of accessing data on a directory with a different namespace is through the use of referrals.

Specifying LDAP Referrals

Referrals are made by specification of a URL of another directory server in response to a query. If a search query is performed on a server that implements referrals, the query can be forwarded to an another server to retrieve additional matching entries.

To specify a referral, a server must be able to bind to the server to which the referral will be sent. Since binding requires authentication, a common authentication method must exist between both servers. An Active Directory server can bind to an iPlanet Directory Server by simple `name/password` authentication. However, binding to the Active Directory requires a more sophisticated authentication method such as Kerberos.

As of this writing, a Kerberos interface to the iPlanet Directory Server is not available although it is being considered. However, even with Kerberos authentication, the access control mechanisms on the Active Directory server could not be used unless the connection were made using the Security Support Provider Interface (SSPI). Otherwise, only anonymous access is allowed.

Using Windows Services in UNIX 2.0

In the latest version of Windows Services for UNIX, Microsoft has included the capability to store NIS map data in the Active Directory and to provide access to NIS clients. Instead of storing NIS data in RFC 2307 format, Windows Services stores the data in a simple keyword-value pair. This means that the data stored in Active Directory cannot be retrieved by an LDAP client expecting to see RFC 2307 format. Also, NIS clients access the data stored in the Active Directory through anonymous authentication, so any client can access it without verification of its identity.

Using Netscape Communicator as an LDAP Client

Setting up a directory server is useless unless you have LDAP clients that can access its data. LDAP clients can be written with several programming and scripting languages including C, C++, Perl, and Java. However, you do not have to write your own client to benefit from the LDAP server you just installed.

The Netscape Communicator Web browser is an LDAP client that can easily be configured to search and retrieve employee information contained in an LDAP directory. This appendix shows you how to configure the Address Book feature of Netscape Communicator and start taking advantage of LDAP technology without writing a single line of code.

Configuration Overview

One of the most important tasks of any directory service is to facilitate the update of the corporation's phone directory. This process includes gathering all the pertinent information (like room number, floor, and extension number) from different sources, compiling this information into an understandable form, printing the information, and finally distributing this information to the correct sources. Not only is this intensive task painful, but it is also out-of-date as soon as it is printed.

Creating a corporate address book is a two-step process. First, the information needs to be placed in a client-accessible portion of the directory information tree (DIT); second, the client needs to be configured to gain access. Once the directory is populated with data, you can decide what level of access you want users to have. For example, you may decide to only allow users to search the directory and not update any data.

Once the directory server is configured, any computer running Netscape Communicator can start using the Address Book, provided the directory server is reachable and LDAP traffic is not blocked by a firewall.

Directory Server Setup

Before setting up an Address Book, you need to populate the directory with employee information. You typically do this by creating a script that converts existing data to an LDIF format that can be imported into the directory. Another way you can populate the directory is through the iPlanet Directory Console, by invoking the **New User** form. While this method is not practical for loading the entire Address Book, it can be useful for creating sample data.

Before you create new user entries, you should create a container to store them in. The iPlanet Directory Server default to create user accounts is in the `ou=People` container, but any container will work. After you create the container, set the permissions to reflect the desired access control level. For testing, allowing read-only access to everyone is probably the easiest course.

For production environments, you can choose to have users authenticated, then set access control based on the user or group to which the user belongs. In the example used here, the default `ou=People` container is used to store employee information, and anonymous read-only access is allowed. The directory server port is set to 389, which is the default LDAP port.

Netscape Communicator Setup

To access the directory server from Netscape Communicator, follow these steps:

1. **Run Communicator.**

2. **Choose Address Book.**

3. **Under File, choose New Directory from the pull-down menu.**

4. **Fill in the form (see** FIGURE A-1**).**

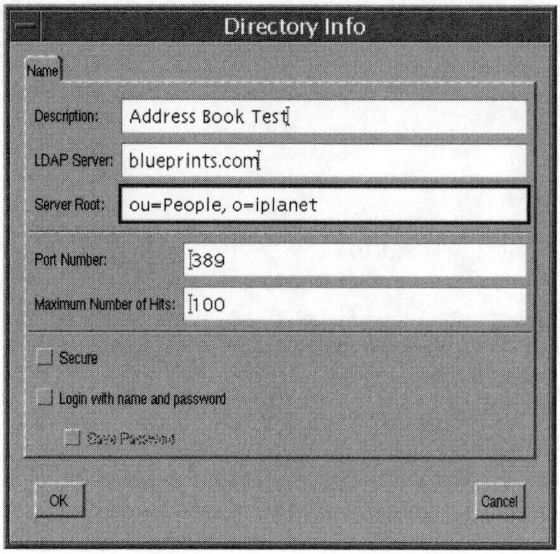

FIGURE A-1 **Directory Info** Form

5. **Click OK.**

You should then see the new directory appear in the left pane of the **Address Book** window.

The directory is now ready to be searched.

Directory Searches

To activate a simple search on Communicator, search the directory with the following steps:

1. **Run Communicator.**

2. **Choose Address Book.**

3. **Highlight the Directory Panel in the newly created directory.**

4. **Type in the Search names containing the desired search string or substring. For example, Johnson, Smith, etc.**

   Matches to your search request are displayed in the right pane. If a common name like Johnson is specified, several matches might be displayed. You can now highlight the correct match, click the right mouse button, then choose **New Message** from the pull-down menu to send that person an email message. You can also add the entry to your personal address book by dragging and dropping it to the **Personal Address** book displayed in the left pane.

Other Features

The Netscape Communicator's Address Book contains many more features than those mentioned here. The layout of the Address Book can be customized and advanced searches can be specified. These and any other features are described in the Netscape Communicator documentation.

LDAP Standards Information

LDAP, like any other standards-based technology, is defined in great detail in a series of documents which are publicly available. As the technology matures and becomes more popular, requests for enhancements are inevitable, necessitating changes to these documents. We could have included copies of the current revision of LDAP documents, but the dynamic nature of LDAP technology would soon make them outdated so, instead of including these documents, we provide information on them and their location.

The following sections provide guidelines to important documents and pointers to where they may be found.

Locating RFCs and Internet Drafts

To locate the specifics of protocols such as LDAP v3, look at RFCs and Internet Drafts. RFC, which stands for Request for Comments, is where each distinct version of an Internet standards-related specification is published as part of the Request for Comments (RFC) document series. This archival series is the official publication channel for Internet standards documents and other publications of the Internet community.

The sites below do not list all the RFCs defining a particular standard; some, are often classified as Experimental, Informational, Historic, or Early (before IETF—standards track). Most RFCs start off as Internet Drafts before being approved as RFCs. When you are searching for a particular RFC or Internet Draft, you will find that it is available at mirrored sites all over the world.

The following sites are not complete but can be used as a starting place for locating your favorite (and most useful) RFCs:

```
http://www.rfc-editor.org/rfcsearch.html
```

```
http://www.ietf.org/rfc/rfc.html
```

```
http://src.doc.ic.ac.uk/computing/internet/rfc/
```

```
ftp://src.doc.ic.ac.uk/computing/internet/rfc/
```

```
http://info.internet.isi.edu:80/in-notes/rfc/files/
```

```
ftp://ds.internic.net/rfc/
```

For example, if you want to access a particular RFC and you know the specific RFC number, say, RFC 2251, you would type 2251 in the box provided. If you do not know the RFC number, use the URL in the following example to locate the RFC you are interested in.

```
http://www.rfc-editor.org/rfcsearch.htm
```

This Web site enables you to specify the RFC number and other information such as the `Title`. You can enter the word `LDAP` and, assuming you have set the maximum number of entries returned high enough, all the LDAP-related RFCs will be returned. Be aware that if you search for an Internet Draft and you are unable to find it, it does not mean that the draft does not exist! You may need to refine your search—try searching for the same draft with a higher number.

Life Cycle of a RFC

The first step toward publication of an RFC is publication of the document as an Internet Draft. Internet Drafts are working documents of the IETF, its areas, and its working groups. You will notice that part of the name has the letters IETF, with a brief description of the RFC followed by a two-digit version number, and the `.txt` extension.

Once an Internet Draft has been submitted, it has a life span of six months; after that time the Internet Draft expires. Expiration means either that a new draft is submitted (which typically means that a new draft is issued with a higher sequential number) or that the Internet Draft has expired and is no longer available. When an Internet Draft expires, it is deleted. Sometimes, you receive a date and timestamp with the information that a particular Internet Draft was deleted.

When the document reaches consensus of the Internet community, it is published as an RFC. RFCs can be of different types, such as the Standards Tracks RFC which include the Proposed Standard, Draft Standard, and Standard. Not all documents are published in the Standards Track; it is also possible to have the documents published as Historical, Experimental, or Informational; these are not Internet Standards.

You can also find Internet Drafts at these sites:

IETF: `ftp://ftp.ietf.org/inte net-drafts/`

Africa: `ftp.is.co.za`

Canada: `ftp.normos.org`

Sweden: `ftp.nordu.net`

Switzerland: `ftp://sunsite.cnlab-switch.ch`

Italy: `ftp.nic.it`

Pacific Rim: `munnari.oz.au`

US West Coast: `ftp.isi.edu`

South America: `ftp.ietf.rnp.br`

LDAP RFCs and Internet Drafts

This section lists some of the LDAP RFCs and provides a sample of LDAP Internet Drafts.

LDAP RFCs

RFC 1823: *The C LDAP Application Program Interface*

RFC 1823 defines the old LDAPv2 interface. This RFC will eventually be replaced by a document that is currently an Internet Draft. This Internet Draft defines the LDAPv3 extensions to the C API for accessing LDAP.

Status: INFORMATIONAL

RFC 2247: *Using Domains in LDAP/X.500 Distinguished Names*

This document defines an algorithm by which a name registered with the Internet Domain Name System (DNS) can be represented as an LDAP-distinguished name.

Status: PROPOSED STANDARD

RFC 2251: *Lightweight Directory Access Protocol (v3)*

This is the main RFC for LDAPv3 and defines the protocol operations, data representation, and data organization.

Status: PROPOSED STANDARD

RFC 2252: *Lightweight Directory Access Protocol (v3): Attribute Syntax Definitions*

LDAP transmits most attribute values as strings, rather than as binary structures. For example, the number 4,000 is transmitted as "4000". This document defines the standard attribute type representations and specifies how attribute values are compared for each standard type during a search operation.

Status: PROPOSED STANDARD

RFC 2253: *Lightweight Directory Access Protocol (v3): UTF-8 String Representation of Distinguished Names*

Each entry in an LDAP directory is uniquely identified by its distinguished name (DN), represented as a string. This document defines the syntax and structure of these names.

Status: PROPOSED STANDARD

RFC 2254: *The String Representation of LDAP Search Filters*

The basic LDAPv3 RFC (RFC 2251) defines a binary format for search expressions passed from a client to a server. However, users of clients compose and submit search requests in an easily readable and printable string format, which is defined in RFC 2254.

Status: PROPOSED STANDARD

RFC 2255: *The LDAP URL Format*

RFC 2255 defines the URL format for expressing an LDAP search. You can enter an LDAP URL in many browsers to perform an LDAP search.

Status: PROPOSED STANDARD

RFC 2256: *A Summary of the X.500(96) User Schema for Use with LDAPv3*

Where possible, LDAP leverages the schema standardization work of X.500, rather than inventing new standards for schema information. This document defines standard attributes for representing a person in an LDAP entry. These attributes are based on the X.500 standard.

Status: PROPOSED STANDARD

RFC 2307: *An Approach for Using LDAP as a Network Information Service*

This document describes an experimental mechanism for mapping entities related to TCP/IP and the UNIX system into X.500 entries so that they can be resolved with the LDAP protocol.

Status: EXPERIMENTAL

RFC 2259: *Internet X.509 Public Key Infrastructure Operational Protocols-LDAPv2*

This document addresses requirements to provide access to public-key infrastructure (PKI) repositories for retrieval and management of PKI information based on LDAP.

Status: PROPOSED STANDARD

RFC 2587: *Internet X.509 Public Key Infrastructure LDAPv2 Schema*

This document defines a minimal schema to support PKIX in an LDAPv2 environment, as defined in RFC 2559.

Status: PROPOSED STANDARD

RFC 2589: *LDAPv3 Extensions for Dynamic Directory Services*

This document defines extended operations to support dynamic (short-lived) directory data storage.

Status: PROPOSED STANDARD

RFC 2596: *Use of Language Codes in LDAP*

This document describes how language codes as defined in RFC 1766 are carried in LDAP and are to be interpreted by LDAP servers.

Status: PROPOSED STANDARD

RFC 2696: *LDAP Control Extension for Simple Paged Results Manipulation*

This document describes an LDAPv3 control extension for simple paging of search results. This control extension allows a client to control the rate at which an LDAP server returns the results of an LDAP search operation.

Status: INFORMATIONAL

RFC 2713: *Schema for Representing Java™ Objects in an LDAP Directory*

This document defines the schema for representing Java™ objects in an LDAP (v3) directory.

Status: INFORMATIONAL

RFC 2714: *Schema for Representing CORBA Object References in an LDAP Directory*

This document defines the schema for representing CORBA object references in an LDAP (v3) directory.

Status: INFORMATIONAL

RFC 2739: *Calendar Attributes for vCard and LDAP*

This document describes a mechanism to locate (URI) an individual user's calendar and free/busy time.

Status: PROPOSED STANDARD

RFC 2798: *Definition of the inetOrgPerson LDAP Object Class*

This document defines a person object class that meets the requirements found in today's Internet and Intranet directory service deployments.

Status: INFORMATIONAL

RFC 2829: *Authentication Methods for LDAP*

This document specifies particular combinations of security mechanisms which are required and recommended in LDAP implementations.

RFC 2830: *Lightweight Directory Access Protocol (v3) Extension for Transport Layer Security*

This document defines the Start Transport Layer Security (TLS) Operation for LDAP [LDAPv3, TLS]. This operation provides for TLS establishment in an LDAP association and is defined in terms of an LDAP extended request.

RFC 2849: *The LDAP Data Interchange Format (LDIF) - Technical Specification*

This document specifies an Internet standards track protocol for the Internet community and requests discussion and suggestions for improvements.

LDAP Internet Drafts

Internet Drafts have a set path that they follow every six months. When you start looking at Internet Drafts, you will be amazed by the number of available drafts that are related to LDAP.

The LDUP (LDAP Duplication Replication Update Protocols) working group is an important working group for LDAP users. This is due to LDAP v3 becoming more widely deployed, and the replication of data across servers running different implementations becomes an important part of providing a distributed directory service. However, the LDAP v3 community to date has focused on standardizing the client-server access protocol. Therefore, this group will standardize master-slave and multimaster LDAP v3 replication.

The LDAPEXT (LDAP Extension) working group is just as important as the LDUP working group by providing LDAP v3 with a standard access control model for the representation and semantic access control information.

The LDAP Bis is a newly created working group whose charter will be to move the LDAP v3 to a Standard, by reissuing the LDAP v3 RFCs and renewing ambiguities.

C API

The C LDAP Application Program Interface (`draft-ietf-ldapext-ldap-c-api-04.txt`)

This document defines a C language application program interface (API) to LDAP. This document replaces the previous definition of this API, defined in RFC 1823, updating this document to include support for features found in version 3 of the LDAP protocol. New extended operation functions were added to support LDAP v3 features (for example, controls). In addition, other LDAP API changes were made to support information hiding and thread safety.

Java API

The Java LDAP Application Program Interface (`draft-ietf-ldapext-ldap-java-api 11.txt`)

This document defines a Java language application program interface to the lightweight directory access protocol (LDAP), in the form of a class library. It complements but does not replace RFC 1823, which describes a C language application program interface. It updates the previous draft in correcting a few minor errors which are listed in Appendix B of RFC 1823. It also includes the asynchronous layer of the API which was previously defined in `draft-ietf-ldapext-ldap-java-api- asynch`.

The Java LDAP Application Program Interface Asynchronous Extension (`draft-ietf-ldapext-ldap-java-api-asynch-ext-05.txt`)

This document defines asynchronous extensions to the Java language application program interface to LDAP defined in `draft-ietf-ldapext-ldap-java-api-11.txt`. Directory SDK for Java implements the API defined by this document and by `draft-ietf-ldapext-ldap-java-api-08.txt`.

Access Control

Access Control Model for LDAP (`draft-ietf-ldapext-acl-model-06.txt`)

This document describes the access control model for the LDAP v3 directory service. It includes a description of the model, the LDAP controls, and the extended operations to the LDAP protocol. The current LDAP APIs are sufficient for most access control operations.

Replication

LDUP Update Reconciliation Procedures, (`draft-ietf-ldup-urp-03.txt`)

This document describes the procedures used by directory servers to reconcile updates performed by autonomously operating directory servers in a distributed, replicated directory service.

LDAP Replication Architecture, (`draft-ietf-ldup-model-04.txt`)

This architectural document outlines a suite of schema and protocol extensions to LDAP v3 that enables the robust, reliable server-to-server exchange of directory content and changes.

LDUP Replication Information Model, (`draft-ietf-ldup-infomod-01.txt`)

This document describes the architectural approach to replication of LDAP directory contents. This document describes the information model and schema elements which support LDAP Replication Services which conform to the LDUP model. Directory schema is extended to provide object classes, subentries, and attributes to describe areas of the namespace which are under common administrative authority, units of replication (i.e., subtrees, or partitions of the namespace, which are replicated), servers which hold replicas of various types for the various partitions of the namespace, which namespaces are held on given servers, and the progress of various namespace management and replication operations. Among other things, this knowledge of where directory content is located will provide the basis for dynamic generation of LDAP referrals for clients who can follow them.

The LDUP Replication Update Protocol, (`draft-ietf-ldup-protocol-02.txt`)

The protocol described in this document is designed to allow one LDAP server to replicate its directory content to another LDAP server. The protocol is designed to be used in a replication configuration where multiple updatable servers are present. Provisions are made in the protocol to carry information that allows the server receiving updates to apply a total ordering to all updates in the replicated system. This total ordering allows all replicas to correctly resolve conflicts that arise when LDAP clients submit changes to different servers that later replicate to one another. All protocol elements described here are LDAP v3 extended operations.

Controls and Extended Operations

Persistent Search: A Simple LDAP Change Notification Mechanism, (`draft-ietf-ldapext-psearch-02.txt`)

This document defines two controls that extend the LDAP v3 search operation to provide a simple mechanism by which an LDAP client can receive notification of changes that occur in an LDAP server. The mechanism is designed to be very flexible yet easy for clients and servers to implement. Since the IETF is likely to pursue a different, more comprehensive solution in this area, this document will eventually be published with Informational status in order to document an existing practice.

LDAP Extensions for Scrolling View Browsing of Search Results, (`draft-ietf-ldapext-ldapv3-vlv-04.txt`)

This document describes a Virtual List View (vlv) control extension for the LDAP Search operation. This control is designed to allow the "virtual list box" feature, common in existing commercial email address book applications, to be supported efficiently by LDAP servers. LDAP servers' inability to support this client feature is a significant impediment to LDAP replacing proprietary protocols in commercial email systems. The control allows a client to specify that the server return, for a given LDAP search with associated sort keys, a contiguous subset of the search result set. This subset is specified in terms of offsets into the ordered list, or in terms of a greater than or equal comparison value.

LDAP Control Extension for Server Side Sorting of Search Results, (draft-ietf-ldapext-sorting-03.txt)

This document describes two LDAP v3 control extensions for server side sorting of search results. These controls allow a client to specify the attribute types and matching rules a server should use when returning the results to an LDAP search request. The controls may be useful when the LDAP client has limited functionality or for some other reason cannot sort the results but still needs them sorted. Other permissible controls on search operations are not defined in this extension. The sort controls allow a server to return a result code for the sorting of the results that is independent of the result code returned for the search operation.

LDAP Control for a Duplicate Entry Representation of Search Results, (draft-ietf-ldapext-ldapv3-dupent-04.txt)

This document describes a Duplicate Entry Representation control extension for the LDAP Search operation. By using the control with an LDAP search, a client requests that the server return separate entries for each value held in the specified attributes. For instance, if a specified attribute of an entry holds multiple values, the search operation will return multiple instances of that entry, each instance holding a separate single value in that attribute.

Returning Matched Values with LDAP v3, (draft-ietf-ldapext-matchedval-02.txt)

This document describes a control for the LDAP v3 that is used to return a subset of attribute values from an entry, specifically, only those values that match a "values return" filter. Without support for this control, a client must retrieve all of an attribute's values and search for specific values locally.

A Taxonomy of Methods for LDAP Clients Finding Servers, (draft-ietf-ldapext-ldap-taxonomy-02.txt)

There are several different methods for an LDAP client to find an LDAP server. This draft discusses these methods and provides pointers for interested parties to learn more about implementing a particular method.

Discovering LDAP Services with DNS, (draft-ietf-ldapext-locate-03.txt)

This document specifies a method for discovering such servers using information in the Domain Name System.

Authentication and Security

X.509 Authentication SASL Mechanism, (`draft-ietf-ldapext-x509-sasl-03.txt`)

This document defines a SASL authentication mechanism based on X.509 strong authentication, providing two-way authentication. This mechanism is only for authentication and has no effect on the protocol encodings and is not designed to provide integrity or confidentiality services.

Information and X.500 Documents

A great deal of the LDAP standards are based on the standards model of X.500. As you may have noticed, the LDAP standards documentation is freely available on the Internet today. This is not the case when dealing with the basic X.500 documentation. If you are interested in gaining access to this documentation, then you must purchase it from the International Telecommunication Union (ITU) or International Organization for Standardization (ISO). Here is the location from which the X.500 documentation may be purchased:

`http://www.itu.int/itudoc/itu-t/rec/x/x500up/`

The following list of documents has been taken from the book *Understanding X.500 The Directory* by David Chadwick.

- The Directory (CCITT REC. X.500-X.521 | ISO/IEC Standard 9594:1993)
- X.500: *Overview of Concepts, Models and Services*
- X.501: *Models*
- X.509: *Authentication Framework*
- X.511: *Abstract Service Definition*
- X.518: *Procedures for Distributed Operations*
- X.519: *Protocol Specifications*
- X.520: *Selected Attribute Types*
- X.521: *Selected Object Classes*
- X.525: *Replication*

The North American Directory Forum (NADF) Documents (April 1993)

- SD-0: *NADF Standing Documents: A Brief Overview*
- SD-1: *Terms of Reference*
- SD-2: *Program Plan*
- SD-3: *Service Description*
- SD-4: *The Directory Schema*
- SD-5: *An X.500 Naming Scheme for National DIT Subtrees and Its Application for C=CA and C=US*

- SD-6: *Guidelines on Naming and Subtrees*
- SD-7: *Mapping the North American DIT onto Directory Management Domains*
- SD-8: *The Experimental Pilot Plan*
- SD-9: *Charter, Procedure, and Operations of the Central Administration for NADF*
- SD-10: *Security and Privacy: Policy and Services*
- SD-11: *Directory Security: Mechanisms and Practicality*
- SD-12: *Registry of ADDMD Names*

EWOS Directory Functional Standards

- A/711 (A/DI1): *Directory Access*, published as ENV 41 210 (also published as ISP 10615 parts 1 and 2)
- A/712 (A/DI2): *Directory System Protocol*, published as ENV 41 212 (also published as ISP 10615 parts 3 and 4)
- A/713 (A/DI32): *Dynamic Behavior of DSAs for Distributed Operations*, published as ENV 41 215 (also published as ISP 10615 part 6)
- A/714 (A/DI31): *Directory User Agents Distributed Operation*, published as ENV 41 217 (also published as ISP 10615 part 5)
- Q/511 (F/DI11): *Common Directory Use*, published as ENV 41 512 (also published as ISP 10616; see also ISO/IEC PDISP)
- Q/512 (F/DI2): *Directory Data Definitions Directory Use by MHS*
- Q/513 (F/DI3): *Directory Data Definitions FTAM Use of the Directory* (to be published as ISP 11190)
- ETG XXX: *Introduction to Directory Profiles* (final draft)
- ETG 017: *Error Handling in the OSI Directory* (final draft, May 1992)
- ETG XXX: *Security Architecture for the Directory* (fifth draft in 1992)

Joint ISO Standards and CCITT Recommendations

- ISO/IEC 8824:1988 | CCITT X.208: *Specification of Abstract Syntax Notation One (ASN.1)*
- ISO/IEC 8824-2 DIS (1993) | CCITT X.208-2: *Abstract Syntax Notation One (ASN.1): Information Object Specification*
- ISO/IEC 8825-1 | CCITT X.209-1: *Part 1: Basic Encoding Rules (BER)*
- ISO/IEC 8825-3 DIS (1993) | CCITT X.209-3: *Part 3: Distinguished Encoding Rules*
- ISO/IEC 9072-1 | CCITT X.219: *Remote Operations Model, Notation and Service Definition*
- ISO 8649:1988 | CCITT X.217: *Service Definition for the Association Control Service Element*

Other ISO Documents

- ISO/IEC JTC 1/SC21 N6063: *Use of Object Identifiers to Access Directory Information* (May 1991)

- ISO 3166:1988: *Codes for the Representation of Names of Countries*
- ISO IS 10162/3: *Documentation Search and Retrieve Service Definition/Protocol Specification*
- ISO 6523:1984: *Data Interchange Structure for the Identification of Organizations*
- ISO/IEC 10646-1:1993: *(E) Information Technology Universal Multiple-Octet Coded Character Set (UCS)*
- ISO/IEC PDISP 10616: *International Standardized Profile FDI11 Directory Data Definitions Common Directory Use* (February 1993)

Additional Information

This appendix presents some additional sources of information available on LDAP. The following categories are covered:

- X.500 books
- General LDAP books and online resources
- Novell Directory Services books and online resources
- DNS books and online resources
- LDAP Server software vendors
- LDAP client SDKs

X.500 Books

Understanding X.500 - The Directory by David Chadwick (Chapman & Hall, 1994).

Unfortunately, the complete book is no longer available. However, parts of the book are available online at

`http://www.salford.ac.uk/its024/Version.Web/Contents.htm.`

X.500 Directory Services by Sara Radicati (International Thompson Computer Press, 1994).

General LDAP Books

The following books will provide you with some general LDAP information.

Introduction to Deploying LDAP

Understanding and Deploying LDAP Directory Services by Timothy A. Howes, Mark C. Smith, and Gordon S. Good (MacMillan Network Architecture and Development Series, 1999).

This comprehensive tutorial provides the reader with a thorough treatment of LDAP directory services. Minimal knowledge of general networking and administration is assumed, making the material accessible to intermediate and advanced readers. It is the first book to explore the design and deployment of directory services, and it contains real-world examples of directory deployments illustrating effective design principles along with practical insight and advice from world-renowned experts.

Implementing Directory Services by Archie Reed (McGraw-Hill, 1999).

This book gives you all the information you'll need for smart and strategic implementation of directory services, on both the business and technical sides. There is a lot more to directory services than just LDAP, and this important resource provides a guide to the various standards available, including LDAP, X.500, Public Key Infrastructure (PKI), and Directory Enabled Networks (DEN), as well as the vendor products available today, including Microsoft Active Directory, Novell eDirectory, and Netscape DS.

Understanding Directory Services by Doug Sheresh, and Beth Sheresh (New Riders Pub., 1999).

This book focuses on directory technology from a networking perspective. Ranging from basic theory and archetypes to current network directory services options, this book provides crucial information for anyone using a directory service on their networks.

LDAP Programming

Programming Directory-Enabled Applications with Lightweight Directory Access Protocol by Tim Howes and Mark Smith (MacMillan Technology Series, 1997).

This book provides a solid introduction to LDAP, including its history and architecture. It also covers LDAP API programming in C and C++ in clear, discrete examples that range from simple searching to filtering, reading, and updating LDAP directories. More advanced topics include asynchronous LDAP programming with threads, as well as a description for building command line tools.

LDAP Programming with Java by Rob Weltman and Tony Dahbura (Addison-Wesley, 2000).

This book comes to you from the designer of the Directory SDK for Java and from a leading implementor of directory-based solutions.

Implementing LDAP by Mark Wilcox (Wrox Press Inc., 1999).

This book is intended for programmers and system administrators who need to install LDAP servers and build LDAP clients.

Online Resources

This is an LDAP Roadmap and FAQ site for Directory Services:

    http://www.kingsmountain.com/ldapRoadmap.shtml

This is Innosoft's (now acquired by Sun) LDAP World site:

    http://www.innosoft.com/ldapworld/

This site is dedicated to bringing you news and information related to LDAP:

    http://www.ldapcentral.com/resources.html

An online encyclopedia, comprised of information and links to LDAP resources:

    http://webopedia.internet.com/TERM/L/LDAP.html

An LDAP schema repository:

    http://www.hklc.com/ldapschema/

This is an article written by a system administrator which gives a perspective on what you'll need in order to reap the benefits of using LDAP. A good understanding of what LDAP can and cannot accomplish. It offers some familiarity with LDAP basics, and ideas on how to make the transition to LDAP.

    http://people.netscape.com/bjm/whyLDAP.html

This is Mark Wilcox's LDAP Root site, which includes LDAP resources:

    http://www.mjwilcox.com/ldap/

This is Mark Wahl's LDAP FAQ site:

    http://www3.innosoft.com/ldapworld/ldapfaq.html

Novell Directory Services Books

Novell's Four Principles of NDS Design by Hughes, Jeff: ISBN: 0764545221.

This guide not only reveals the principles of Novell Directory Services design but also offers the practical, step-by-step information you need to be able to put them into action. From trees to synchronization, from objects to partitions, *Novell's Four Principles of NDS Design* provides the authoritative, high-level guidance every Novell professional needs.

Administering NDS: Corporate Edition by Nancy Cadjan and Jeffrey Harris: ISBN: 0072122080.

This all-inclusive resource covers everything from server and client installation, to design principles for maximizing the efficiency and scalability of NDS trees in a mixed environment, to basic step-by-step instructions for installing NDS.

Novell's NDS Developer's Guide by Chris Andrew and Karl Bunnell: ISBN: 0764545574.

This book will enable developers to leverage the power of Novell Directory Service and develop NDS-aware ActiveX controls and javaBeans, use Delphi to create a password administration application, build reports using the NDS ODBC Driver and Crystal Reports, learn the fundamentals of JavaScript and CGI scripting for web programming, manipulate NDS using cross-platform APIs and the LDAP APIs, master NetBasic NDS library calls and other related libraries, access NDS using JNDI and ADSI, and find out how to extend NetWare Administrator and ConsoleOne.

Novell's Guide to Troubleshooting NDS by Peter Kuo and Jim Henderson: ISBN: 0764545795.

An advanced network administrator's guide to managing the performance of Novell Directory Services, which has over 40 million users. The focus is on resolving and/ or preventing problems that may occur with NDS, including discussions on diagnostic tools and techniques, recovery tools, programming for NDS disaster recovery, and error codes.

Online Resources

NDS eDirectory Online Documentation:

```
http://www.novell.com/documentation/lg/ndsse/docui/index.html/
```

NDS eDirectory Development:

```
http://www.developer.novell.com/nds/
```

NDS Schema Registration:

```
http://www.developer.novell.com/support/schreg2c.htm
```

DNS Books

DNS and BIND, third edition by Paul Albitz and Cricket Liu: ISBN: 1565925122.

This book discusses one of the Internet's fundamental building blocks: the distributed host information database that's responsible for translating names into addresses, routing mail to its proper destination, and many other services. The third edition covers BIND 4.9, on which most commercial products are currently based; and BIND 8, which implements many important new features and will be the basis for the next generation of commercial name servers.

Online Resources

DNS Resources Directory:

```
http://www.dns.net/dnsrd/
```

LDAP Server Software Vendors

iPlanet Directory Server:

```
http://www.iplanet.com/downloads/download/detail_8_213.html
```

IBM SecureWay Directory:

```
http://www-4.ibm.com/software/network/directory/
```

OpenLDAP Directory:

```
http://www.openldap.org/
```

Linux Directory Services:

```
http://www.rage.net/ldap/
```

Oracle Directory Services:

```
http://www.oracle.com/database/oid/
```

LDAP Client SDKs

The Java Naming and Directory Interface™ (JNDI) is a standard extension to the Java™ platform, providing Java technology-enabled applications with a unified interface to multiple naming and directory services in the enterprise. As part of the Java Enterprise API set, JNDI enables seamless connectivity to heterogeneous enterprise naming and directory services. Developers can now build powerful and portable directory-enabled applications using this industry standard.

```
http://java.sun.com/products/jndi/
```

At the location below, you will find the directory SDKs for C, Java, and Perl. These SDKs are precompiled. If you wish to obtain the source code version's then go to the mozilla.org Web site.

```
http://www.iplanet.com/downloads/developer/index.html
```

This is the mozilla.org site which is the location where the Open Source for the LDAP SDKs for C, Java, and Perl programming can be found. In addition, to the SDKs you will find some useful LDAP tools.

```
http://www.mozilla.org/directory/
```

LDAP v3 Result Codes

This appendix explains some of the LDAP error codes that can be returned by your LDAP server. It is not a complete list and does not discuss the mechanism of why an LDAP server gives a particular error. To find out additional information on error codes refer to RFC 2251, which defines these error codes. Also, as another very useful resource, see Internet Draft `draft-just-ldapv3-rescodes-02.txt`, which details exact descriptions of these error codes. Finally, you may also want to refer to the `ldap.h` file, which in the case of the Solaris Operating Environment can be found in `/usr/include`.

In addition to reviewing the RFC 2251, review the access and error log files, which are located by default under `/usr/netscape/server4/`*slapd-instance*`/logs`. These files can help you debug certain problems with your directory server.

The error codes in TABLE D-1 apply to the iPlanet Directory Server, and possibly to other LDAP servers, but not to all. This list is not comprehensive. Codes without comments in the third column are not currently returned to clients by Netscape Directory Server or generated by the SDK.

TABLE D-1   LDAP Error Codes

0	**0x00**	`LDAP_CONNECTION SUCCESS`	The operation completed successfully.
1	**0x01**	`LDAP_OPERATIONS_ERROR`	Invalid syntax for ACI or schema, or inappropriate control for the operation.
2	**0x02**	`LDAP_PROTOCOL_ERROR`	Invalid filter expression on search, or DN on add, modify, or delete.
3	**0x03**	`LDAP_TIME_LIMIT_EXCEEDED`	Either the server's or the client's specified search time limit was exceeded.

4	**0x04**	LDAP_SIZE_LIMIT_EXCEEDED	Either the server's or the client's specified limit on number of search results was exceeded.
5	**0x05**	LDAP_COMPARE_FALSE	A compare operation returns mismatch.
6	**0x06**	LDAP_COMPARE_TRUE	A compare operation returns match.
7	**0x07**	LDAP_STRONG_AUTH_METHOD_NOT_SUPPORTED	The server does not support the requested authentication method.
8	**0x08**	LDAP_STRONG_AUTH_REQUIRED	The server requires an authentication method stronger than unencrypted user name and password.
9	**0x09**	LDAP_PARTIAL_RESULTS	The client has bound with LDAP v2, or the server supports only LDAP v2, and the base DN specified by the client is not among the naming contexts of the server.
10	**0x0a**	LDAP_REFERRAL	The server is configured to return a referral or search reference when an operation is directed toward this DN. This is an LDAP v3 error ONLY.
11	**0x0b**	LDAP_ADMIN_LIMIT_EXCEEDED	To satisfy the search request, the server would need to process too many entries; the search may need to be narrowed, or the server's lookthrough limit raised.
12	**0x0c**	LDAP_UNAVAILABLE_CRITICAL_EXTENSION	A control was provided with request; the control was tagged as critical, but the server doesn't support it.

13	**0x0d**	LDAP_CONFIDENTIALITY_REQUIRED	This error code is new in LDAPv3. This error code may be returned if the session is not protected by a protocol which provides session confidentiality. For example, if the client did not establish a TLS connection using a cipher suite which provides confidentiality of the session before sending any other requests, and the server requires session confidentiality then the server may reject that request with a result code of confidentialityRequired.
14	**0x0e**	LDAP_SASL_BIND_IN_PROGRESS	SASL authentication is being negotiated between the client and the server.
16	**0x10**	LDAP_NO_SUCH_ATTRIBUTE	An attribute to be modified or deleted was not present in the entry.
17	**0x11**	LDAP_UNDEFINED_ATTRIBUTE_TYPE	Applicable operations: Modify, Add. This error may be returned if the specified attribute is unrecognized by the server, since it is not present in the server's defined schema. If the server doesn't recognize an attribute specified in a search request as the attribute to be returned, the server should not return an error in this case - it should just return values for the requested attributes it does recognize. Note that this result code applies only to the Add and Modify operations
18	**0x12**	LDAP_INAPPROPRIATE_MATCHING	The value specified doesn't adhere to the syntax definition for that attribute.

19	0x13	LDAP_CONSTRAINT_VIOLATION	Invalid attribute for this entry, or new password does not meet password policy requirements
20	0x14	LDAP_ATTRIBUTE_OR_VALUE_EXISTS	Attempt to add an identical attribute value to an existing one.
21	0x15	LDAP_INVALID_ATTRIBUTE_SYNTAX	
32	0x20	LDAP_NO_SUCH_OBJECT	Attempt to bind with a nonexistent DN, to search with a nonexistent base DN, or to modify or delete a nonexistent DN.
33	0x21	LDAP_ALIAS_PROBLEM	Applicable operations: Search. An alias has been dereferenced which names no object.
34	0x22	LDAP_INVALID_DN_SYNTAX	Invalid DN or RDN specified on adding an entry or modifying an RDN.
35	0x23	LDAP_IS_LEAF	
36	0x24	LDAP_ALIAS_DEREFERENCING_PROBLEM	Applicable operations: Search. An alias was encountered in a situation where it was not allowed or where access was denied. For example, if the client does not have read permission for the aliasedObjectName attribute and its value, then the error aliasDereferencing Problem should be returned.
48	0x30	LDAP_INAPPROPRIATE_AUTHENTICATION	Applicable operations: Bind. This error should be returned by the server when the client has tried to use a method of authentication that is inappropriate.

49	**0x31**	`LDAP_INVALID_CREDENTIALS`	Invalid password or other credentials supplied on bind.
50	**0x32**	`LDAP_INSUFFICIENT_ACCESS_RIGHTS`	Give the user the proper privileges. Check the ACL rules to make sure they are correct.
51	**0x33**	`LDAP_BUSY`	Applicable operations: All. This error code may be returned if the server is unable to process the client's request at this time. This implies that if the client retries the request shortly, the server will be able to process it then.
52	**0x34**	`LDAP_UNAVAILABLE`	Returned by SDK if server is not accessible.
53	**0x35**	`LDAP_UNWILLING_TO_PERFORM`	User not allowed to change password, password expired, operation not implemented (`moddn`), attempt to modify read-only attribute, attempt to delete all schema elements, attempt to delete an object class that has derived object classes, attempt to delete a read-only schema element, the database is read-only, no back end (database) is available for the operation, or other uncategorized error.
54	**0x36**	`LDAP_LOOP_DETECT`	Applicable operations: All. This error may be returned by the server if it detects an alias or referral loop and is unable to satisfy the client's request.

64	**0x40**	LDAP_NAMING_VIOLATION	Applicable operations: Add, ModifyDN. The attempted addition or modification would violate the structure rules of the DIT as defined in the directory schema and X.501. That is, it would place an entry as the subordinate of an alias entry, or in a region of the DIT not permitted to a member of its object class, or would define an RDN for an entry to include a forbidden attribute type.
65	**0x41**	LDAP_OBJECT_CLASS_VIOLATION	Invalid attribute specified for modify operation on an entry. Update the schema.
66	**0x42**	LDAP_NOT_ALLOWED_ON_NONLEAF	Attempt to delete an entry that has child nodes.
67	**0x43**	LDAP_NOT_ALLOWED_ON_RDN	Applicable operations: Delete, ModifyDN. Attempt to modify the value of the attribute which is the RDN of the entry.
68	**0x44**	LDAP_ENTRY_ALREADY_EXISTS	No need to update the directory server, since it already has this value/ entry.
69	**0x45**	LDAP_OBJECT_CLASS_MODS_PROHIBITED	Applicable operations: Modify. An operation attempted to modify an object class that should not be modified, e.g., the structural object class of an entry.
70	**0x46**	LDAP_RESULTS_TOO_LARGE	
71	**0x47**	LDAP_AFFECTS_MULTIPLE_DSAS	
80	**0x50**	LDAP_OTHER	

81	0x51	LDAP_SERVER_DOWN	SDK could not connect to server. Start the directory server.
82	0x52	LDAP_LOCAL_ERROR	
83	0x53	LDAP_ENCODING_ERROR	
84	0x54	LDAP_DECODING_ERROR	
85	0x55	LDAP_TIMEOUT	
86	0x56	LDAP_AUTH_UNKNOWN	
87	0x57	LDAP_FILTER_ERROR	
88	0x58	LDAP_USER_CANCELLED	
89	0x59	LDAP_PARAM_ERROR	No modifications on a modify operation, no attributes on an add operation, invalid scope or empty search filter on search, or other invalid argument to an SDK method.
90	0x5a	LDAP_NO_MEMORY	
91	0x5b	LDAP_CONNECT_ERROR	SDK reports unexpected error connecting to server.
92	0x5c	LDAP_NOT_SUPPORTED	
93	0x5d	LDAP_CONTROL_NOT_FOUND	
94	0x5e	LDA_NO_RESULTS_RETURNED	
95	0x5f	LDAP_MORE_RESULTS_TO_RETURN	
96	0x60	LDAP_CLIENT_LOOP	
97	0x61	LDAP_REFERRAL_LIMIT_EXCEEDED	SDK reports hop limit exceeded on referral processing.

Schema Information

This appendix looks at the LDAP schema, especially the schema required to support the Solaris 8 LDAP Client. LDAP schemas are defined by Internet Engineering Task Force (IETF), the revised RFC 2307 Network Information Service Schema draft, and the LDAP Mailgroups Internet draft. Solaris 8-specific schemas and predefined schema elements, especially in the area of managing user information, are also discussed.

LDAP has well-defined schema elements so you can add data without any modifications to the LDAP server.

LDAP schemas are an arrangement of attribute-value pairs. Which attributes are required and allowed is controlled by the content rules defined on a per-server basis or by a special attribute called the `objectclass`. The values of this attribute identify the type of entry (person, organization, etc.) and determine which attributes are required and which are optional.

Support for Solaris LDAP Naming clients requires Solaris-specific schemas and schemas defined by IETF.

IETF Schemas

IETF defines two required LDAP schemas:

- Revised RFC 2307 Network Information Service schema draft
- LDAP mailgroups Internet draft

RFC 2307 Network Information Service Schema

The LDAP servers must be configured to support the revised RFC 2307 draft.

Note – Internet-Drafts are draft documents valid for a maximum of six months and might be updated, replaced, or made obsolete by other documents at any time.

TABLE E-1 lists RFC 2307 draft attributes.

TABLE E-1   RFC 2307 Draft Attributes

Schema	Description	Equality	Syntax
nisSchema.1.0 NAME 'uidNumber'	An integer uniquely identifying a user in an administrative domain	integerMatch	'INTEGER' SINGLE-VALUE
nisSchema.1.1 NAME 'gidNumber'	An integer uniquely identifying a group in an administrative domain	integerMatch	'INTEGER' SINGLE-VALUE
nisSchema.1.2 NAME 'gecos'	The GECOS field; the common name	caseIgnoreIA5Match SUBSTRINGS caseIgnoreIA5Subst ringsMatch	'IA5String' SINGLE-VALUE
nisSchema.1.3 NAME 'homeDirectory'	The absolute path to the home directory	caseExactIA5Match	'IA5String' SINGLE-VALUE
nisSchema.1.4 NAME 'loginShell'	The path to the login shell	caseExactIA5Match	'IA5String' SINGLE-VALUE
nisSchema.1.5 NAME 'shadowLastChange'		integerMatch	'INTEGER' SINGLE-VALUE
nisSchema.1.6 NAME 'shadowMin'		integerMatch	'INTEGER' SINGLE-VALUE
nisSchema.1.7 NAME 'shadowMax'		integerMatch	'INTEGER' SINGLE-VALUE
nisSchema.1.8 NAME 'shadowWarning'		integerMatch	'INTEGER' SINGLE-VALUE
nisSchema.1.9 NAME 'shadowInactive'		integerMatch	'INTEGER' SINGLE-VALUE
nisSchema.1.10 NAME 'shadowExpire'		integerMatch	'INTEGER' SINGLE-VALUE
nisSchema.1.11 NAME 'shadowFlag'		integerMatch	'INTEGER' SINGLE-VALUE
nisSchema.1.12 NAME 'memberUid'		caseExactIA5Match SUBSTRINGS caseExactIA5Substr ingsMatch	IA5String

Schema	Description	Equality	Syntax
nisSchema.1.13 NAME'memberNisNetgroup'		caseExactIA5Match SUBSTRINGS caseExactIA5SubstringsMatch	IA5String
nisSchema.1.14 NAME'nisNetgroupTriple'	Netgroup triple		nisNetgroupTripleSyntax
nisSchema.1.15 NAME'ipServicePort'		integerMatch	'INTEGER' SINGLE-VALUE
nisSchema.1.16 NAME'ipServiceProtocol'SUP name			
nisSchema.1.17 NAME'ipProtocolNumber'		integerMatch	'INTEGER' SINGLE-VALUE
nisSchema.1.18 NAME'oncRpcNumber'		integerMatch	'INTEGER' SINGLE-VALUE
nisSchema.1.19 NAME'ipHostNumber'	DESC'IP address as a dotted decimal, e.g., 192.9.25.1 omitting leading zeros'SUP name		
nisSchema.1.20 NAME'ipNetworkNumber'	'IP network as a dotted decimal, e.g., 192.168, omitting leading zeros' SUP name SINGLE-VALUE		
nisSchema.1.21 NAME'ipNetmaskNumber'	IP netmask as a dotted decimal, e.g., 255.255.255.0, omitting leading zeros	caseIgnoreIA5Match	'IA5String{128}' SINGLE-VALUE
nisSchema.1.22 NAME'macAddress'	MAC address in maximal, colon separated hex notation, e.g., 08:00:20:01:01:01	caseIgnoreIA5Match	IA5String{128}
nisSchema.1.23 NAME'bootParameter'	rpc.bootparamd parameter		bootParameterSyntax

Schema	Description	Equality	Syntax
nisSchema.1.24 NAME'bootFile'	Boot image name	caseExactIA5Match	IA5String
nisSchema.1.26 NAME'nisMapName' SUP name			
nisSchema.1.27 NAME'nisMapEntry'		caseExactIA5Match SUBSTRINGS caseExactIA5Substr ingsMatch	'IA5String{1024 }' SINGLE-VALUE
nisSchema.1.28 NAME'nisPublicKey'	NIS public key		nisPublicKeySyn tax
nisSchema.1.29 NAME'nisSecretKey'	NIS secret key		nisSecretKeySyn tax
nisSchema.1.30 NAME'nisDomain'	NIS domain		IA5String

RFC 2307 Draft Objectclasses

TABLE E-2 lists of the RFC 2307 objectclasses.

TABLE E-2   RFC2307 Objectclasses

Schema	Description	Must	May
nisSchema.2.0 NAME'posixAccount' SUP top	Auxiliary - Abstraction of an account with POSIX attributes	(cn $uid $uidNumber $gidNumber $home Directory)	(userPassword $loginShell $gecos $description)
nisSchema.2.1 NAME'shadowAccount' SUP top	Auxiliary - Additional attributes for shadow passwords	uid	(userPassword $shadowLastChange $shadowMin shadowMax $shadowWarning $shadowInactive $shadowExpire $shadowFlag $description)
nisSchema.2.2 NAME'posixGroup' SUP top	Structural - Abstraction of a group of accounts	(cn $gidNumber)	(userPassword $memberUid $description)
nisSchema.2.3 NAME'ipService' SUP top	Structural - Abstraction of an Internet Protocol service. Maps an IP port and protocol (such as tcp or udp) to one or more names; the distinguished value of the cn attribute denotes the service's canonical name.	(cn $ipServicePort $ipServiceProtocol)	(description)
nisSchema.2.4 NAME'ipProtocol' SUP top	Structural - Abstraction of an IP protocol. Maps a protocol number to one or more names. The distinguished value of the cn attribute denotes the protocol's canonical name.	(cn $ipProtocolNumber)	(description)

Schema	Description	Must	May
nisSchema.2.5 NAME'oncRpc' SUP top	Structural - Abstraction of an Open Network Computing (ONC) [RFC1057] Remote Procedure Call (RPC) binding. This class maps an ONC RPC number to a name. The distinguished value of the cn attribute denotes the RPC service's canonical name.	(cn $ipHostNumber)	(1 $description $manager $userPassword)
nisSchema.2.6 NAME'ipHost' SUP top	Auxiliary - Abstraction of a host, an IP device. The distinguished value of the cn attribute denotes the host's canonical name. Device *should* be used as a structural class.	(cn $ipHostNumber)	(1 $description $manager $userPassword)
nisSchema.2.7 NAME'ipNetwork' SUP top	Structural - Abstraction of a network. The distinguished value of the cn attribute denotes the network's canonical name.	ipNetworkNumber	(cn $ipNetmaskNumber $1 $description $manager)
nisSchema.2.8 NAME'nisNetgroup' SUP top	Structural - Abstraction of a netgroup. May refer to other netgroups.	cn	(nisNetgroupTriple $memberNisNetgroup $description)
nisSchema.2.9 NAME'nisMap' SUP top	Structural - A generic abstraction of an NIS map	nisMapName	description
nisSchema.2.10 NAME'nisObject' SUP top	Structural - An entry in an NIS map	(cn $nisMapEntry $nisMapName)	description

Schema	Description	Must	May
nisSchema.2.11 NAME'ieee802Device' SUP top	Auxiliary-A device with a MAC address; device *should* be used as a structural class.		macAddress
nisSchema.2.12 NAME'bootableDevice' SUP top	A device with boot parameters; device *should* be used as a structural class.		(bootFile $bootParameter)
nisSchema.2.14 NAME'nisKeyObject' SUP top	Auxiliary - An object with a public and secret key	(cn $nisPublicKey $nisSecretKey)	(uidNumber $description)
nisSchema.2.15 NAME'nisDomainObject ' SUP top	Auxiliary - Associates an NIS domain with a naming context	nisDomain	

Mail Alias Schema

LDAP servers must be configured to support mail alias information. Mail alias information uses the schema defined by the LDAP Mailgroups Internet draft, formerly known as the `draft-steinback-ldap-mailgroups` draft. Since the introduction of the Solaris LDAP client functionality, this Internet draft has expired and is no longer a valid Internet draft. Unfortunately, no available standard provides a schema with the same information. For now, Solaris LDAP clients need to continue to use this schema for mail alias information until a new schema becomes available.

The original LDAP Mailgroups schema contains a large number of attributes and object classes. Only three of them are used by Solaris clients. These are listed in the following sections.

Attributes/Syntax

TABLE E-3 lists mail alias attributes and syntax.

TABLE E-3   Mail Alias Schemas

Schema	Description	Equality	Syntax
0.9.2342.19200300.10 0.1.3 NAME'mail'	RFC822 email address for this person	caseIgnoreIA5Match	IA5String(256) SINGLE-VALUE
2.16.840.1.113730.3. 1.30 NAME'mgrpRFC822MailM ember'	RFC822 mail address of email only member of group	CaseIgnoreIA5Match	IA5String(256)

Object Class

This is a mail alias object class.

Schema: `2.16.840.1.113730.3.2.4 NAME'mailGroup' SUP top`

Structural Must: mail

May: (cn $mailAlternateAddress $mailHost $mailRequireAuth $mgrpAddHeader $mgrpAllowedBroadcaster $mgrpAllowedDomain $mgrpApprovePassword $mgrpBroadcasterModeration $mgrpDeliverTo $mgrpErrorsTo $mgrpModerator $mgrpMsgMaxSize $mgrpMsgRejectAction $mgrpMsgRejectText $mgrpNoMatchAddrs $mgrpRemoveHeader $mgrpRFC822MailMember)

Solaris-Specific Schemas

The schemas required for the Solaris operating environment are:

- Extended user accounting
- Role-based access control
- Solaris client naming profile

Extended User Accounting Schema

`/etc/user_attr` is a local source of extended attributes associated with users and roles. TABLE E-4 lists the attributes. For additional information, see `user_attr(4)`.

TABLE E-4 Extended User Accounting Attributes

Schema	Description	Equality	Syntax
1.3.6.1.4.1.42.2.27.5.1.1 NAME'SolarisProjectID'	Unique ID for a Solaris Project entry	integerMatch	INTEGER SINGLE
1.3.6.1.4.1.42.2.27.5.1.2 NAME'SolarisProjectName'	Name of a Solaris Project entry	caseExactIA5Match	IA5String SINGLE
1.3.6.1.4.1.42.2.27.5.1.3 NAME'SolarisProjectAttr'	Attributes of a Solaris Project entry	caseExactIA5Match	IA5String

The extended user accounting `Objectclass` is:

Schema: `1.3.6.1.4.1.42.2.27.5.2.1 NAME'SolarisProject' SUP top`

Structural Must: `(SolarisProjectID $SolarisProjectName)`

May: `(uidNumber $gidNumber $description $SolarisProjectAttr)`

Role-Based Access Control Schema

`/etc/user_attr` is a local source of extended attributes associated with users and roles. TABLE E-5 is a list of the role-based access control attributes. For additional information, see `user_attr(4)`.

TABLE E-5 Role-Based Access Control Attributes

Schema	Description	Equality	Syntax
1.3.6.1.4.1.42.2.27.5.1.4 NAME'SolarisAttrKeyValue'	Semicolon-separated key=value pairs of attributes	caseIgnoreIA5Match SUBSTRINGS caseIgnoreIA5Match	'IA5String' SINGLE-VALUE
1.3.6.1.4.1.42.2.27.5.1.5 NAME'SolarisAuditAlways'	Always audited attributes per user	caseIgnoreIA5Match	'IA5String' SINGLE-VALUE
1.3.6.1.4.1.42.2.27.5.1.6 NAME'SolarisAuditNever'	Never audited attributes per user	caseIgnoreIA5Match	'IA5String' SINGLE-VALUE)

Schema	Description	Equality	Syntax
1.3.6.1.4.1.42.2.27.5.1.7 NAME'SolarisAttrShortDesc '	Short description about an entry, used by GUIs	caseIgnoreIA5Match	'IA5String' SINGLE-VALUE
1.3.6.1.4.1.42.2.27.5.1.8 NAME'SolarisAttrLongDesc'	Detail description about an entry	caseIgnoreIA5Match	'IA5String' SINGLE-VALUE
1.3.6.1.4.1.42.2.27.5.1.9 NAME'SolarisKernelSecurit yPolicy'	Solaris kernel security policy	caseIgnoreIA5Match	'IA5String' SINGLE-VALUE
1.3.6.1.4.1.42.2.27.5.1.1 0 NAME'SolarisProfileType'	Type of object defined in profile		
1.3.6.1.4.1.42.2.27.5.1.1 1 NAME'SolarisProfileId'	Identifier of object defined in profile	caseExactIA5Match	'IA5String' SINGLE-VALUE
1.3.6.1.4.1.42.2.27.5.1.1 2 NAME'SolarisUserQualifier '	Per user login attributes	caseIgnoreIA5Match	'IA5String' SINGLE-VALUE
1.3.6.1.4.1.42.2.27.5.1.1 3 NAME'SolarisReserved1'	Reserved for future use	caseIgnoreIA5Match	'IA5String' SINGLE-VALUE
1.3.6.1.4.1.42.2.27.5.1.1 4 NAME'SolarisReserved2'	Reserved for future use	caseIgnoreIA5Match	'IA5String' SINGLE-VALUE

TABLE E-6 lists role-based access control `objectclasses`.

TABLE E-6   Role-based Access Control Objectclasses

Schema	Description	Must	May
1.3.6.1.4.1.42.2.27.5.2. 2 NAME'SolarisAuditUser' SUP top	Auxiliary - Per user audit attributes		(SolarisAuditAlways $SolarisAuditNever)
1.3.6.1.4.1.42.2.27.5.2. 3 NAME'SolarisUserAttr' SUP top	Auxiliary - User attributes		(SolarisUserQualifier $SolarisAttrReserved1 $\ SolarisAttrReserved2 $SolarisAttrKeyValue)

TABLE E-6   Role-based Access Control Objectclasses (*Continued*)

Schema	Description	Must	May
1.3.6.1.4.1.42.2.27.5.2.4 NAME'SolarisAuthAttr' SUP top	Structural - Authorizations data	cn	(SolarisAttrReserved1 $SolarisAttrReserved2 $\SolarisAttrShortDesc $SolarisAttrLongDesc $\SolarisAttrKeyValue)
1.3.6.1.4.1.42.2.27.5.2.5 NAME'SolarisProfAttr' SUP top	Structural - Profiles data	cn	(SolarisAttrReserved1 $SolarisAttrReserved2 $\ SolarisAttrLongDesc $SolarisAttrKeyValue)
1.3.6.1.4.1.42.2.27.5.2.6 NAME'SolarisExecAttr' SUP top	Auxiliary - Profiles execution attributes		(SolarisKernelSecurityPolicy $SolarisProfileType $\SolarisAttrReserved1 $SolarisAttrReserved2 $\SolarisProfileId $SolarisAttrKeyValue)

Solaris Client Naming Profile Schema

/etc/user_attr is a local source of extended attributes associated with users, roles, and profiles. For additional information, see user_attr(4).

/etc/security/prof_attr is a local source for execution profile names, descriptions, and other attributes of execution profiles. For additional information, see prof_attr(4).

To support simplified client setup with client profile, the LDAP servers must support the client profile schema shown in TABLE E-7.

TABLE E-7   Solaris Client Naming Profile Attributes

Schema	Description	Equality	Syntax
`1.3.6.1.4.1.42.2.27.5.1.15` `NAME'SolarisLDAPServers'`	LDAP Server address, e.g., 76.234.3.1:389	`caseIgnoreIA5Match`	`SolarisLDAPServerSyntax`
`1.3.6.1.4.1.42.2.27.5.1.16` `NAME'SolarisSearchBaseDN'`	Search Base Distinguished Name	`distinguishedNameMatch`	`DN SINGLE-VALUE`
`1.3.6.1.4.1.42.2.27.5.1.17` `NAME'SolarisCacheTTL'`	TTL value for the Domain information, e.g., 1w, 2d, 3h, 10m, or 5s	`caseIgnoreMatch`	`IA5String SINGLE-VALUE`
`1.3.6.1.4.1.42.2.27.5.1.18` `NAME'SolarisBindDN'`	DN to be used to bind to the directory as proxy	`distinguishedNameMatch`	`DN SINGLE-VALUE`
`1.3.6.1.4.1.42.2.27.5.1.19` `NAME'SolarisBindPassword'`	Password for `bindDN` to authenticate to the directory	`caseExactIA5Match`	`OctetString SINGLE-VALUE`
`1.3.6.1.4.1.42.2.27.5.1.20` `NAME'SolarisAuthMethod'`	Authentication method to be used, e.g., `NS_LDAP_AUTH_NONE`, `NS_LDAP_AUTH_SIMPLE` or `NS_LDAP_AUTH_SASL_CRAM_MD5`	`caseIgnoreIA5Match`	`IA5String`
`1.3.6.1.4.1.42.2.27.5.1.21` `NAME'SolarisTransportSecurity'`	Transport Level Security method to be used, e.g., `NS_LDAP_SEC_NONE` or `NS_LDAP_SEC_SASL_TLS`	`caseIgnoreIA5Match`	`IA5String SINGLE-VALUE`
`1.3.6.1.4.1.42.2.27.5.1.22` `NAME'SolarisCertificatePath'`	Path to certificate file/device	`caseExactIA5Match`	`IA5String SINGLE-VALUE`
`1.3.6.1.4.1.42.2.27.5.1.23` `NAME'SolarisCertificatePassword'`	Password or PIN that grants access to certificate.	`caseExactIA5Match`	`OctetString SINGLE-VALUE`

Schema	Description	Equality	Syntax
1.3.6.1.4.1.42.2.27.5.1.24 NAME'SolarisDataSearchDN'	Search DN for data lookup in *"database*: (DN0), (DN1), ..." format	caseIgnoreIA5Match	IA5String
1.3.6.1.4.1.42.2.27.5.1.25 NAME'SolarisSearchScope'	Scope to be used for search operations, e.g., NS_LDAP_SCOPE_BASE, NS_LDAP_SCOPE_ONELEVEL or NS_LDAP_SCOPE_SUBTREE	caseIgnoreIA5Match	IA5String SINGLE-VALUE
1.3.6.1.4.1.42.2.27.5.1.26 NAME'SolarisSearchTimeLimit'	Time limit in seconds for search operations	integerMatch	INTEGER SINGLE-VALUE
1.3.6.1.4.1.42.2.27.5.1.27 NAME'SolarisPreferredServer'	Preferred LDAP Server address or network number	caseIgnoreIA5Match	IAString
1.3.6.1.4.1.42.2.27.5.1.28 NAME'SolarisPreferredServerOnly'	Boolean flag for use of preferredServer or not	booleanMatch	BOOLEAN SINGLE-VALUE
1.3.6.1.4.1.42.2.27.5.1.29 NAME'SolarisSearchReferral'	Referral chasing option, e.g., NS_LDAP_NOREF or NS_LDAP_FOLLOWREF	caseIgnoreIA5Match	IA5String SINGLE-VALUE

The Solaris client naming profile object class is:

Schema: 1.3.6.1.4.1.42.2.27.5.2.7 NAME'SolarisNamingProfile' SUP top

Structural Description: Solaris LDAP Naming client profile object class

Must: (cn $SolarisLDAPServers $SolarisSearchBaseDN)

May: (SolarisBindDN $SolarisBindPassword $SolarisAuthMethod $SolarisTransportSecurity $SolarisCertificatePath $SolarisCertificatePassword $SolarisDataSearchDN $SolarisSearchScope $SolarisSearchTimeLimit $SolarisPreferredServer $SolarisPreferredServerOnly $SolarisCacheTTL $SolarisSearchReferral)

Glossary

Access Control Entry (ACE) An entry in Active Directory that contains a security identifier which identifies the principles who are granted access to a directory object.

Access Control Instruction (ACI) An instruction that grants or denies permissions to entries in the directory server.

Access Control List (ACL) The list from which Windows NT authorization checks the client's SID.

Access Control Rule (ACR) Collective permissions and bind rules that are set as a pair.

ACE See Access control entry.

ACI See Access Control Instruction.

ACL See Access Control List.

ACR See Access Control Rule.

Active Directory Microsoft's directory service used by the core operating system to store user account and system resource data and by the BackOffice suite of products as their data store.

Active Directory Service Interface (ADSI) A set of APIs through which Windows 2000 clients and services access the Active Directory.

administration domain A domain that allows a common login to work across several servers.

ADSI See Active Directory Service Interface.

ASN.1 Abstract Syntax Notation One (ASN.1) describes objects within a management information database.

Backup Domain Controller (BDC) A backup mechanism that maintains a read-only copy of the SAM database.

BDC	See Backup Domain Controller.
Broadcast method	A way in which to locate an NIS server to bind to. The method sends out a broadcast message and binds to the first server that responds.
CA	Certificate Authority. A trusted third party that issues digital certificates.
Cold Start File method	A way to provide a file to a client. The method contains information about how to locate directory objects and also a set of credentials. This is the preferred NIS+ method because it provides additional security.
CRAM-MD5	One of the SASL mechanisms (RFC 2222) that was at one point proposed as a required mechanism for LDAP v3. CRAM stands for Challenge Response Authentication Mechanism, Message digest 5, and it uses the MD5 hash algorithm developed by Ron Rivest for generating a message digest, which in turn is used for authentication.
DAP	Directory Access Protocol (X.500).
DEN	Directory Enabled Networks.
DES	Data Encryption Standard.
DHCP	See Dynamic Host Configuration Protocol.
Directory Information Tree (DIT)	An arrangement of directory entries in a treelike structure.
directory naming context	A method to map to the DNS domain name of a company and its subdomains. Termed Active Directory by Microsoft.
Directory Specific Entry (DSE)	A naming context that defines the root entry of the directory server.
directory service	A specific type of naming service in which the objects bound to names are directory entries.
Directory System Agent (DSA)	The core program of Microsoft's Active Directory implementation.
Distinguished Name (DN)	A unique identifier of each entry in the DIT.
DIT	See Directory Information Tree.
DN	See Distinguished Name.
DNS	See Domain Name System.
domain forests	A set of domains or domain trees that do *not* form a contiguous namespace, but they do have an implicit trust relationship among them.

Domain Name System (DNS)	A method to solve the problem of locating computers on ArpaNet, the forerunner of the Internet. DNS is the de facto standard naming service of the Internet.
domain trees	A set of domains that form a contiguous namespace through a set of hierarchal relationships.
DSA	Directory Services Agent.
DSE	See Directory Server Entry.
Dynamic Host Configuration Protocol (DHCP)	A procedure by which IP-related information is provided to new clients.
Extensible Storage Engine (ESE)	A database that has built-in indexing features, along with other database features such as transaction logging and recovery. All Active Directory data resides in this database.
flat namespace	An area (domain) in which one NIS domain is not related to another.
Global Catalog	A list that provides a way to centrally maintain information about users and universal groups for access control.
GMT	Greenwich Mean Time.
GSSAPI	Generic Security Service API. Used to provide a standard interface to different authentication methods.
heartbeat signal	Client access to the directory service itself. If the heartbeat or communication channels fail, then the cluster will not function properly.
http	Hypertext Transport Protocol.
IANA	Internet Assigned Numbers Authority.
Indexed Sequential Access Method (ISAM)	A database modeled after the ESE and similar to the one in which Microsoft Exchange stores data.
ISO	International Standards Organization.
JNDI	Java Naming and Directory Interface.
KCC	See Knowledge Consistency Checker.
KDC	See Key Distribution Center.
Kerberos	A network authentication protocol that provides strong authentication for client-server applications by using secret-key cryptography.

Key Distribution Center (KDC)	A clearinghouse required by Kerberos.
KM	See Knowledge Module.
Knowledge Consistency Checker (KCC)	An Active Directory process that is responsible for mapping out the Active Directory domain controller topology and determining how replication should be performed.
Knowledge Module (KM)	A utility that monitors the iPlanet Directory Server. KM continually monitors and automatically reacts to critical infrastructure information.
LAN	Local Area Network.
LDAP	Lightweight Directory Access Protocol. The newest addition to the list of Solaris naming services. It is an optional naming service that can coexist with legacy Solaris naming services. LDAP shares some characteristics with NIS and NIS+, but it is more sophisticated in how stored data is structured and accessed.
LDAP access model	A model that defines how LDAP clients communicate with LDAP servers.
LDAP Data Interchange Format (LDIF)	A common method for importing data from legacy data sources such as NIS maps.
LDAP information model	A model that defines how entries are organized in a directory.
LDAP naming model	A model that defines how objects are named and the type of information which can be stored in the directory.
LDAP referral	A mechanism used to instruct an LDAP client searching the directory to continue the search on another directory server.
LDAP replication model	The mechanism by which directory data is automatically copied from one directory server to another. Using replication, you can copy everything from entire directory trees to individual directory entries between servers.
LDAP security model	A model that defines how information in the directory is protected from unauthorized access.
LDIF	See LDAP Data Interchange Format.
Lightweight Directory Access Protocol	See LDAP.

Management Information Base (MIB)	A data structure used to define network devices and objects that SNMP accesses.
naming service	In a general sense, a facility that organizes and names objects. It provides an association, often referred to as a binding, between a name and an object.
NDS	Netware Directory Server.
Network Information Service	See NIS.
Network Information Service +	See NIS+.
NIS	The first UNIX-based distributed naming service. It replaced text files as the repository for storing information.
NIS+	A successor to NIS that corrected a number of flaws in the NIS architecture.
NMS	Network Management Servers.
NTLM	A SAM agent that provides backward compatibility to Windows clients by using NT Lan Manager (NTLM) style authentication.
Object Identifier	A number assigned to child object classes to ensure they will not conflict with another object class.
OID	See Object identifier.
OSI stack	Open Systems Interconnection that allows network devices to read, write, and act upon management data.
PAM	See Pluggable Authentication Module.
PDC	See Primary Domain Controller.
Pluggable Authentication Module (PAM)	A framework that allows new authentication technologies to be "plugged in" without changing commands such as `login`, `ftp`, and `telnet`.
Primary Domain Controller (PDC)	A controller that has write privileges on the SAM database.
PSL	A language that enables users to write their own KMs.
Public key technology	Security feature that uses a mathematically related pair of encryption keys called the public and private key. Data encrypted with the public key can only be decrypted with the associated private key.
RDN	Relative Distinguished Name. The leftmost portion of a directory entry name.

Remote Procedure Calls (RPC)	A programming mechanism that enables NIS clients and servers to communicate with each other.
Replication	The mechanism by which directory data is automatically copied from one directory server to another.
RFC	Request for Comments, A means by which each distinct version of an Internet standards-related specification is published as part of the RFC document series.
RPC	See Remote Procedure Calls.
SAM	See Security Account Manager.
SASL	See Simple Authentication and Security Layer
SDK	Software Development Kit.
Secure Socket Layer (SSL)	An authentication method developed by Netscape as a way to create a secure connection between a web client and a web server.
Security Account Manager (SAM)	A database of user account information maintained on special Windows NT servers called Domain Controllers, of which there are two varieties: primary (PDC) and backup (BDC).
Service Resource Records (SRV RR)	An Active Directory service that clients search to locate the nearest controller.
shared nothing architecture	An architecture wherein at any time a resource is owned by only one of the cluster nodes.
SID	Security ID. An identification, the generation of which is specific to Microsoft's Active Directory implementation and not a standard LDAP concept.
Simple Authentication and Security Layer (SASL)	A standard proposed for pluggable authentication methods to be used for adding authentication support to connection-based protocols such as LDAP. SASL allows negotiation about multiple authentication schemes between a client and a server. SASL is beneficial as a modular security layer.
Simple Network Management Protocol (SNMP)	A widely deployed protocol originally designed to manage network devices, SNMP can also be used to manage other items such as applications and services.
Single sign-on	The ability to authenticate a user once upon login so that user is automatically authenticated for all applications the user accesses.

SNMP	See Simple Network Management Protocol.
Solaris Naming Service Switch	A tool to cope with the coexistence of multiple directory services present in the Solaris operating environment.
Solaris Resource Manager (SRM)	A utility that assigns shares of system resources to different applications, thereby maintaining a minimum threshold of performance.
Specified Server Method	A mechanism that specifies an NIS server or list of servers to bind to.
SQL	Structured Query Language. Standard used for database queries.
SRV RR	See Service Resource Records.
SSL	See Secure Socket Layer.
SSPI	Security Support Provider Interface.
TCP/IP	Transmission Control Protocol/Internet Protocol.
TGT	See Ticket-Granting Ticket.
Ticket-Granting Ticket (TGT)	A Kerberos method for application servers to grant service tickets to an authenticated user.
TLS	See Transport Layer Security.
Transport Layer Security (TLS)	The new standard for secure socket layers. A public-key-based Transport Layer Security protocol.
URL	Uniform Resource Locator.
Wide Area Network (WAN)	Wide area network.
X.500	The first incarnation of LDAP.

Index

A

abbreviations, PAM, 63
access control policies, 237
    ACI, 238
    LDAP security model review, 238
access control process, 299
access control, Internet drafts, 316
access log, 219
    Access Log tab and parameter settings, 223
    Access Log tab and resulting details, 222
    command line, viewing, 221
    configuration options, 222
    Directory Server Console, viewing, 221
    enabling, 223
    log creation policies, setting, 223
    viewing, 221
access model, 299
access rights, ACI, 239
ACI, 238
    access rights, 239
    adding new, 241
    best practices, 242
    bind rules, 239
    creating, 240
    format, 239
Active Directory
    access model, 299
    applications access, 302
    architecture, 294
    architecture, DNS integration, 296
    clients interaction, 301
    Extensible Storage Engine (ESE), 295

    Global Catalog, 298
    information model, 296
    Kerberos, 298
    Kerberos Ticket-Granting Ticket (TGT), 299
    Knowledge Consistency Checker (KCC), 300
    LDAP referrals, 303
    major components, 295
    namespace, 297
    naming, 297
    replication model, 300
    security model, 298
    single sign-on, 303
    Solaris interactions, 302
    transport layer security (TLS), 298
Active Server Model, 218
`admin` login account, 69
`admin` password, changing, 88
administration domains, 68
Administration Server Console, 68
alternative authentication mechanisms, 41
    CRAM-MD5, 42
    Kerberos, 45
    LDAP, 41
    Secure Socket Layer (SSL), 49
appending to the database, 91
architecture
    Active Directory, 294
    evolution of Solaris naming services, 11
    iPlanet Directory Server, 67
    LDAP overview, 27
    NIS extensions, 148
    NIS overview, 16

Solaris DNS, 25
Solaris naming service switch, 14
Solaris naming services, 11
asymmetric high availability model, 217
asymmetric model, 216
attribute update test, 174
audit log, 225
audit log, configuration, 226
authenticate tests, 174
authentication and security, Internet drafts, 319
authentication method, 115
authentication performance of the directory
    server, 177
authentication tests, 177
authentication vs. authorization, 37
authentication, PAM, 64

B

backing up and restoring directory database, 229
backing up database from
    command line, 230
    directory server console, 230
basic iPlanet Directory PATROL architecture, 268
basic PATROL
    Agent, 266
    architecture, 266
    Console, 267
    Event Manager, 267
    Knowledge Modules, 267
basic referrals mechanism, 208
benchmarks, 172
benefits of consolidation, 273
bind rules, ACI, 239
BMC PATROL, introduction
    Agent, 266
    architecture, 268
    Console, 267
    Event Manager, 267
    Knowledge Modules, 267
Broadcast method, 17, 25
building a Sun Cluster with HA LDAP data
    services, 212
    configuring for Netscape data services, 215
    iPlanet Directory Server installation, 214

LDAP fault monitor, 213

C

C API, 315
caching for performance, 184
    cache parameters, 189
    data design considerations, 193
    Database tab statistics, 189
    directory caches, 184
    entry cache size, 186
    LDAP client design, 195
    Performance tab information, 192
    Plugins icon, expanded, 196
    removing unnecessary plug-ins, 195
    setting
        all IDs threshold, 190
        database cache size, 186
        search limit parameters, 191
    sizing database and entry caches, 187
    sizing factors, 185
    tuning
        all IDs threshold value, 191
        cache sizes, 188
        import performance, 199
        write performance, 196
calculating directory database size, 164
    backups, 167
    log files, 167
    sizing example, 165
capacity planning
    caching for performance, 184
    directory considerations, 162
    methodology, 164
    performance tuning, 178
    qualitative observations based on test
        results, 177
    results of experimentation, 174
    server sizing, 161
    troubleshooting checklist, 200
Certificate Setup Wizard
    certificate request, generating, 100
    running, 99
    server certificate, installing, 101, 102
Change Trust DB Password window, 103

changing
  DB backing files location, 85
  DB files location, 83
  transaction log location, 84
  trust DB password, 103
client configuration, 140
  initialization, 140
  LDAP create Client, 144
client-side certificates, 49
coexistence
  NIS and DNS, 13
  NIS and files, 12
Cold Start File method, 25
commands
  domainname, 76
  dsexport, 160
  dsimport, 139
  hadsconfig(1M), 215
  ldag_gen_profile, 134
  ldap_gen_profile(1M), 114
  ldaplist, 143
  ldapmodify, 91, 157
  ldapsearch, 134, 159
  ldif2db, 90
  make, 156
  makedbm, 156
  ns-slapd, 89
  passwd, 39
  restoreconfig, 93
  setup, 73
  startconsole, 69, 80
  tar, 72
  ypcat, 158
  ypcat hosts, 159
common installation configuration parameters,
  changing, 87
comparison with legacy naming services, 35
configuration, 174
configuration data, 68
configuring the Sun Cluster HA for Netscape data
  services, 215
connection status, 250
consolidation, 273
  approaches, 274
  benefits, 273
  iPlanet Directory Access Router (iDAR), 284
  LDAP gateways, 276

  LDAP synchronization, 276
  LDAP-enabled applications, 274
  unified login and single sign-on, 281
controls and extended operations, Internet
  drafts, 317
CRAM-MD5, 42
CRAM-MD5, authentication diagram, 43
Create Attribute window, 246
Create Object Class window, 247
creating
  attributes from Directory Server Console, 246
  LDIF file, 97
  object classes from Directory Server
    Console, 247
  subtree, 157
crypt
  benefits and drawbacks, 40
  UNIX, 39
current resource usage, 249

D

data design considerations, 193
  design of directory hierarchy, 194
  design of entries, 194
  design of security rules, 194
data services for Sun Cluster, 212
data synchronization, 149
database
  appending to, 91
  backups, deleting, 232
  cache sizing, 186
  connector, 279
  entry cache, 170
  Import Database window, 91
  index cache, 171
  initialization, 89
database cache information, 254
database performance metrics, 253
database servers vs. directory service, 3
Database tab statistics, 189
database transaction log
  database checkpoint interval, changing, 228
  durable transactions, enabling, 228
  location, changing, 227
  managing, 226

`db2ldif` script, 235
debugging, 144
default NIS mappings, 153
deleting database backups, 232
deploying HA LDAP data services, 203
   building a Sun Cluster, 212
   iPlanet Directory Services architecture
      models, 203
   LDAP cluster deployment options, 216
   overview of Sun Cluster 2.2 software, 210
   redirecting LDAP Client requests, 218
deploying LDAP, 9
directory backups, 167
directory caches
   database cache, 184
   entry cache, 184
Directory Connector
   Lotus Notes, 280
   Microsoft Exchange, 280
directory considerations, 162
   directory access, 163
   directory size, 162
   replication strategy, 164
   security requirements, 163
directory data, importing, 89
directory database, backing up and restoring, 229
directory information tree (DIT), 117
directory information tree structure, 152
directory log files, 219
   access, 219
   audit log, 225
   error log, 224
`Directory Manager`
   login account, 69
   password, changing, 87
directory objects and attributes, 29
directory replication, 93
   Consumer Settings tab, 95
   LDIF file, creating, 97
   planning, 93
   setting up, 94
   Source and Destination form, 96
   SSL, using, 104
   Supplier Settings tab, 95
   troubleshooting, 98
   verifying, 98

directory schema, 30
directory schema update, 123, 155
directory server
   asymmetric high availability model, 217
   monitoring, 248
directory service
   overview, 2
   proliferation, 3
   vs. database servers, 3
directory sizing example, 165
Directory tab, 159
disk storage
   partitioning and layout, 71
   requirements, 168
disk throughput, increasing, 198
displayed parameters, 258
distinguished names, 31
DIT, 117
   sample tree, 28
   structure, 152
   subtree, creating, 157
   support entry creation, 123
DNS
   client architecture, 26
   high availability features, 27
   integration, 296
   introduction, 6
   server architecture, 26
`domainname` command, 76
`dsexport` command, 160
`dsimport` command, 139
`dsservd` process, 148
`dsypserv` process, 170

E

effects of additional CPUs, 176
Encryption tab, 102
entry add/delete test, 174
entry cache size, 186
Entry table, 263
error log, 224
error log, viewing, 224
estimating CPU usage, 172
evolution of Solaris naming services, 11

NIS and DNS coexistence, 13
NIS and files coexistence, 12
service switch, 13
EWOS directory functional standards, Internet
drafts, 320
example simple SNMP environment, 259
exporting and importing database with LDIF, 233
exporting databases to LDIF from command
line, 234
Extensible Storage Engine (ESE) database, 295

F

file navigation, 82
files
    `nis.mapping`, 153
    `nsswitch.conf`, 14
    `pam.conf`, 57
    `pam_ldap`, 62
    `slapd.ldbm.conf`, 187
file-specific table, 255

G

generic mappings, 153
generic `pam.conf` file, 57
Global Catalog, 298

H

`hadsconfig(1M)` command, 215
high availability
    architecture models, 203
    asymmetric model, 216
    hot standby model, 216
    referral models, 208
    replication models, 204
    strategy, 204
    typical Sun Cluster HA configuration, 211
high-performance single-master directory-
replication architecture, 206
history of LDAP, 7
hot standby model, 216

I

iDAR, 284
    feature set, 285
        client-server compatibility, 287
        firewall-like security, 286
        high availability, 285
    overview, 284
Import Database window, 91
importing databases from LDIF, 235
importing directory data, 89
    appending to the database, 91
    database initialization, 89
importing LDIF files from command line, 123
indexing, 178
    administration, 183
    automatically created indexes, 181
    built-in system indexes, 180
    cost, 183
    default indexes, 180
    determining importance, 182
    importance, 178
    optimize, 197
    relative costs of index types, 197
    Select Attribute window, 183
    summary, 184
    system indexes, 180
    types, 179
    viewing, 179
information and X.500 documents, Internet
drafts, 319
information model, 296
initialization
    checklist, 157
    NIS extensions, 154
    NIS extensions overview, 154
    procedure, 158
installation
    custom, 78
    defaults, 78
    differences, 80
    disk storage partitioning and layout, 71
    express, 78
    file navigation, 82
    layout diagram, 82
    NIS extensions, 108
    planning, 70
    post, procedures, 83

procedure, 72
restarting administration and directory
   servers, 82
starting Netscape Console, 80
troubleshooting tips, 92
type, 74
typical, performing, 74
verifying, 81
installation scripts, NIS vs. DNS, domain name, 76
Interaction table, 263
Internet drafts
   access control, 316
   authentication and security, 319
   C API, 315
   controls and extended operations, 317
   EWOS directory functional standards, 320
   information and X.500 documents, 319
   Java API, 316
   joint ISO standards and CCITT
      recommendations, 320
   LDAP specific, 315
   locating, 309
   NADF documents, 319
   other ISO documents, 320
   replication, 316
interoperability
   Windows 2000, 294
   Windows NT, 289
iPlanet Directory Access Router (iDAR), 284
iPlanet Directory Server
   installation, 214
   reinstalling, 92
   SASL, 50
   script generation program, 105
   startup files, 104
iPlanet Directory Services architecture models
   HA strategy, 204
iPlanet Meta-Directory Server, 278
ISO documents, 320 ·
ISO standards, joint and CCITT
   recommendations, 320

J

java API, 316

K

Kerberos, 45, 281, 298
Kerberos Ticket-Granting Ticket (TGT), 299
Knowledge Consistency Checker (KCC), 300

L

layout of `NetscapeRoot` portion of directory
   tree, 69
LDAP
   architecture overview, 27
   authentication, 41, 115
   choosing, 274
   client
      configuration, 140
      create, 144
      design, 195
      initialization, 140
      profiles, 113
      requests, redirecting, 218
      verification, 144
   cluster deployment options, 216
   comparison with legacy naming services, 35
   connector, 279
   consolidating enabled applications, 274
   deployment, factors, 9
   directory objects and attributes, 29
   directory schema, 30
   directory topology model, 27
   distinguished names, 31
   DIT, 117
   error codes, 329
   fault monitor, 213
   functional model, 31
   gateways, 276
   goals, 8
   history, 7
   implementation, native configuration, 112
   loading data, 118
   managing with BMC PATROL, 264
   MIB (management information base), 260
   naming context, 118
   naming model, 29
   NIS domain, 114
   NIS information, storing, 150
   overview, native configuration, 111
   `pam_ldap` authentication, 116

`pam_unix` authentication, 115
proxy agent authentication, 116
replication
    full tree, 34
    subtree, 34
replication model, 33
RFCs and Internet drafts, 311
schema information, 337
security model, 32
security model review, 238
Solaris implementation, 8
specifications, 8
standards information, 309
synchronization, 276
test suite, 172
vs. SSL, 50
LDAP cluster deployment options
    active server model, 218
    hot standby model, 216
LDAP synchronization
    database connector, 279
    deploying iPlanet Meta-Directory, 280
    iPlanet Meta-Directory Server, 278
    LDAP connector, 279
    Meta-Directory connectors, 279
    NIS extensions for Solaris, 277
    NT synchronization service, 277
    password synchronization, 277
LDAP test suite
    attribute update, 174
    authenticate, 174
    entry add/delete, 174
    sample test matrix, 173
    simple read, 173
`ldap_cachemgr` daemon, 142
`ldap_gen_profile` command, 134
`ldap_gen_profile(1M)` command, 114
`ldaplist` command, 143
`ldapmodify` command, 91, 157
`ldapsearch` command, 134, 159
LDIF (LDAP Data Interchange Format)
    creating a file, 97
    `db2ldif` script, 235
    exporting and importing the database, 233
    exporting databases from command line, 234
    importing databases, 235
`ldif2db` command, 90

loading data, 118
log creation policies, setting, 223
log files, 167
login accounts, 69
    `admin`, 69
    `Directory Manager`, 69
login does not work, 145
    `ldapclient` cannot bind to server, 146
    lookup too slow, 146
login program text string converting to a hashed string, 39
login to directory window, 88

M

maintenance, preventive, 219
`make` command, 156
`makedbm` command, 156
`Makefile` examination and modification, 156
Manager tab, 88
managing database transaction logging, 226
managing directory schema
    files, 243
    modifying, 245
    reading schema files, 245
managing directory services, 237
    access control policies, 237
    managing LDAP directory server using BMC PATROL, 264
    managing the directory schema, 242
    monitoring the directory server, 248
    SNMP-based management, 258
managing LDAP directory server using BMC PATROL, 264
    checking memory usage with `pmap`, 270
    introduction, 265
    KM overview, 264
managing the directory schema, 242
    Create Attribute window, 246
    Create Object Class window, 247
    creating attributes from Directory Server Console, 246
    creating object classes from Directory Server Console, 247
mapping, NT to LDAP, 291

master and replication directory hub
  architecture, 207
memory sizing, 170
  database entry cache, 170
  database index cache, 171
  estimating, 172
  server executables, 170
  Solaris file system cache, 171
  typical usage, 171
  usage summary, 171
Meta-Directory
  connectors, 279
  deploying, 280
  how it works, 278
methodology, capacity
  calculating directory database size, 164
  estimating CPU usage, 172
  LDAP test suite, 172
  memory sizing, 170
  summary of disk storage requirements, 168
  summary of memory usage, 171
Microsoft Windows interoperability, 289
  Active Directory Services Architecture, 294
  Solaris Directory services and Active Directory
    services interactions, 302
  Windows 2000, 294
  Windows NT, 289
minimize write traffic, 198
modify tests, 176
modify tests, effects of additional CPUs, 176
monitoring database activity, 253
  cache information, 254
  file-specific, 255
  performance metrics, 253
monitoring the directory server
  connection status, 250
  current resource usage, 249
  database from command line, 256
  database from Directory Server Console, 255
  database output example, 256
  displayed parameters, 258
  monitoring database activity, 253
  performance counters, 251
  performance from command line, 251
  performance from Directory Server Console, 251
  server performance, 249

N
NADF documents, Internet drafts, 319
naming context, 118
naming services
  NIS, 12
  NIS and DNS coexistence, 13
  overview, 1
  Solaris evolution, 11
  Solaris switch, 13
  Solaris switch architecture, 14
  Solaris switch functions, 14
native LDAP configuration, 111
  client configuration, 140
  implementation, 112
  introduction, 111
  overview, 111
  server configuration procedure, 119
  troubleshooting, 144
native LDAP implementation, 112
  authentication method, 115
  directory information tree, 117
  loading data, 118
  naming context, 118
  NIS domain, 114
  pam_ldap, 116
  pam_unix, 115
  proxy agent, 116
  Solaris LDAP client profiles, 113
Netscape Communicator
  configuration overview, 305
  other features, 308
  using, 305
Netscape Console, 69
  diagram of component interactions, 70
  starting, 80
NIS
  architecture overview, 16
  Broadcast method, 17
  client failover
    broadcast method, 19
    specified server method, 20
  client server architecture, 16
  clients bind to NIS server, 17
  DNS coexistence, 13
  domain, 114
  files coexistence, 12
  high availability architecture features, 19
  introduction, 4

major components, 16
maps, 17
maps, creating, 18
specific attributes, 150
Specified Server method, 17
NIS extensions
architecture, 148
configuration, 147
creating the subtree, 157
data accessibility, 149
data synchronization, 149
default NIS mappings, 153
directory schema, update, 155
Directory tab, 159
DIT structure, 152
generic mappings, 153
initialization, 154
checklist, 157
overview, 154
procedure, 158
installing, 108
`Makefile` examination and modification, 156
maps
importing, 157
propagating, 160
updating, 159
object classes, new, 151
overview, 147
postinstallation and verification, 158
slave server mode, 150
Solaris, 277
specific attributes, 150
storing NIS information in LDAP, 150
typical subtree, 152
NIS maps
defaults, 153
generic, 153
importing, 157
propagating, 160
updating, 159
NIS+
architecture, 22
architecture overview, 20
Broadcast method, 25
client server architecture, 21
clients bind to the NIS+ server, 22
Cold Start File method, 25
credentials, 40

high availability architecture features, 25
interaction with DNS, 24
introduction, 5
security process, 23
Specified Server method, 25
tables, 23
`nis.mapping` file, 153
`ns-admin` process, 93, 170
`ns-dssync` process, 291
`ns-slapd` command, 89
`ns-slapd` process, 76, 170
caution, 77
changing owner, 87
`nsswitch.conf` file, 14
NT
Lan Manager (NTLM) authentication, 295
synchronization service, 277
synchronization service, installation, 292
to LDAP mapping, 291
user account information, 290

O
object classes, new, 151
OIDs, obtaining, 246
Operations table, 261
overview of Sun Cluster 2.2 software, 210
data services, 212

P
PAM (Pluggable Authentication Module)
abbreviations, 63
authentication, 64
configuration file, 54
configuration file syntax, 55
configuration, control flags, 56
configurations, 55
error reporting, 60
framework, 52
generic `pam.conf` file, 57
how to add a module, 59
LDAP module, 61
module types, 52
module verification, 60
modules, 54

preventing unauthorized access, 60
relationship between applications, library, and
    modules, 54
update of password, 64
using, 53
pam_ldap, 116
pam_ldap file, 62
pam_unix, 115
passwd command, 39
password synchronization, 277
Password tab, 129
PEM (PATROL Event Manager), 267
performance counters, 251
performance counters, resetting, 189
performance optimization, 124
Performance tab information, 192
performance tuning, 178
    automatically created indexes, 181
    built-in system indexes, 180
    caching for performance, 184
    cost of indexing, 183
    default indexes, 180
    determining index importance, 182
    importance of indexing, 178
    index administration, 183
    index types, 179
    indexing, 178
    indexing summary, 184
    Select Attribute window, 183
    system indexes, 180
    viewing indexes, 179
Plugins icon, expanded, 196
posixAccount attributes, 30
postinstallation and verification, 158
postinstallation procedures, 83
    DB backing files location, changing, 85
    DB files location, changing, 83
    saving the configuration, 83
    transaction log location, changing, 84
preventive maintenance, 219
    backing up and restoring directory
        database, 229
    directory log files, 219
    exporting and importing the database with
        LDIF, 233
    managing database transaction logging, 226

processes
    dsservd, 148
    dsypserv, 170
    ns-admin, 170
    ns-dssync, 291
    ns-slapd, 170
    ypserv, 148
product architecture, 67
    administration domains, 68
    configuration data, 68
    diagram of component interactions, 70
    installation planning, 70
    layout of NetscapeRoot portion of the
        directory tree, 69
    login accounts, 69
    Netscape Console, 69
Property Editor, 121
proxy agent, 116

Q

qualitative observations based on test results, 177

R

read test with nonpersistent connection, 175
redirecting LDAP Client requests, 218
referral models, 208
    basic referrals mechanism, 208
    replication referrals mechanism, 209
    search beyond the local division, 210
referral search beyond the local division, 210
reinstalling iPlanet
    Directory Server, 92
    ns-slapd vs. root, 77
removing unnecessary plug-ins, 195
replication models, 204
    high-performance single-master directory
        architecture, 206
    master and replication directory hub
        architecture, 207
    single-master directory architecture, 205
    Windows 2000, 300
replication referrals mechanism, 209
replication, directory, 93

Consumer Settings tab, 95
  LDIF file, creating, 97
  planning, 93
  setting up, 94
  Source and Destination form, 96
  Supplier Settings tab, 95
  troubleshooting, 98
  using SSL, 104
  verifying, 98
replication, Internet drafts, 316
Request for Comments (RFC)
  LDAP specific, 311
  life cycle, 310
  locating, 309
restarting
  administration server, 82
  directory server, 82
restoreconfig command, 93
restoring database
  from command line, 231
  from directory server console, 231
  including replicated entries, 232
results of experimentation, 174
  authentication tests, 177
  configuration, 174
  modify tests, 176
  read test with nonpersistent connection, 175
  simple read test with persistent connection, 175
Rights pop-up menu in the Set Access Permissions
  window, 241

S
samples
  /var/ldap/ldap_client_cred file, 142
  /var/ldap/ldap_client_file, 141
  directory information tree (DIT), 28
  test matrix, 173
SASL, 50
saving the configuration, 83
schema files
  directory, 243
  modifying, 245
  obtaining OIDs, 246
  reading, 245

schemas
  checking, 199
  checking, import, 200
  information, 337
script generation program, 105
search limit parameters
  lookthrough limit, 192
  size limit, 191
  time limit, 191
secure server
  Certificate Setup Wizard
    generating certificate request, 100
    installing a certificate, 102
    running, 99
  planning configuration, 99
  rebooting, 103
  setting up, 98
  trust database password or PIN, changing, 103
Secure Socket Layer (SSL) authentication, 49
secure system, planning configuration, 99
security infrastructure, 50
  iPlanet Directory Server SASL, 50
  PAM configuration file, 54
  PAM framework, 52
  PAM LDAP module, 61
  PAM module types, 52
  using PAM, 53
security models, 37
  alternative authentication mechanisms, 41
  authentication vs. authorization, 37
  infrastructure, 50
  traditional Solaris authentication, 38
  Windows NT, 290
Select Attribute window, 183
Select Attributes window, 122
sendmail fails to deliver/receive mail to/from
  remote users, 145
server configuration, 174
server configuration procedure, 119
  adding new containers, 129
  adding proxy agent entry, 134
  changing password store to unix_crypt
    format, 128
  creating indexes, 137
  creating virtual list view indexes, 137
  generating the client profile, 135
  importing LDIF files from command line, 123

modifying
    self-entry modification, 133
    `slapd.oc.conf`, 125
    `slapd.user_at.conf`, 124
    `slapd.user_oc.conf`, 126
    populating the LDAP data, 139
    setting password read permission for
      `proxyagent`, 135
    setting VLV control ACI, 133
    summary of steps required, 123
    tools and techniques, 119
server executables, 170
server performance monitoring, 249
server setup
    creating an LDAP client, 144
    debugging, 144
    directory information tree, 117
    `ldap_cachemgr` daemon, 142
    `ldaplist` command, 143
    loading data, 118
    naming context, 118
    NIS domain, 114
    proxy agent, 116
    sample `/var/ldap/ldap_client_cred`
      file, 142
    sample `/var/ldap/ldap_client_file`, 141
server sizing, capacity planning, 161
server-side certificates, 49
Set Access Permissions window, 121
setting
    all IDs threshold, 190
    cache sizes, 200
    database cache size, 186
    search limit parameters, 191
    search limit parameters, changing, 192
`setup` command, 73
simple authentication, see LDAP authentication
simple read test, 173
simple read test with persistent connection, 175
single sign-on, Windows 2000 interoperability, 303
single-master directory-replication
    architecture, 205
SiteMinder, 281
    how it works, 282
    limitations, 283
    single sign-on, 283
sizing database and entry caches, 187

sizing factors, 185
`slapd.ldbm.conf` file, 187
SNMP-based management, 258
    Entry table, 263
    example of simple SNMP environment, 259
    Interaction table, 263
    LDAP MIB, 260
    Operations table, 261
Solaris
    CRAM-MD5 authentication, 42
    directory services, historical, 4
    DNS architecture, 25
    file system cache, 171
    Kerberos authentication, 45
    LDAP authentication, 41
    LDAP client profiles, 113
    LDAP implementation, 8
    LDAP vs. SSL authentication, 50
    PAM framework, 52
    SSL authentication, 49
    traditional authentication, 38
    UNIX crypt, 39
Solaris and Active Directory interactions, 302
Solaris naming service switch, 13
    architecture, 14
    functions, 14
    introduction, 6
Solaris naming services
    architecture, 11
    evolution, 11
    overview, 1
Source and Destination form, 96
Specified Server method, 17, 25
SSL
    client-side certificates, 49
    enabling on server, 102
    Encryption tab, 102
    replication, using, 104
    secure port, 291
    server-side certificates, 49
    specification of, 104
    vs. LDAP, 50
`startconsole` command, 69, 80
startup files, iPlanet Directory Server, 104
storage considerations
    directory database, 169
    directory database backups, 169

log files storage, 169
storing NIS information in LDAP, 150
summary of disk storage requirements, 168
summary of memory usage, 171
summary of steps required
   directory schema update, 123
   DIT and support entry creation, 123
   loading data, 124
   performance optimization, 124
Sun Cluster
   building with HA LDAP data services, 212
   configuring for Netscape data services, 215
   data services, 212
   iPlanet Directory Server installation, 214
   LDAP cluster deployment options, 216
   LDAP fault monitor, 213
   overview, 210
   typical HA configuration, 211
synchronization service, 291
   installation, 292
   SSL, 291

T

`tar` command, 72
tools and techniques, 119
   adding object to DIT, 120
   importing LDIF files from Directory
     Console, 122
   setting permissions by creating ACI entries, 121
traditional Solaris authentication, 38
   NIS+ credentials, 40
   UNIX crypt, 39
Transport Layer Security (TLS), 298
troubleshooting, 144
   checklist, capacity planning, 200
   login does not work, 145
   replication problems, 98
   sendmail fails to deliver/receive mail to/from
     remote users, 145
   tips on installation, 92
   unable to reach systems in the LDAP domain
     remotely, 145
   unresolved host name, 145
tuning
   all IDs threshold value, 191

cache sizes, 188
tuning import performance, 199
   schema checking, 200
   setting cache sizes, 200
tuning write performance, 196
   increase disk throughput, 198
   minimize write traffic, 198
   optimize indexes, 197
   schema checking, 199
typical
   memory usage, 171
   subtree, 152
   Sun Cluster HA configuration, 211

U

unified login and single sign-on, 281
   Kerberos, 281
   SiteMinder, 281
Universal Connector, 280
UNIX crypt, 39
UNIX crypt, benefits and drawbacks, 40
unresolved host name, 145
using Netscape Communicator, 305

V

viewing error log, 224

W

Windows 2000
   access control process, 299
   access model, 299
   Active Directory
     access, 302
     client interaction, 301
   Active Directory Services, 294
   interoperability, 294
   LDAP referrals, 303
   replication model, 300
   security model, 298
Windows NT
   interoperability, 289
   Security Account Manager (SAM) database, 290

security model, 290
synchronization service, 291
synchronization service, installation, 292
to LDAP mapping, 291
user account information, 290

Y

ypcat command, 158
ypcat hosts command, 159
ypserv process, 148